Milton's Inward Liberty

Milton's Inward Liberty

*A Reading of Christian Liberty
from the Prose to* Paradise Lost

FILIPPO FALCONE

With a Foreword by Marialuisa Bignami

PICKWICK *Publications* · Eugene, Oregon

MILTON'S INWARD LIBERTY
A Reading of Christian Liberty from the Prose to *Paradise Lost*

Pickwick Publications
An Imprint of Wipf and Stock Publishers
199 W. 8th Av.e, Suite 3
Eugene, OR 97401

www.wipfandstock.com

ISBN 13: 978-1-62564-190-8

Cataloging-in-Publication data:

Falcone, Filippo.

    Milton's inward liberty : a reading of Christian liberty from the prose to *Paradise Lost* / Filippo Falcone ; with a foreword by Marialuisa Bignami.

    xviii + 196 p. ; 23 cm. Includes bibliographical references and index.

    ISBN 13: 978-1-62564-190-8

    1. Milton, John, 1608–1674. Paradise lost. 2. Milton, John, 1608–1674—Allegory and symbolism. 3. Milton, John, 1608–1674—Political and social views. I. Bignami, Marialuisa. II. Title.

PR3562 .F35 2014

Manufactured in the U.S.A.

For him whom to know is
Life eternal

For Sandra, Miriam, Benjamin, and Ryan
My associate souls

Contents

Notes on the Text

All quotations of *Paradise Lost* are from Kerrigan, Rumrich, and Fallon's 2007 edition.

All quotations of Milton's prose works are from Wolfe's 1953–82 editions, unless otherwise indicated.

All texts originally in languages other than English have been cited in translation, or supplied in both original and translation if pertinent. The spelling of early modern sources is left unmodernized.

References to multivolume works or collections in the notes follow the volume-book-page pattern or, alternatively, the volume-page pattern.

References to *Paradise Lost* and *Paradise Regained* follow the book-line pattern.

Foreword

I HAVE BEEN SUPERVISING Filippo Falcone's work on John Milton over the years and I want to offer as my opening statement that it has been a pleasure throughout, from his very beginnings to the achievement of the present book, the outcome of his doctoral dissertation: I have supervised his strictly-speaking academic work (in collaboration with other colleagues), but I also had frequent occasions to discuss with him the issues—indeed sometimes argue and fight over them—of the path of research he started conducting of his own accord on the Miltonic topics of his choice, sailing closer to theology than to literature. This meant enquiring into theological issues next to literary ones, which double perspective would eventually lead to the present work.

The issue of liberty in Milton and of its source always came first and foremost for him, as he himself states in the acknowledgments pages of the present book. Such was the notion of "inner," or "inward" liberty, which he maintains was his first interest in any case, as is immediately made clear to the reader by the title itself Filippo has thought fit to choose for his book. Thus it will be a pleasure for the reader, as it has been for the present writer, to discuss his peculiar literary as well as theological topics with Filippo Falcone and to hear from him the reports of how he was fearlessly opening up to discussions with Milton scholars from a wide variety of universities (to avoid the provincialism of sticking simply with his own institution); as with human beings, it has been equally captivating to hear him report about the books he was all the time reading: I have seldom met a young scholar so passionately fond of setting his eyes on anything available on his chosen topic and of leaving no stone unturned to make sure his would be the best "library" on the topic available, and so its bibliography is—and all first hand in collecting and reading, in understanding and making use of. Moreover, in the abovementioned acknowledgments pages, our author, in sending out his thanks into the world, moves from men to books *via* a hint ("If a book is the quintessence of a man . . .") at a passage from *Areopagitica*.

The present book in any case is never far from a theological outlook. Altogether it deals with how the gospel frees humankind from the rule of the law and of men and frequent are the cases in which the author argues with other critics on points of theology and on the way in which this discipline and field of study conditions the book's reading of Milton's poetical works. This may also be the place where to remind the reader that, before starting to write the present book, its author felt the appropriateness—indeed the necessity—to go back on a topic frequently tackled by critics with uncertain results, that of *De Doctrina Christiana* and its attribution, for which he is in favor of Milton himself.

The book which results from such a big effort painstakingly digs into Milton's early prose writings to begin with, in which the attention to liberty on Milton's part seems to be as strong as any other revolutionary's in the unsettled atmosphere of the early and middle Forties, but in any case it is remarked that very soon Milton started equating inward liberty with Christian liberty, thus defining Milton's libertarian revolution as an inherently inward one.

Filippo then moves on to look at Milton's poetry and at the role played there by light to mean Christian liberty. This device, that corresponds to a poetic transposition of Christian liberty, is used in the first place in order to define Satan, but also of course Adam and Eve, thus generating a very original reading of the main characters in *Paradise Lost*. Thus Filippo's reading of the crucial book 9 proves particularly thought-provoking. At the end of this very particular reading of all the aspects and the development of Milton's work the book leads us to the conclusion that (to employ the author's own words) "*Paradise Lost* teaches the lesson that the true Eden is within."

Marialuisa Bignami
University of Milan

Preface

As I first approached the theme of liberty in Milton, little room seemed to be left for further study and definition. In moving deeper into my research, however, it became clear to me that the Milton community had to a large extent read liberty through the spectacles of liberalism. In so doing, Milton studies had largely failed to tackle liberty from the point of view of Milton's Christian beliefs. The latter show that the Christian paradigm of liberty speaks of an inward microcosm, a place of freedom whose precincts are defined by man's fellowship with God. All other forms of freedom relate to the outer world, be they freedom to choose the good, absence of external constraint and oppression or freedom of alternatives. All of these are not true liberty, but they are pursued by Milton in concert with true liberty. This driving concept prompted me to read Milton's work from the inside out, that is, from the inward dimension to the outward. Theology suddenly became key to this progress. Yet what theology? If it is anything but simple to make one's way through the many and various nuances of seventeenth-century theology, it is even harder to try to relate Milton's personal theological synthesis to its broader theological milieu. Nevertheless, a few striking analogies stand out which align Milton's thought with strains of Independency as well as with General Baptist and Quaker theology. This work does not concern itself with settling matters of influence. What it does attempt to do is interact with texts that appear to shed light on Milton. It attempts to engage in a hermeneutical circle that intersects Milton and his theological background with the Bible. The Bible itself proves the ultimate crossroads and the final synthesis for a world seeking liberty. It is there that Milton found it.

Acknowledgments

I<small>T WAS</small> M<small>ARIALUISA</small> B<small>IGNAMI</small> who first inspired me to pursue Milton studies. It was Marialuisa who also threw me in the water so I could learn how to swim. Much like a Daniel in the lions' den, I was committed to present a paper in Oxford at the very outset of my doctoral studies. Marialuisa was my king Darius. I have copiously drawn from her scholarly insight and kindness ever since.

Oxford was where I first met Edward Jones. He has been my Vergil through the Inferno of turning research into writing. If my seminal reflections on Milton and liberty could first translate into a dissertation and subsequently take the present form, I largely owe it to his gracious guidance and rigorous scholarship.

Giuliana Iannaccaro has provided whatever was missing. Her fresh input has shed light on a number of weaknesses in the initial drafts of my research and it has been a constant reminder that my work was in literature, and not in theology only.

Although he was not directly involved in my doctoral dissertation, Alessandro Vescovi has himself left an indelible impression on this work. His stimulating conversation has opened new doors, new venues, and possibilities far greater than he will ever know.

Other scholars and teachers from whose insight and feedback I have variously drawn and benefitted include Alida Franca, Noam Reisner, Dennis Danielson, Regina Schwartz, David Urban, Gordon Campbell, Stephen Fallon, and John Rogers.

If a book is the quintessence of a man, then many more are those to whom I am indebted through their works. Of these works the following significantly inform this book in their respective areas: Charles Ryrie's books in theology and biblical exegesis constitute an underlying theological foundation for the present work; for Paul's thought, I primarily turn to the work of F. F. Bruce; to Garrett's *Baptist Theology: A Four-Century Study* and Lumpkin's *Baptist Confessions of Faith* for the Baptist movement; to Barbour's *The Quakers in Puritan England* and Endy's *William Penn and Early Quakerism* for early Quaker life and thought. Coffey's *John Goodwin and the Puritan Revolution: Religion and Intellectual Change in Seventeenth-Century England*, "Puritanism and Liberty Revisited: The Case for Toleration in the English Revolution" and Davis' *The Moral Theology of Roger Williams* shed light on John Goodwin and Roger Williams' thought; likewise Loewenstein's "Toleration and the Specter of Heresy in Milton's England" and Corns' "John Milton, Roger Williams and the Limits of Toleration" (in Achinstein and Sauer, eds., *Milton and Toleration*, respectively chs. 2, 3, and 4, pp. 23–44, 45–71, and 72–85) define Goodwin's and Williams' relation to Milton. With regard to Milton's connection to Free-Gratians John Saltmarsh and William Dell, Bennet's *Reviving Liberty* (especially ch. 4, "Milton's Antinomianism and the Separation Scene in *Paradise Lost*," 94–118) provides helpful insight. For biographical aspects relating to Milton's connections to these divines and thinkers, Campbell and Corns' *John Milton: Life, Work and Thought* is to date the most accurate and comprehensive reference work. I variously take the *Yale Prose* introductions to Milton's prose works into account in the pertinent notes. For Amyraut's background and theology I am indebted to Schaff's *Creeds of Christendom*, vol. 1, 483ff.; Muller's *Post-Reformation Reformed Dogmatics*, vol. 1, 79ff.; and Armstrong, *Calvinism and the Amyraut Heresy: Protestant Scholasticism and Humanism in Seventeenth-Century France*.

Many would still be left to acknowledge, but to list them all the length of this book would not suffice. I will have to limit myself to a scant, if notable, few. Special thanks to Adrian Bright for proofreading the text and providing both linguistic and theological feedback. Many thanks also to Brad Sewell at the Milton Quarterly library at Oklahoma State University, Richard Carhart at Northeastern State University, both faculty and staff at the Department of English of the Università degli Studi di Milano, and everyone at Wipf and Stock Publishers.

An affectionate thought goes to Adrian, Jenni, Natalie, Matthew, and Daniel.

My parents, Davide and Alida, my brother Federico, Daniele, and Samuele, and my sisters, Maria Noemi, Marta, Rebecca, and Rachele, have been a fortress and a lighthouse along my journey.

Last but foremost, the highest debt of gratitude is that which I owe my wife Sandra and my children, Miriam, Benjamin, and Ryan. It is a debt immense that cannot be repaid. And yet I find myself in the position of the person who, as Milton would have it, is at once indebted and discharged. My highest debt of gratitude is a debt of love.

Abbreviations

CM	Frank A. Patterson et al., eds., *The Works of John Milton*
CPW	Don M. Wolfe et al., eds., *The Complete Prose Works of John Milton*
De Doctrina	Milton's *De Doctrina Christiana*
PL	*Paradise Lost*
PR	*Paradise Regained*
SA	*Samson Agonistes*

Permissions

Unless otherwise indicated, Scripture quotations are from The Authorized (King James) Version. Rights in the Authorized Version in the United Kingdom are vested in the Crown. Reproduced by permission of the Crown's patentee, Cambridge University Press.

Other quotations are from The Holy Bible, English Standard Version® (ESV®), copyright © 2001 by Crossway, a publishing ministry of Good News Publishers. Used by permission. All rights reserved.

Chapter 1 of the present volume contains a revision of parts of the paper "The Dialectic of Poetical Aspiration and the Service of God in John Milton," presented at the Young Milton Conference, Worcester College, Oxford (UK), in March 2009.

Chapter 3 of the present volume contains a revision of parts of the article "More Challenges to Milton's Authorship of De Doctrina Christiana," ACME 63/1 (2010) 231–50, http://www.ledonline.it/acme/allegati/Acme-10-I-08-Falcone.pdf. Copyright © 2010 Filippo Falcone.

Chapter 5 of the present volume contains a revision of parts of the paper "'From strict laws to large grace': Gleanings from Milton's Theology of History in Book XII of Paradise Lost," presented at the Newton: Milton, Two Cultures? Conference, University of Sussex, Brighton (UK), in July 2009.

Chapter 5 of the present volume also contains reworded parts of the article "Il Bosco come Utopia: A Midsummer Night's Dream e Comus a Confronto." In Il Fascino Inquieto dell'Utopia: Percorsi Storici e Letterari in Onore di Marialuisa Bignami, edited by Lidia De Michelis, Giuliana Iannaccaro and Alessandro Vescovi, 73–82. Milan: Di/segni, 2014. Copyright © 2014 Filippo Falcone.

Introduction

The years 2011 and 2012 were years of revolution in Northern Africa and the Middle East. Rising in Tunisia, the revolutionary wave has spread through Egypt, Libya, Syria and other countries. The common denominator of all insurgencies has been the people's desire to shake off a long-endured yoke of tyranny which had resulted in a stagnant economy, poor life conditions and poorer public liberties. The word *democracy* has become the catalyst of all aspirations. However, where the overthrowing of the dictator has succeeded, reform has been slow to come to pass, opening the door to new, potentially worse, forms of tyranny.

The revolution John Milton envisioned during the years of England's Interregnum was itself one of liberty. Toward such end he worked tirelessly. He worked to see liberty projected in all areas of social and political life. Criticism has largely read this as the result of Milton's apprehension of individual liberty as only fully definable within the context of public liberties. The present work argues that true individual liberty is more appropriately defined in Milton as Christian liberty. Liberal laws and institutions might afford relative liberties, through negotiation of individual and collective freedom,[1] but never true liberty. The latter, in fact, resided within. The man who was inwardly a slave, a slave must remain, irrespective of outward liberties. The man who was inwardly free, free must remain, irrespective of outward restraint. Inasmuch as it entails the restoration of mind and conscience from sin to inward liberty, Christian liberty is found setting the terms for the creation of an inward microcosm of rest and authority. This microcosm is in turn the forge of liberal conclusions. In due course, Rationalism would retain these very conclusions, not so their Christian source.

1. See n. 5.

1

Theo Hobson has recently reasoned from Milton's liberal conclusions in an attempt to make them argue for the ultimate compatibility of Christian liberty and secular liberalism. Hobson's end is to underscore that no dichotomy exists between the two. The two did coexist and indeed may coexist, for Hobson, today. Even more so, in "the liberal Protestant tradition that he [Milton] helped to launch, secular liberalism and Christianity are allies rather than enemies. They need each other."[2]

The present work reasons from the causes in an attempt to show that in Milton Christian liberty *is* true freedom and the sole ground in which full outward liberties may be born and thrive. Hence I intend to show that in Milton liberal effects cannot be disjoined from their cause. In fact, liberty—both inward and outward—cannot be disjoined from Christianity.

In the final analysis, while Hobson reads Milton's work as an endeavor to free the gospel from the rule of law and of men, the present work deals with how the gospel frees man from the rule of the law and of men.

If the work of Milton's prose, his left hand, is best read as his attempt at actualizing liberty in the domestic, ecclesiological and political realms, failure to see freedom reflected in his temporal community would alert the poet to the need for man to individually appropriate it. In the conclusion to his extensive study of Christian liberty, Arthur Barker first pointed to a similar movement:

> As he had feared, his hopes had "passed through the fire only to perish in the smoke"; but that tempering experience bore its fruit in his great poems. In them the ideal of Christian liberty was translated, by a process already under way in the prose, into a contemplation of the freedom to be obtained through obedience to eternal law, not in a temporal community which should make possible the achievement of something like the happiness enjoyed by Adam in his natural perfection and promised the saints in Christ's Kingdom, but in "a Paradise within thee happier far" (*PL* 12.587).[3]

Barker here identifies a substantial shift from an outward to an inward-based dimension of Christian liberty in the passage from the prose to

---

2. Hobson, *Milton's Vision*, ix.

3. Barker, *Milton and the Puritan Dilemma*, 333.

Paradise Lost. If in the latter Christian liberty unfolds as an inward reality, Barker contends with respect to the former that

> the end and good of a people free by nature could not be achieved otherwise than through the real and substantial liberty fully to be enjoyed in a commonwealth modelled on that only just and rightful kingdom . . . [4]

Moving from such premises with respect to the prose, subsequent criticism has largely failed to picture true liberty as a fully defined inward reality, hence also falling short of its poetical representation in *Paradise Lost.* The general attitude is well represented in Joan Bennett's *Reviving Liberty.* For Bennett, Milton "shares with Marxism and other calls to continual social reform a commitment to see the private good as definable only in the public, or community's good—to do as Milton, on the eve of his political imprisonment in 1659, exhorted the readers of his last attempt to avert the monarchy's restoration—'to place every one his privat welfare and happiness in the public peace, libertie and safetie' (*Ready and Easy Way, CPW* 7:443)."[5]

---

4. Ibid., 332.

5. Bennett, *Reviving Liberty*, 2. Inscribed in this same rationale, ever since Roland Bainton's *The Travail of Religious Liberty* (1958) scholarship has largely equated liberty in Milton with domestic and public liberties. A recent example of this is *Milton and Toleration* (2007), a collection of sixteen essays edited by Achinstein and Sauer aiming to contextualize Milton's idea of toleration. Following in the same strain, eds. Parry and Raymond's *Milton and the Terms of Liberty* (2002) features twelve essays, six of which relate to political facets of liberty, and the remaining six to elements of Milton's persona, life, work, language and theology which are only relevant to the discussion on inward liberty in terms of contiguity. In turn addressing political liberties, eds. Armitage, Himy and Skinner's *Milton and Republicanism* (1995) encompasses thirteen essays on Milton's political thought and the neo-classical approach to the role of law and government with respect to freedom. This work largely hinges on Skinner's lesson in liberty. In *Liberty Before Liberalism* (1998), Skinner examines the dialectic between individual and collective freedom in the political writings of the *Interregnum*, not least Milton's prose: if individual freedom amounts to the unrestrained expression of one's will, external restraint is indispensable where contrasting wills are expressed, namely within the context of a society. Hence, for the neo-roman theory of free states, laws, as opposed to monarchs, are called to uniformly limit individual freedom in order to enhance the shared ground of individual and collective liberties. The philosophical work of Isaiah Berlin, *Two Concepts of Liberty* (in *Four Essays on Liberty*, 1958), variously underlies Skinner's depiction of liberty in the seventeenth century and supplies a helpful synthetic categorization. Berlin divides liberty into the two categories of negative and positive liberty. The former is that kind of freedom which the individual experiences insofar as he is not "prevented by other persons from doing what [he wants]"

In depicting the prose as purposing the integration of external freedom and Christian liberty in a free commonwealth shaped after the principles of God's kingdom, scholarship has maintained the interdependence of outward and inward liberty in the pursuit of individual freedom. Nevertheless, in his *Defensio Secunda* Milton claims that the keystone to his entire engagement with public liberties is to be traced to "true and substantial liberty, which must be sought, not without, but within."[6] The identification of true and substantial liberty as an inward principle in turn implicitly points to the moral and spiritual dimension of liberty which underlies action, namely that which Northrop Frye identifies as the "condition in which genuine action is possible."[7] If so, inward liberty is not seen as dependent on outward liberties. The latter are rather seen as resulting from the former.

Ever since *Of Reformation* Milton identifies inward liberty as Christian liberty, but it is only in *De Doctrina Christiana* that a full definition transpires. In the Latin treatise Milton understands liberty as that reality whereby

CHRIST OUR LIBERATOR FREES US FROM THE SLAVERY OF SIN AND THUS FROM THE RULE OF THE LAW AND OF

(Berlin, *Four Essays on Liberty*, 56–57). In other words, negative liberty is absence of external coercion in the expression of one's will. External coercion is exerted, in Berlin's words, "by other persons." Once again, individual liberty can only be prevented by external restraint, thus amounting to that space of opportunity which is left in between the individual and the outward source of limitation. In his philosophical approach, Berlin need not distinguish between 'persons' and 'laws,' since the latter are but the expression of the former's will. This is true of both human and divine law. This is where the second concept of liberty comes in. Positive liberty amounts, in Skinner's words, to "self-realization" (Skinner, *Liberty Before Liberalism*, 114). Or, to put it in plain terms, if negative liberty is tantamount to being able to do what one wants to do, positive liberty is the freedom to act in a moral way, that is to say, to act in accordance with a moral law. A notion of quality is therefore attached to one of neutral possibility. Hence Skinner: "Rather than connecting liberty with opportunities for action—as in the neo-roman as well as in the liberal analysis—the 'positive' view connects liberty with the performance of actions of a determinate type." Skinner goes on to argue that "whether the understanding of liberty as . . . an 'exercise' and not merely an 'opportunity' concept can be vindicated is a separate question, and one with which I am not concerned" (Skinner, *Liberty Before Liberalism*, 114). In that they explore the results of Milton's public appropriation of liberty, the above works shed light on the extent and practical limitations of Milton's idea of liberty. The present work concerns itself with that same question of positive liberty which the above works variously discard.

6. *CPW* 4.624.

7. Frye, *Return of Eden*, 94.

MEN, AS IF WE WERE EMANCIPATED SLAVES. HE DOES THIS SO THAT, BEING MADE SONS INSTEAD OF SERVANTS AND GROWN MEN INSTEAD OF BOYS, WE MAY SERVE GOD IN CHARITY THROUGH THE GUIDANCE OF THE SPIRIT OF TRUTH.[8]

In light of this definition the present work resolves to construe Milton's libertarian revolution as inherently inward. To this end, also, it seeks to identify two conflicting principles around which Milton's entire production revolves: the way of self, or the way of inner slavery hinging on law-empowered self-complacency and self-assertion, and the way of grace, or the way of the cross resulting in freedom and love. Whereas the prose expands on the contingency of this dialectic, *Paradise Lost* is given to project it in its characters only to hand the human characters over to true freedom as the prototypes of all that would choose to become children of liberty.

In the final analysis, in envisioning Christian liberty as sole true liberty, this study aims to reassess the concept in Milton's work leading up to *Paradise Lost* only to confront its explicit theological synthesis and poetical translation in the poem.

Chapter 1 identifies the substantial Pauline underpinnings of Milton's formulation of Christian liberty against the backdrop of Reformed thought and overtones of Independent, General Baptist and Quaker belief. The chapter largely deals with the ways in which the inward microcosm of Christian liberty is projected outwardly in a constant dialectic of love and liberty. This same dialectic turns in the prose into a process of negotiation which must run through the institutional channels, calling for laws that reflect the terms of Christian liberty.

Chapter 2 expands on Milton's theology of Christian liberty in the poem. Essential continuity is found in Milton's apprehension of the concept from *Of Reformation* to *Paradise Lost*. Its movement, as opposed to its substance, is shown to differ. Even so, a linear, if nuanced, progress from rationalism to spiritualism variously surfaces which is best defined within the context of Amyraldism and Quaker as well as Independent and General Baptist thought.

Chapter 3 focuses on the poet and on light as the poetical transposition of Christian liberty. Like Satan, the poet wanders in inward darkness. Unlike Satan, he ultimately turns to the celestial light. Active

8. *CPW* 6.537. See Egan, *Inward Teacher*, 1.

in creation, the light of heaven is life which descends from heaven to make a new creation and thus lay the foundation for the poetical one. The light is identified with the Son, whose grace frees and gives the poet a knowledge of God that overcomes the bounds of nature. Falling short of poetical expectations, the ability to tell of God's will and nature must be seen as unfolding in spiritual terms. Overtones of Quakerism appear here to be intertwined with Johannine symbolism only to magnify certain traits of Milton's Pauline vision.

Against the backdrop of the tragic denial of inward liberty in the ultimate choice of self on the part of Satan—chapter 4—it is given to the human characters in the poem to illustrate and embody the terms of inward liberty in the progressive unfolding of an inaugurated eschatology—chapter 5.

If in outlining the intent of the book I have already pointed to critical stances and trajectories, I shall now turn more specifically to the critical context against whose backdrop this work stands and with which it is bound to come to terms.

Paramount though the attention toward liberty in Milton has been, I have noted how criticism has largely neglected its defining unfolding as an inward reality. Much of the emphasis on the latter, in fact, dates back to the Thirties and early Forties. The intuition that Christian liberty was foundational to Milton's very apprehension of public liberties is to be ascribed to A. S. P. Woodhouse. In *Puritanism and Liberty: Being the Army Debates* (1638) Woodhouse refers to Christian liberty as "the very corner-stone of his [Milton's] theory of toleration."[9]

It was Arthur Barker, however, who defined and extensively read the concept in the prose. For Barker Milton's idea of Christian liberty largely hinged on Calvin's three tenets of liberty: 1. "the law of works is abrogated by the gospel of faith, and Christians are freed from the impositions of the Mosaic Law, though the moral part of the Law is still in force . . ." 2. "Depraved mankind is manifestly incapable of fulfilling the law of righteousness; but the elect, freed from the necessity by Christ's vicarious suffering, 'cheerfully and alertly' follow God's guidance in the Law as the spontaneous result of grace." 3. "All things concerning which there is no gospel prohibition are sanctified to the Christian use."[10]

---

9. Woodhouse, *Puritanism and Liberty*, 65. See also Woodhouse, "Milton, Puritanism and Liberty," 395–404, 483–513.

10. Woodhouse, *Puritanism and Liberty*, 101.

For all the foundational significance of Calvin's tri-fold reading of Pauline liberty in Milton, arguments of continuity and discontinuity variously contributed to a redefinition of its boundaries. Woodhouse traces the general bearing of the concept in Milton's prose back as early as 1642.[11] For his part, Sewell argues for a germinal stage of Milton's elaboration of the doctrine up to 1659, when it fully develops along heterodox lines in an ultimate revision of Picard's manuscript of *De Doctrina Christiana*.[12] Barker provides the middle ground by envisioning an earlier date (some time between 1643 and 1645) for Milton's heterodox commitment.

The crux of the matter is the identification of Milton's shift to the understanding of the moral law as abrogated in its Mosaic formulation. While the antiprelatical tracts insist that the moral portion of the law is still in force after Christ, *De Doctrina* makes an extensive case for the abrogation of the law in its entirety, only to then maintain the subsistence of the essence of the law, or the law of love, as an eternal law. Barker detects a progressive shift to the latter view in the 1644 additions to *The Doctrine and Discipline of Divorce* and in *Tetrachordon* (1645). Diverting Barker's trajectory, Lowell W. Coolidge, in his introduction to the divorce pamphlets in the *Yale Prose* edition, argues that "much of the new matter [in the 1644 additions] is brought to reinforce the contention that Christ did not abrogate the Mosaic law of divorce."[13] Rather, for Coolidge, the evolution of Milton's argument is to be traced to his subordination of Christ's ruling to the natural law.[14]

The present work will contend that, when seen in light of *De Doctrina*'s definition above, discontinuity in the definition of the moral law in the antiprelatical tracts, the divorce tracts and the Latin treatise appears less than substantial—ever grounded in liberty, love is indeed the essence and the end of God's eternal moral law. Nevertheless, the work of divinity seems to make it more than formal by turning the abrogation of the law into a cause of Christian liberty. In so doing, the treatise's extensive discussion contradicts the premise of its initial formulation. While in light of this and other idiosyncrasies the debate on the authorship of the Latin treatise is not without merit, I have chosen

11. Ibid., 66.
12. Sewell, *Study of Milton's Christian Doctrine*, 51–53.
13. *CPW* 2.150. "Introduction to the Divorce Tracts."
14. *CPW* 2.150–58. "Introduction to the Divorce Tracts."

to analyze divergences in terms of continuity and discontinuity with the Miltonic *corpus*.

In regarding freedom by nature and spiritual freedom as ultimately integrated as "the right only of those who will act in accordance with that perfect law which is being cleared in their hearts by the Spirit,"[15] Barker is once again setting the stage for subsequent criticism. For Michael Schoenfeldt, "Milton . . . wishes to gear the achievement of liberty to the performance of obedience."[16] Along the same lines, Joan Bennett resorts to the definition "humanist antinomianism" to "characterize John Goodwin and John Milton and to indicate that these thinkers descend in the Christian humanist line that reaches from Saint Thomas Aquinas through Richard Hooker into the seventeenth century where, with these thinkers, the traditional beliefs were radicalized."[17] All such contentions work to the effect of making Christian liberty out to be an effect rather than a cause of compliance with divine eternal law. Nonetheless, if freedom by nature and spiritual freedom must be understood as ultimately impaired by sin, their assimilation in Milton can only be regarded as effected under the banner of grace, in the strain of the Reformed tradition. Accordingly, man is not free because he obeys, but he obeys because he is free.

Though largely subscribing to mainstream stances and only marginally turning to the poetical representation of liberty in *Paradise Lost*, the following contributions to the bibliography of liberty in Milton have their place here:

James Egan's *The Inward Teacher: Milton's Rhetoric of Christian Liberty* (1980) appears to revive the discussion on the foundational significance of inward liberty in the prose. Even so, the vast majority of the book expands on rhetoric without engaging liberty.

In *Milton and the Pauline Tradition: A Study of Theme and Symbolism* (1982), Timothy J. O'Keeffe helps shed light on Milton's significant adherence to Paul and his ties to the Augustinian, Thomist and Reformed traditions. In tracing patterns of Pauline thought in Milton, however, this work only partially commits Milton's libertarian ideas to the unifying foundation of Christian liberty. Also, the author mistakenly views faith in Milton in Thomist terms, as obedience, that is, resulting

---

15. Barker, *Milton and the Puritan Dilemma*, 118.

16. Schoenfeldt, "Obedience and Autonomy in *Paradise Lost*," 366.

17. Bennett, *Reviving Liberty*, 99.

from love. Scholastic and Reformed theology end up being juxtaposed in a dialectic which finds little synthesis. Finally, the book's reading of Paul in *Paradise Lost* is scarcely a reading of Christian liberty therein.

As we enter the domain of theological studies, we are immediately confronted with a number of works on the fall and Milton's divinity which are yet little more than contiguous to the theme of Christian liberty. Will Poole's *Milton and the Idea of the Fall* (2005) is undoubtedly the most relevant recent accomplishment in this respect and provides helpful references.

A direct theological reading of liberty in *Paradise Lost* is, on the other hand, found in Benjamin Myers' *Milton's Theology of Freedom* (2006). Like O'Keeffe, Myers defines Milton's idea of liberty against the backdrop of traditional theological categories. He aptly traces the roots of the theological debate on freedom back to Augustine and patristic theology, only to lead us through Aquinas and Scholasticism and ultimately address the Reformed and post-Reformed tradition. He then attempts to read liberty in Milton in light of his overview. For all the lucidity of his analysis, Myers fails to see Milton's personal theology past the backdrop of *De Doctrina Christiana*'s anti-trinitarian and Episcopian outlook and the fixed categories of post-Reformed Scholasticism. In this respect, the relation between Scholastic tenets of reason and will and Reformed soteriological apprehensions of faith and grace remains in part unsorted. Myers regards Milton's true liberty as freedom to choose amongst alternatives, with prevenient grace as the pivotal factor. The present work reverses this perspective to view the freedom of reason and will to choose among alternatives as a consequence of true liberty. As regards Milton's soteriology, Myers is bound to leave postlasparian Adam and Eve to struggle in the mire of dynamic achievements. In so doing, he overlooks overtones of Independent, Quaker and General Baptist theology that are largely looming in the years prior to and concomitant with *Paradise Lost* and which work to the effect of magnifying certain traits of Milton's Johannine and Pauline theology. In the final analysis, Myers does not in fact trace Milton's theology of freedom back to the Pauline conception of Christian liberty.

In attempting to mend theological misapprehensions, critical imbalances and omissions, the present work accords the poem conclusive emphasis. As it graphically outlines the reality which the prose builds upon, *Paradise Lost* teaches the lesson that the true Eden is within.

1

Christian Liberty towards *Paradise Lost*

Pauline Christian Liberty

In *Defensio Secunda* Milton claims that the keystone to his entire engagement with public liberties is to be traced to "true and substantial liberty, which must be sought, not without, but within."[1] The identification of true and substantial liberty as an inward principle in turn implicitly points to the moral and spiritual dimension of liberty which underlies action. Ever since *Of Reformation* (1641) such a dimension is consistently identified by Milton as Christian liberty, but it is only in *De Doctrina Christiana* (1658?) that a full theological definition surfaces:

> CHRISTIAN LIBERTY means that CHRIST OUR LIBERATOR
> FREES US FROM THE SLAVERY OF SIN AND THUS FROM
> THE RULE OF THE LAW AND OF MEN, AS IF WE WERE
> EMANCIPATED SLAVES. HE DOES THIS SO THAT, BEING
> MADE SONS INSTEAD OF SERVANTS AND GROWN MEN
> INSTEAD OF BOYS, WE MAY SERVE GOD IN CHARITY
> THROUGH THE GUIDANCE OF THE SPIRIT OF TRUTH.[2]

The Pauline underpinnings in the passage cannot be overstated. In fact, these words distinctly rephrase the very contents of Galatians 4:1–7; 5:1–6. Christian liberty is the principle of inward moral and spiritual freedom produced by the terms of that which Paul of Tarsus labels "the gospel of God." In F. F. Bruce's words, for Paul the

1. *CPW* 4.624.
2. *CPW* 6.537.

law might declare the will of God, but could not impart the power to do it or break the thralldom of sin. It was therefore possible to be under law, recognizing its divine majesty and authority, and under the control of sin at the same time. But the same act of grace that broke the chains of sin simultaneously freed those who were under the constraint of law. A dangerous doctrine, many must have thought; but Paul makes his meaning plain: the grace of God liberates those who are bound by sin, but law can never do so: paradoxically, law may serve to bind the chains of sin more securely on the sinner.[3]

A single act of grace, the cross signified the substitutionary provision of righteousness for man, with the transfer of the believer from a condition of slavery to self-seeking compulsion to the freedom of love-informed adult sonship. He who believes is so identified with Christ that the latter's death and resurrection become the former's death and resurrection to new life. As he is dead in Christ, he is free from the domain and power of sin and thus from the constraining capacity of the law. The believer, that is, is free from his former self to the extent that he no longer lives, but Christ lives in him. A shift is thus marked from the rule of law to the rule of grace.

In Romans 8:1–4, Paul echoes the content of the prophetic utterances of Jeremiah 31:31–34 and Ezekiel 11:19; 36:26–7.[4] No essential difference is found here between the law which Israel failed to observe

---

3. Bruce, *Paul*, 330.

4. Jer 31:31–34: "Behold, the days come, saith the LORD, that I will make a new covenant with the house of Israel, and with the house of Judah: Not according to the covenant that I made with their fathers in the day *that* I took them by the hand to bring them out of the land of Egypt; which my covenant they brake, although I was an husband unto them, saith the LORD: But this *shall be* the covenant that I will make with the house of Israel; After those days, saith the LORD, I will put my law in their inward parts, and write it in their hearts; and will be their God, and they shall be my people. And they shall teach no more every man his neighbour, and every man his brother, saying, Know the LORD: for they shall all know me, from the least of them unto the greatest of them, saith the LORD: for I will forgive their iniquity, and I will remember their sin no more." Ezek 11:19–20; 36:26–27: "And I will give them one heart, and I will put a new spirit within you; and I will take the stony heart out of their flesh, and will give them an heart of flesh: That they may walk in my statutes, and keep mine ordinances, and do them: and they shall be my people, and I will be their God'. 'A new heart also will I give you, and a new spirit will I put within you: and I will take away the stony heart out of your flesh, and I will give you an heart of flesh. And I will put my spirit within you, and cause you to walk in my statutes, and ye shall keep my judgments, and do *them*."

and the law which God resolves to write upon his people's hearts. "The difference lies between their once knowing the law as an external code and their knowing it henceforth as an inward principle." "The will of God had not changed; but whereas formerly it was recorded on tablets of stone it was now engraved on human hearts, an inward impulsion . . . [carrying out] what external compulsion could not." Accordingly, "Doing the will of God . . . [was] not a matter of conformity to outward rules but of giving expression to inward love, such as the Spirit begets."[5]

This new reality is of grace, as it is solely for the inward liberty produced by grace to afford the ground for the life of the Spirit to fulfill the law of love. Unlike the old rule, the law of love is not enforced by the dynamics of fear and coercion but it responds to the prompting of inner love and freedom. The law of love is itself the sum of the law or the law of Christ (Gal 6:2), as both "the law Christ exemplified" and "the law which Christ laid down" in terms of love for God and one's neighbor (Matt 22:40).[6]

The commandments Paul lays down in his epistles cannot themselves be seen as a new code, but as a reflection and expression of the law of love with respect to the ramifications of a diversified reality. It is no wonder, then, if the written Pauline imperatives invariably concern the Christian's relation to God and his neighbor. And if a written blueprint remains as an objective earnest of the inner law of the Spirit of life in Christ Jesus, the person who is led by the Spirit is no longer under a legal code. A son by unconditional grace, the Spirit-led believer is no longer a child who needs rules and regulations, but an adult who is free to discern and choose God's eternal law.

Grace is, in Bruce's words, "the source and principle of their liberation [that of men and women] from all kinds of inward and spiritual bondage, including the bondage of legalism and moral anarchy."[7] Sole possible response to such new source and principle, faith cannot be anything other than renouncing the self to embrace this grace and live it out.

5. Bruce, *Paul*, 199–200.

6. Ibid., 201

7. Ibid., 18.

Freedom from the Slavery of Sin and thus from the Rule of the Law

When seen against its biblical background, the extended quotation of *De Doctrina* above marks a singular internal contradiction with the Latin treatise's extensive argument for the abrogation of the law as a theological necessity with respect to Christian liberty. "thus," as in "Christ our liberator frees us from the law of slavery and *thus* from the rule of the law," has a final function, which turns what follows into a consequence of what precedes. In other words, liberation from the rule of the law does not come by doing away with the law, as the treatise, on the contrary, extensively argues, but through redemption from the slavery of sin. Where the old self is dead in Christ, the rule of the law is no more, because it is deprived of the principle upon which it operates. Much to this effect, emancipation from the slavery of sin does not result in freedom from the moral demands of the law, but from the *rule* of the law. Likewise, in *Paradise Lost* the passage from the covenant of works to the covenant of grace is not a passage from law to antinomianism, but from the "*imposition* of strict laws to free / Acceptance of large grace" (12.304–5). It is evident that the poem and the words of the quotation envision the effects, specifically the constraint, of the law, as opposed to the moral law itself, as superseded in Christ.[8]

---

8. By making liberty dependent upon the termination of the law, *De Doctrina* fails to fully understand the position which finds in Calvin its fountain-head. So Polanus: "the fact that one is not under the law does not mean that one does not owe obedience to the law, but that one is free from the curse and constraint of the law and from its provocation to sin" (*Syntagma* 6.10.351. Trans. Kelley, *CPW* 6.535). Here the law metonymically stands for what we may call the domain of the law, from which the gospel frees the believer. *De Doctrina*'s reply to a similar argument is revealing: "But if this is so, what do believers gain from the gospel? For believers, even under the law, were exempt from its curse and its provocation to sin. Moreover what, I ask you, can it mean to be free from the constraint of the law, if not to be entirely exempt from the law, as I maintain we are? For so long as the law exists, it constrains, because it is a law of slavery" (*CPW* 6.535). From these words, one may infer that believers do not gain from the gospel exemption from the law's curse and provocation to sin, namely the very capacities the author has been arguing to be sources of slavery, but the extinction of the written code. Thus the treatise gets caught in a circular inconsistency as it maintains that freedom from the constraint of the law only comes by getting rid of the law altogether. Also, if that same law is what produced curse and provocation to sin, how could believers under the law be exempt from these principles, given the law was there to enforce them? It goes without saying that the constraining power of the law, curse and provocation to sin all vanish when the believer is clothed in Christ's righteousness and passes from the necessity to the desire and possibility to observe the law. What do

In light of this, a clarification is in order: Milton never intends the moral law as the letter of the Mosaic formulations. Consistently through-out his work, he refers to the moral law as perpetual and universal truth running through the Mosaic code yet never exhausted in its letter. In fact, God's eternal law is also reflected in nature and in the individual conscience, and finds in love its paramount fulfillment.

Both Barker and Coolidge envision a radical development of Milton's thought in the divorce tracts with respect to the abrogation of the law, but their trajectories prove contrary. While for Coolidge the Mosaic law was portrayed as superseded by the gospel in *The Reason of Church-government* only to be reaffirmed and subordinated to the natural law in the divorce tracts, Barker saw in the additions to the first edition of *The Doctrine and Discipline of Divorce*[9] the germs of that col-lapse of the law into love that would be more explicitly formulated in *Tetrachordon* and later in *De Doctrina*.[10]

The critical contrast largely accounts for substantial continuity in Milton. In fact, both critics fail to see Milton's progressive hermeneutical stances as the linear unfolding of his apprehension of the law as char-ity resulting from Christian liberty. In *Tetrachordon* Milton argues that through his gospel God "redeemed us to a state above prescriptions by dissolving *the whole law* into charity."[11] Charity in turn is to be measured and defined "by the rules of nature and eternall righteousness which no writt'n law extinguishes and the Gospel least of all."[12] The gospel of

believers gain from the gospel? They gain everything, for it is not through the removal of the law that inward liberty is achieved, but through the removal of sin. Where there is no sin, the law has no jurisdiction. Where there is no sin, the law loses its prerogative to stir sin's enslaving affections. The gain is in clarity and freedom, along with the fulfill-ment of the very core of the law through works of faith.

9. Four editions of *The Doctrine and Discipline of Divorce* appeared during Milton's lifetime. The second edition presented conspicuous, albeit of little consequence, ad-ditions to the original, whereas the third and fourth—ones Milton seems not to have overseen—did not vary from the second as to content.

10. After going to great length to emphasize the unity and abrogation of the law in its entirety, *De Doctrina* specifies that "in reality the law, that is the substance of the law, is not broken by this abolition. On the contrary its purpose is attained in that love of God and of our neighbour which is born of faith, through the spirit" (*CPW* 6.531). Bewilderment is perceptible in Maurice Kelley's respective note as he has to consent, if parenthetically, that of this "substance of the law" "indeed the Moral Law [which *De Doctrina* regards as abrogated] was itself a formulation" (endnote 15).

11. *CM* 4.76.

12. *CM* 4.134.

Christian liberty is rather that new rule which enhances love as sole true representation of the laws of nature and eternal righteousness in man:

> For what can be more opposite and disparaging to the cov'nant of love, of freedom, & of our manhood in grace, then to bee made the yoaking pedagogue of new severities, the scribe of syllables and rigid letters . . . If the law of Christ shall be writt'n in our hearts, as was promis'd to the Gospel, Jer. 31, how can this in the vulgar and superficial sense be a law of Christ, so farre from being writt'n in our hearts, that it injures and dissallowes not onely the free dictates of nature and morall law, but of charity also and religion in our hearts. Our Saviours doctrine is, that the end, and the fulfilling of every command is charity . . .[13]

Three tenets here portray Christian liberty and, in so doing, shed light on the nature of true law:

1. The Christian is under a new covenant of grace which is characterized by love, freedom and adulthood.

2. The law of Christ differs from a prescriptive code insofar as it is an inward law. While under the principle of legal righteousness prescriptions prove to have no part in man, but are observed out of fear and necessity, the law of Christ is a constitutive part of the regenerate and is that which is observed out of love and desire.

3. The law of Christ is in tune with and indeed matches the "free dictates of nature, the moral part of the Mosaic law, charity and religion in our heart [conscience]." All such expressions of the divine nature find an ultimate fulfillment in charity so that the inward law of Christ may be said to coincide with *the law of love.*

   Whereas Barker correctly identifies the close match between these statements and *De Doctrina*, he fails to acknowledge that much the same understanding underlies the antiprelatical tracts. So *The Reason of Church-government*:

> For the imperfect and obscure institution of the Law, which the Apostles themselves doubt not oft-times to vilifie, cannot give rules to the compleat and glorious ministration of the Gospell,

13. *CM* 4.134–35.

which looks on the Law, as on a childe, not as on a tutor . . . How then the ripe age of the Gospell should be put to schoole againe, and learn to governe her selfe from the infancy of the Law . . . will be a hard undertaking to evince . . . [The law is] morall, which containes in it the observation of whatsoever is substantially, and perpetually true and good, either in religion, or course of life. That which is thus morall, besides what we fetch from those unwritten lawes and Ideas which nature hath ingraven in us, the Gospell, as stands with her dignity most, lectures to us from her own authentic hand-writing, and command, not copies out from the borrow'd manuscript of a subservient scrowl.[14]

The gospel and the law are here meaningfully contrasted. The law is to the gospel what a child is to the adult. As the child cannot teach the adult anything, neither can the law govern the economy of the gospel. The child needs the constriction of rules, but the adult can be his own chooser. So the gospel need not go back to the school of the law, but is itself the teacher and interpreter of the law. While the law could not produce conformity to the moral law, but only served to bind the chains of lawlessness more securely on man, the gospel, having freed man from sin and thus from the deleterious prerogatives of the law, teaches man the moral law apart from the logic of outward prescriptions and works of law. It does so by directly inscribing it into the heart as an inward autograph. The incumbent necessity to fulfill the moral law, epitomized by the external scroll, is infinitely inferior to the large desire produced by the freedom and love of the gospel.

But what is then the moral law? The moral law is defined by all that is substantially and perpetually true and good, including that which matches the purest dictates of nature graven in us. As such, the moral law cannot be supplanted or superseded, but it is preserved under the gospel. In fact, it is only apprehended and fulfilled under the gospel through love. From the start, then, law is seen as abrogated as a means to righteousness, but perpetual in all those facets which reflect the eternal character of God.

While the moral law is found in essence in God's written commands and nature, its teaching, as noted, is not their sole prerogative. Although insufficient and precarious, due to the impairment produced by sin, conscience and reason themselves testify to it. To this very effect,

14. *CPW* 1.762–64.

God's moral law can be said to amount to all that is "just and good to every wise and sober understanding."[15] Regina Schwartz views the claim as possessing a radical quality,[16] yet its unexceptionable character is accounted for by its inscription in Paul's Epistle to the Romans:

> For when the Gentiles, which have not the law, do by nature the things contained in the law, these, having not the law, are a law unto themselves: which shew the work of the law written in their hearts, their conscience also bearing witness, and *their* thoughts the mean while accusing or else excusing one another.[17]

Albeit his argument is devised in such a way as to demonstrate that both Gentiles and Jews are justly liable to God's condemnation, Paul makes clear that in a relative sense the human being without the law bears in himself the witness of God's nature.[18] Eternal and perpetual, the moral law is thus also universal. That is, it applies and speaks to all people and ages through nature and reason "ingraven in us."

One would not have to look far for philosophical and theological ground shaping much the same contention. In commenting on the light that "enlighteneth every man that cometh into the world" (John 1:9), Calvin had argued that "men have this peculiar excellence which raises them above other animals, that they are endued with reason and intelligence, and that they carry the distinction between right and wrong engraven on their conscience. There is no man, therefore, whom some perception of the eternal *light* doesn't reach."[19] This understanding was shared by the Cambridge Platonists. In Cambridge Milton had been exposed to the noetic concept of eternal moral truths instilled in the minds of all men as the innate moral blueprint of heaven.[20] Though not referring to a natural faculty, the Quaker doctrine of the inner light would itself work to much the same effect by extending to all individuals the benefit of that light of heaven which only expresses itself in terms of the

---

15. *CPW* 2.297–98, *The Doctrine and Discipline of Divorce.*

16. Schwartz, "Milton on the Bible," 40.

17. Rom 1:14.

18. In commenting on the verses above, Calvin offers as examples of such match man's observance of religious rites, laws against adultery, theft, and murder, and the commendation of good faith in business affairs.

19. Calvin, *Commentaries: John,* 17.2.38. All references from Calvin's *Commentaries* refer to the 2003 Baker publication. Cf. *CPW* 6.132.

20. Cf. Willey, *The Seventeenth Century Background,* 78.

moral law. In Barclay's words, echoing John Smith and the Cambridge Platonists (while also yielding parallels with the latitudinarian light of nature), "this divine revelation and inward illumination is that which is evident and clear of itself, forcing, by its own evidence and clearness, the well-disposed understanding to assent, irresistibly moving the same thereunto, even as the common principles of natural truths do move and incline the mind to a natural assent; as, that the whole is greater than its part; that two contradictories can neither be both true, nor both false."[21]

The distillation of the essence of the law from its written formulations comes therefore as little surprise as it occurs "not otherwise then to the law of nature and of equity imprinted in us seems correspondent."[22] A problem yet remains which is implicitly addressed in Barclay's words and which calls for the inner light to be more than natural: sin impairs understanding and, more than that, it defiles natural man's ability to fulfill that which he knows to be just and right. On 1 August 1643, Milton anonymously published *The Doctrine and Discipline of Divorce: Restor'd to the Good of Both Sexes, From the Bondage of Canon Law, and other mistakes, to Christian freedom, guided by the Rule of Charity, Wherein also many places of Scripture, have recover'd their long-lost meaning: Seasonable to be now thought on in the Reformation intended.*[23] Significantly, the extended title suggests that the two poles of Milton's discussion are the bondage of the canon law and Christian freedom. Divorce can either be regulated by one or the other. To follow the dictates of the canon law is to be under bondage, for, as an external code, the canon law relentlessly exacts its formal demands irrespective of their conformity to love. In so doing, it reveals its human origin. To this effect, any kind of law will not do. Beza's opinion "that a politick law . . . may regulate sin" does nothing but replicate the faults of the canon law, as "the essence of it [sin] cannot consist with rule; and if the law fall to regulate sin, and not to take it utterly away, it necessarily confirms and establishes sin."[24]

---

21. Endy, *William Penn*, 151–52.

22. *CPW* 2.297, *The Doctrine and Discipline of Divorce*.

23. *The Doctrine and Discipline of Divorce* was followed by *The Judgement of Martin Bucer* (1644), *Tetrachordon: Expositions upon The foure chief Places in Scripture which treat of Mariage, or nullities in Mariage* (1645) and *Colasterion: A Reply to a Nameless Answer against The Doctrine and Discipline of Divorce* (1645).

24. *CPW* 2.321.

The heavenly alternative is not a Christian code, but Christian freedom. In pronouncing man free from sin and thus from the demands of any form of external prescription, the latter, as we have noted, binds him to love as the new driving force and the element which correctly interprets the moral law and defines the extent of freedom. Hence when it comes to confront the biblical teaching on marriage and divorce, a whole new hermeneutic is in place. The ruling text can no longer be traced among prescriptive passages, but among ones indicating charitable finality. This text is identified by Milton in Genesis 2:18, 24:

> And the LORD God said, It is not good that man should be alone; I will make him an help meet for him . . . Therefore shall a man leave his father and his mother, and shall cleave unto his wife: and they shall be one flesh.

Fit society is the *natural* and *charitable* end of the divine institution of marriage. Whereas all Scriptural prescriptions concerning marriage must ultimately concur to this end, the Bible proves most abused when "resting in the mere element of the Text," that is, when not "consulting with charitie, the interpreter and guide of our faith."[25] To this effect, Jesus' apparently restrictive expansion on the Mosaic law of divorce[26] must be so interpreted as "to preserve those his fundamental and superior laws of nature and charitie."[27] Charitie is described by the result it produces, that is, mercy, peace and liberty.[28] Nature, on the other hand, is seen in "that which is good and acceptable and friendly," as opposed to "what is

---

25. *CPW* 2.236.

26. Deut 24:1, Matt 5:32; 19:9 are the scriptural texts around which Milton's arguments for divorce revolve. The Mosaic ruling provided the blueprint for Jesus' teaching in the words, "When a man hath taken a wife, and married her, and it come to pass that she find no favour in his eyes, because he hath found some uncleanness in her: then let him write her a bill of divorcement, and give it in her hand, and send her out of his house." In the Gospel narrative, however, Jesus appears to overrule Moses along restrictive lines, "But I say unto you, That whosoever shall put away his wife, saving for the cause of fornication, causeth her to commit adultery: and whosoever shall marry her that is divorced committeth adultery." And challenged with the Mosaic background by the Pharisees after stating the divine sanction on the marital union, Jesus reiterates, "And I say unto you, Whosoever shall put away his wife, except it be for fornication, and shall marry another, committeth adultery: and whoso marrieth her which is put away doth commit adultery."

27. *CPW* 2.325.

28. *CPW* 2.229.

disagreeable, displeasing and unlike."[29] Milton need not refer to nature
alongside love in his title, for the former is but encompassed in the ministry of love. All such interpretive guidelines find a more manifest match
in the Mosaic blueprint so that Jesus can be said "not so much [to be]
interpreting the Law with his words, as referring his owne words to be
interpreted by the Law."[30] The specific perilous exegesis of the biblical
passages in which Milton engages is of little relevance here, yet it testifies
to his recourse to entirely new hermeneutical keys.

Along the same lines, in his preface to *The Judgement of Martin
Bucer, Concerning Divorce*, Milton argues that "it . . . may well seem more
then time to apply the sound and holy persuasions of this Apostolic
man," given the resort of many to the *"Papistical way of a literal apprehension against the direct* analogy *of sense, reason, law and the Gospel."*[31]
This statement well summarizes Milton's previous polemic engagement.
A literal reading of formulaic prescriptions is here contrasted to a direct
analogical reading of the same: the sieve of direct analogy is afforded by
a sober sense and reason, namely those very functions of man's faculties which apprehend the truthful and perpetual character of the law, in
fact, its charitable and natural end, as it is impressed in the spirit of the
gospel. It is once again given to *Tetrachordon* to tie it all together:[32]

> Christ having "cancelled the handwriting of ordinances which
> was against us," Col. ii. 14, and interpreted the fulfilling of all
> through charity, hath in that respect set us over law, in the free
> custody of his love, and left us victorious under the guidance of
> his living Spirit, not under the dead letter; to follow that which
> most edifies, most aides and furders a religious life, makes us
> holiest and likest to his immortall Image.[33]

In that he holds to love as both end and means and to the indwelling
Spirit as the agent of love, Milton never substantially departs from
Calvin. In accounting for the believer's prerogative to rise above the external demands of the law, however, Milton is ever so close to the likes
of Saltmarsh, for whom "the reborn Christian was not to be exhorted

29. *CPW* 2.345–46.
30. *CPW* 2.301.
31. *CPW* 2.431.
32. See Sanchez, "The Middling Temper of Nourishment."
33. *CM* 4.75.

to perform duties or to measure himself by the outworn law,"[34] but by the inward law of the Spirit. In this sense, the New Testament imperatives are but mirror and confirmation of the inward impulse of the Spirit, never a constraining law. Accordingly, Milton regards the Christian as no longer being disposed of by law, but as disposing of it as it appears more suitable with respect to charity. The law is thus contrasted to the oxymoronic "free custody of his love." The freedom that is produced by the secure embrace of divine love gives man over from the oppressive grip of outward prescriptions to the inward guidance of the Spirit, who interprets "the fulfilling of all through charity." In the final analysis, nature and intuitive reason are for the gospel of Christian liberty to encompass and uphold and that which they respectively suggest and identify still for Christian liberty to teach and produce.

Adult Sonship

Interposing the sequence of divorce tracts, in November 1644, *Areopagitica*[35] proves itself deeply rooted in Christian liberty. Christian liberty here entails, once more, the liberation of mind and conscience from the slavery of sin and thus from the yoke of outward prescriptions. More than this, however, the ensuing liberty results in adulthood and in full freedom to choose the good amongst alternatives.

In the opening of *Areopagitica*, Milton appeals first to "the strong assistance of God our deliverer," and next "to your faithful guidance and undaunted wisdom, Lords and Commons of England."[36] Milton is thus sketching the background for his argument by pointing to the two sides of but one coin. He first associates with his audience by stating that they can count on the assistance of the God whose deliverance they share (*our* deliverer), next he turns to the second person plural to emphasize human responsibility being placed in the hands of his audience. He is speaking as a Christian to Christians whose faithful guidance

---

34. Endy, *William Penn*, 29.

35. *Areopagitica* addressed the parliament to argue against its Licensing Order of 1643. The uncontrollable and indiscriminate proliferation of literature in the early Forties had induced the parliament to regulate its flow, by producing a system of oversight and censorship. If the licensers had changed from Charles' court of Star Chamber to appointees of the Long Parliament, the basic aim to restrain and deter the spreading of radical ideas remained. Total freedom of print was still equated with instability and anarchy.

36. *CPW* 2.487.

and undaunted wisdom must ultimately concede the ensuing argument and pursue it: while the title refers to the liberty of unlicensed printing, *Areopagitica*'s ultimate emphasis is not so much on the freedom of publishing, but on the freedom of reading.[37]

In what is the backbone of its discussion, *Areopagitica* comes to compare books to the life of man, to the extent of equating the suppression of a book to a kind of murder. Even more so, a book is the quintessence of man, his purest extraction, for it is the essence of reason, namely the very image of God impressed on the human being:

> We should be wary therefore . . . how we spill that seasoned life
> of man, preserved and stored up in books; since we see a kind
> of homicide may be thus committed, sometimes a martyrdom,
> and if we extend it to the whole impression, a kind of massacre;
> whereof the execution ends not in the slaying of an elemental life,
> but strikes at that ethereal and fift essence, the breath of reason
> itself, slays an immortality rather than a life.[38]

Reason is portrayed here as that distinctive element which assimilates man to God and differentiates him from animals. In a way that closely parallels Aristotelian and Thomist propositions, Milton comes to distinguish between "an elemental life" (*animal soul*) and "the breath of reason" (*rational* or *intellective soul*). In cutting off the latter, "an immortality rather than a life" is destroyed, for the very rational *pneuma*, as opposed to the biological breath of life, lives on on paper. Hence Milton speaks of "a kind of homicide," the murder, that is, of the immanent expression of man's rational soul. In the final analysis, the overarching scope of the intellective soul corresponds in Milton to reason seen as both intuitive and discursive.

In his subsequent overview of the lessons of history ranging from Greece to the Reformation and the Inquisition through Rome and Christian history, Milton sheds light on the liberating function of reason with respect to inward contamination. In so doing, he is sure to resort, in due course, to his ultimate *auctoritas*, the Bible:

> For those actions which enter into a man, rather than issue out of
> him, and therefore defile not, God uses not to captivate under a

37. Marialuisa Bignami first pointed out this emphasis to me.
38. *CPW* 2.493.

perpetual childhood of prescription, but trusts him with the gift of reason to be his own chooser.[39]

As in *The Reason of Church-government*, Milton knows here to turn to the dispensational rupture with the law which the covenant of grace has ushered in. He knows to turn to the words of Jesus to show that the food prescriptions of the Mosaic law did not amount to a restraint from moral defilement, but pertained to a condition of childhood. Christian liberty brings about adulthood and adulthood signifies investment with authority and reason. In other words, adulthood brings about the freedom to choose the good. The adult does not need external rules, but can allow reason to be its own chooser. Books do not defile man more than food does, unless he choose not to obey the voice of reason and misuse the knowledge he attains. The words of Paul of Tarsus to the Thessalonians next yield Milton's argument:

> "Prove all things, hold fast that which is good." And . . . another remarkable saying of the same author: "To the pure, all things are pure;" not only meats and drinks, but all kind of knowledge whether of good or evil; the knowledge cannot defile, nor consequently the books, if the will and conscience be not defiled.[40]

A line is drawn here between theoretical knowledge and the involvement of "will and conscience" in the knowledge of evil. The latter is not *per se* detrimental so long as it does not affect will and conscience. In other words, it is the experience of evil, as opposed to the theoretical knowledge thereof, which defiles man. Hence the adult Christian need not fear proving all things, for his reason is sufficient to inform the will, and the latter, in turn, to discard what is evil and store what is good. Not only so, but the knowledge of evil ultimately proves beneficial and instrumental to the knowledge of good when governed by reason:

> . . . perhaps this is the doom which *Adam* fell into of knowing good and evill, that is to say of knowing good by evil. As therefore the state of man now is; what wisdom can there be to choose, what continence to forebeare without the knowledge of evill? He that can apprehend and consider vice with all her baits and seeming pleasures, and yet abstain, and yet distinguish, and yet prefer that which is truly better, he is the true warfaring Christian.[41]

39. *CPW* 2.513–14.
40. *CPW* 2.511–12.
41. *CPW* 2.515.

Milton here challenges that good which does not result from free choice amongst alternatives. Evil affords the alternative, which ultimately amounts to a form of temptation. Before the fall Eve could not understand or see evil, hence no temptation could exert its negative power on her. Even so, an alternative to good remained in the form of that which was contrary to God's single command. The fall opened the door to man's experiential comprehension of evil and made him subject to its attractive force. Far from entertaining a version of the *felix culpa*,[42] Milton speaks of a *doom* which can be reversed by reason through the positive appropriation of man's completeness through grace. Whereas Milton can in no way advocate the experience of evil, he does adumbrate the work of grace as that which ennobles such experiential knowledge and thus restores it to man as an element of maturity.

The true significance of good is only given by that measure of evil which reason is willing to discard. The person who, being exposed to all evil, can abstain, discern the good and choose it is the true *warfaring Christian*. Positive freedom therefore appears to be more than spontaneous determination[43] or lack of coercion in the choice of the good.[44] It rather amounts to reason's discernment and resulting choice of the chief good among equally apprehended options. Underlying all such liberating functions of man's faculties, the freedom of reason alone stems from the inward liberty produced by the gospel of grace.

Education and learning, for their part, would relate to Christian liberty in a functional sense. While education may be expected to inform reason's choice of the good, reason must first be restored to the freedom of its functions. Education, therefore, will only prove beneficial if it first contributes to the appropriation of Christian liberty through the knowledge of God.

When *Of Education* appeared in 1644, Britain was largely familiar with efforts to favor education due to the legacy of Bacon and Comenius.[45]

---

42. Cf. Poole, *Milton and the Idea of the Fall*, 138–39. Poole contends that "Milton's argument is a version of the *felix culpa*, because felicity and culpability are both accepted as components of the Fall."

43. See Aquinas, *Summa*, 1a.83.1.

44. Ibid., 1a.82.1. Cf. *CPW* 6.352–3.

45. In developing his philosophy and program of education, Milton moved from the solid ground of preceding and concomitant theorization. Francis Bacon's influential *Two Bookes of the Proficience and Advancement of Learning* (London, 1605) had laid the foundation for a rational, empirical and functional view of education and

Both had strongly advocated learning as a means to the advancement of man. While Comenius had stressed the importance for education to be extended in its entirety to all social classes and individuals (*omnia omnibus omnino*) for the pursuit of the ongoing making of man in both the spiritual realm and the civil, Bacon had attempted to restore knowledge from the caution and limitation that surrounded it based on its association with original sin. To this end, he had magnified the role of reason and empirical observation in discarding vainglory and pride while appropriating, as a reflecting mirror, "the image of the universal world" along with solace.[46] Even so, a number of limitations still restricted the scope of learning:

> . . . if any man shall think by view and inquiry into these sensible and material things to attain that light, whereby he may reveal unto himself the nature or will of God, then indeed is he spoiled by vain philosophy; for the contemplation of God's creatures and works produceth (having regard to the works and creatures themselves) knowledge; but having regard to God, no perfect knowledge, but wonder, which is broken knowledge.[47]

For Bacon, the light of the knowledge of God, that is, the light of the knowledge of his will and nature, could not be attained through empirical inquiry. Bacon reasons in absolute terms: God is too high for the creature to know him. Tackling the issue from an opposite angle, Milton sees what of God could be known by the creature as spoiled by the fall.[48] Regaining that measure of the knowledge of God which was accorded to the creature then becomes the end of learning:

knowledge in seventeenth-century England. However, a more immediate context for Milton's involvement in the pedagogical debate is found in the writings of Johannes Amos Comenius. The Czech reformer had written extensively on the need for universal education and the pedagogical means to attain to it. His ideas were circulated in England by a group of pedagogical reformers that revolved around Samuel Hartlib, a German immigrant to whom Milton's epistolary tract *Of Education* is addressed. Three subsequent events involving Comenius and Hartlib paved the way for Milton's writing: Thomas Horne's translation *Janua linguarum reserata: or a seed-plot of all languages and sciences* appeared in London in 1636. London in turn hosted Comenius in 1641 and the printing of Hartlib's translation of Comenius' work on the reformation of education, *A Reformation of Schooles*, in 1642.

46. Bacon, *The Advancement of Learning*, edited by James Spedding et al., 265.

47. Ibid., 267.

48. Poole argues that "if Milton read Bacon, he had a decided more gloomy estimation of a sin-damaged cosmos than the latter" ("Milton and Science," 18).

> The end, then, of learning is to repair the ruins of our first parents
> by regaining to know God aright, and out of that knowledge to
> love him, to imitate him, to be like him, as we may the near-
> est, by possessing our souls of true virtue, which being united to
> the heavenly grace of faith makes up the highest perfection . . .
> because our understanding cannot in this body found itself but
> on sensible things, nor arrive so clearly to the knowledge of God
> and things invisible as by orderly conning over the visible and
> inferior creature, the same method is necessarily to be followed
> in all discreet teaching.[49]

To be sure, Milton is not saying that learning may yield the full knowledge of God more than Bacon is saying that "no perfect knowledge" is
no knowledge. Rather, Milton is pointing to the limitations of the body
as dictating the method to attain to the end of learning. Since man only
understands what he can know through his senses, a process of progressive accommodation has to inform his trajectory.

    At a first glance, Thomist nuances seem to underlie a similar
outlook inasmuch as a direct correlation is drawn between education
and the restoration of man. To this effect, Aquinas insists that a proper
knowledge of the good is inevitably to result in reason's choice thereof.[50] Nonetheless, we next learn that education can only serve its higher
purpose insofar as it leads man "to know God aright." We also learn that
love for God, the imitation of God and the likeness of God, namely all
good, are produced by virtue and faith "out of that knowledge." It follows
the knowledge of God must precede the manifestation of the good in
man. Schuler argues to much the opposite effect that "Milton's general

---

49. *CPW* 2.366–69. In addition to this initial statement of purpose, *Of Education*
appears to present the reader with a second one, "I call therefore a compleate and generous Education that which fits a man to perform justly, skilfully and magnanimously all
the offices both private and publike of peace and war" (2.377–79). After a cursory overview of the criticism concerning the apparent dialectic between the two purposes of
education in the pedagogical treatise, in "Sanctification in Milton's Academy" Schuler
traces a synthesis to the distinction between a general goal and a concrete objective
working towards the life-long process of sanctification. As I argue further along, however, that which has been identified as a second end of learning is no end at all. Rather,
it is the result of proper learning, namely the result of that education which has in the
knowledge of God its end. In other words, a complete and generous education is that
which leads man to the knowledge of God and by that knowledge prepares him for all
offices, both private and public, of peace and war.

50. The good "as soon as known, must also be willed" (Gilson, *The Philosophy of St.
Thomas Aquinas*, 120).

goal and practical objective involve different aspects of sanctification, and he gives priority to Milton's 'repair the ruins' over phrases such as 'regaining to know God aright,' 'possessing our souls of true vertue,' and 'highest perfection.' All suggest that Milton is describing the long process of sanctification rather than the instantaneous moment of justification."[51] Whether Milton has sanctification or justification in mind, in disjoining as it does the phrase "repair the ruins" from "regaining to know God aright" the argument disjoins the course of mending from the source of mending. Far from subordinating the knowledge of God to the repairing of our first parents' ruins, Milton is pointing to the knowledge of God as the way to restoration and to learning as instrumental in the process.

A question arises as to what measure of God may be apprehended through man's impaired natural senses and faculties. To answer this question, Milton's assessment of the effects of the fall must first be considered. If for Aquinas Adam's primitive innocence was but a gift whose loss did not deprive him of his rational being and the resulting good nature, for Augustine, and Calvin, sin thwarts and impairs both reason and will, thus producing total corruption. While the adjective *total* is not to be intended here as *absolute*, but as *pervasive*, the pervasive corruption of reason and will is such that fallen man has both lost his original integrity and his unclouded faculty of discerning both inward and outward reality according to its naked truth.[52]

---

51. Schuler, "Sanctification in Milton's Academy," 45–46.

52. Myers supplies a list of Reformed stances which pertinently illustrate and define this difference as follows (*Milton's Theology of Freedom*, 136): "Theodore Beza writes that 'man's understanding and will' are 'blind and forward' respectively" (*A booke of Christian questions and answers*, 27). "Stephen Charnock speaks of human nature's 'darkened wisdom' and 'enslaved will'" (*The Works* 3.169). "Johannes Wollebius writes that 'the intellect . . . is beclouded,' while 'the will . . . has lost its rectitude'" (*Compendium* 1.10.1). "Arminianism followed Reformed orthodoxy in this respect, also denying that fallen human beings can either 'think' (*cogitare*) or 'will' (*velle*) anything good (*Articuli Arminiani sive remostrantia*, 3; in *The Creeds* 3.546–7) since sin both 'darken[s] our Minds' and 'pervert[s] our Wills'" (Episcopius, *The confession*, 121). Again in Charnock's words, "Sin hath made its sickly impressions in every faculty" (*The Works* 3.171) so that it can be said to have affected "the whole man" (Ames, *The substance*, 15). "Calvin had asserted that 'the whole person' is 'so deluged, as it were, that no part remains exempt from sin,' and William Perkins speaks similarly of 'the whole body and soule' as corrupted by original sin" (*Symbole*, 112). Significantly, also, Calvin turns to Augustine in insisting that to do truth before coming to the light of the gospel (see John 3:21) is "to acknowledge that we are miserable and destitute of all power of doing good." (*Commentaries: The Gospel According to John* 17.2.129).

Milton appears to align himself in this respect with Calvinism as early as the anti-prelatical tracts.[53] While retaining the idea of a pervasive impairment of both intellect and will, *The Doctrine and Discipline of Divorce*, for its part, redefines the negative emphasis informing mainstream stances. Here Milton decries that theology which depresses

> . . . the high and Heaven-born spirit of Man, farre beneath the condition wherein either God created him, or sin hath sunke him.[54]

Whereas Augustine's premises about the elevation of undefiled Adam and Eve are embraced,[55] Milton departs from the church father's stress on loss. In fact, *because* Augustine's premises are embraced, Milton departs from absolute concepts of human depravity. The result of human choice is contrasted to the origin of the human spirit. If the spirit of man is the stuff of heaven, sin cannot *completely* spoil its nature. God himself, metonymically signified by the word "Heaven," is the term against which the fall is to be measured. The fall of man is not from magnificent height to absolute depths, but from magnificent height, and however unconfirmed worth, to relative depths. Calvin, in his own right, is sure to indicate that "the mind of man, how much so ever it be perverted and fallen from the first integrity, is yet still clothed and garnished with excellent gifts."[56] Man's impaired senses and faculties still have the possibility to fulfill their function, though in a relative sense, on the horizontal level. What they cannot do is fully overcome the bounds of spiritual loss and derivation. Along the same lines, *An Orthodox Creed*[57] epitomizes the

---

53. So Poole, *Milton and the Idea of the Fall*, 133, "At this stage . . . Milton has nothing unexpected to say about the Fall, and his polemical slur that Arminians were sure to deny original sin—they did not—shows well where his tastes lay."

54. *CPW* 2.223.

55. For Augustine, prelapsarian Adam and Eve were endowed with the highest intelligence (*Contra secundam Juliani responsionem*, ca. 429–30, *Patrologia Latina*, vol. 45, col. 1432) and were subject to no human perturbation, there being in them "no gloom at all, no unreal gaiety" (*De Doctrina Christiana* 14.10.26).

56. Calvin, *Institutes*, 2.2.15.

57. While dating back to 1678, *An Orthodox Creed* serves our purpose in that it formulates General Baptist tenets as they are expounded in previous confessions (esp. *The Standard Confession*, 1660) in more articulate theological language, its general purpose being "to unite and confirm all true protestants in the fundamental articles of the Christian religion" (in Lumpkin, ed., *Baptist Confessions*, 297) against the spreading of Hoffmannite Christology particularly in the Midlands.

General Baptist position by envisioning the effects of the fall as absolute with sole relation to "any spiritual good" and "eternal salvation."[58]

In the final analysis, Milton appears to be arguing for both justification and sanctification to come alongside the knowledge of God. Learning—bear in mind the study of the Scriptures is, to this effect unsurprisingly, the coronation of Milton's educational program—can lead to the knowledge of God, but only the latter can elevate to the "highest perfection" by the concurrence of "the grace of faith." Inasmuch as it is a gift of grace, faith comes from heaven and constitutes the basic channel for that light whose full blaze Bacon, and Aquinas with him, ultimately denies man. For Aquinas man's natural reason proves limited in its scope to the sole knowledge of God's existence, whereas it cannot tell him anything about his essence. Faith, on the other hand, while it does not give access to the knowledge of God's essence, allows man to comprehend that God is beyond all that is known through natural means.[59] Though concurring with the argument for natural reason's impotence in rising to the knowledge of God's nature and will, Milton also points to an opposing motion whereby God reaches down to man and makes himself known in the Son. If so, faith must no longer be intended as tension toward God, but as reception of the knowledge of God which descends from heaven.[60]

Far from referring to intellectual knowledge alone, the complement of "the grace of faith" and the nature of our first parents' knowledge to be regained is reminiscent of its personal and relational character. A breach is found here with both the Augustinian and the Scholastic tradition. In Aquinas the *infusion* of special grace, as it is afforded by the mediation of the church and the sacramental system, empowers the natural faculties of man, thus enabling him to attain to salvation.[61] For his part, Augustine views grace as wholly prevenient. He does not, however, distinguish between justification and sanctification. In other words, the divine of Hippo regards life as a journey of sanctification which leads to God and grace as the divine ransom of man's will which empowers him to live in accordance with God's will. He then comes to conceive of

58. Lumpkin, ed., *Baptist Confessions*, art. XX, 312.

59. See Irene Zavattero, "Fede e Ragione in Tommaso D'Aquino," at http://www.treccani.it/scuola/tesine/.

60. See chapter 3.

61. Aquinas, *Summa*, in *The Basic Writings*, q. 81, art. 1; q. 85, art. 2; q. 85, art. 3.

libertas, or true freedom, as the freedom to obey God. Though original sin has extinguished this freedom, God's grace restores it, so that man can experience the full extent of freedom in his compliance with divine righteousness.[62]

For all the differences between Augustine and Aquinas as to the extent of grace, both regard it as that element which fully enables one's inner faculties to choose the good. In so doing, both ultimately bind true freedom to obedience. In Milton true liberty departs from this idea of liberty in that it rests on an entirely new foundation. Grace is no longer an enabling element, but a position which comes to coincide with the liberating knowledge of God in the Son. Due to such position and knowledge, man is no longer free insofar as he obeys, but he obeys because he is free. True liberty, that is, is no longer freedom to choose the good. The latter freedom rather results from true liberty, which is the knowledge of God. It is only such freedom which allows him "to love him, to imitate him, to be like him," the end of learning.

Freedom from the Slavery of Sin and thus from the Rule of Men

The direct result of Christian liberty in Milton can be said to be the projection of love and liberty as the new coordinates of *all* life and thought. To this effect, for Milton emancipation from the slavery of sin does not only produce freedom from the yoke of the law, but also from "the rule of men." It is sin that has subjected a people once free by nature to the tyranny of man. Grace not only restores man to his original freedom by doing away with the source of enslavement, but it grants even greater freedom by according the status of God's adult son to the believer. The terms of his emancipation from the rule of men could not be any stronger, but the contextual association with the rule of the law makes it clear that it is the tyranny of men Milton has in mind, as opposed to a form of government which complies with love and liberty.

Both Calvin and Luther drew a sharp line between the spiritual realm, to which matters of conscience also belonged, and the visible realm of history, which primarily characterized itself as ecclesiastical, civil and political. Calvin insisted that Christian liberty pertained to the former dimension and was abused by those "who think there is no lib-

---

62. Augustine, *In evangelium Ioannis tractatus*, in Schaff, ed., *A Select Library of the Nicene and Post-Nicene Fathers*, 7.5.1.

erty unless it be used in the presence of men."[63] While considering both the ceremonial and the judicial portion of the Mosaic law as abrogated by the advent of Christ, the Genevan divine advocated the present bearing of its moral portion on the judicial systems of nations.[64] Luther, for his part, while envisioning the Mosaic code as entirely abrogated and merely useful after Christ for self-examination,[65] pictured the macro-division into spiritual and earthly as two kingdoms operating simultaneously. He thus identified love as the sole legitimate limitation to negative liberty with respect to the spiritual kingdom, "A Christian man is a most free lord of all, subject to none. A Christian man is a most dutiful servant of all, subject to all." "Subject to none," with respect to liberty, "subject to all," with respect to love.[66] In relation to the kingdom of history, however, the Reformer saw earthly authority as autonomous and operating by divine right.

Far from entertaining the thought that there is no liberty unless it be used in the presence of men, Milton himself regarded the inward liberty produced by the gospel as man's true liberty. Unlike the Reformers, though, he saw inward liberty as yielding the emancipation of man from all outward restraint in sole concert with charity, just as he saw charity as projecting liberty through all aspects of reality in sole obedience to grace. The civil and political laws contained in the Mosaic code were themselves "but the arme of the moral lawe."[67] That is to say, they only reflected or amounted to the expression of the moral law in both the civil and the political domain.

While projecting divisions in terms of formal theological categorization,[68] Calvin himself appears to adumbrate unity under the banner of the moral law, seen as a law of love. The Reformer, however, embraces Augustinian replacement theology, thus subscribing to the transfer of all Israel's theonomic prerogatives unto the church.[69] For Milton under the new covenant the moral law is to maintain the pre-

---

63. Calvin, *Institutes* 2.135.

64. Ibid., 14–21.

65. Luther, *A Treatise on Christian Liberty*, 2.312–48.

66. Luther, *Tractatus de libertate Christiana*, cited in Bruce, *Paul*, 202.

67. *CPW* 2.322.

68. Calvin, *Institutes* 2.135.

69. See Diprose, *Israel and the Church*, 87–89. See also Ryrie, *Basic Theology*, 460–63, 520, 592; idem, *Dispensationalism*, 64, 127–31.

rogative to direct the civil and political course of a community and a nation, yet, as the expression of the inward microcosm of Christian liberty, it is bound to differentiate itself from the strictures of Israel's theonomic prescriptions:

> The whole Judaick law is . . . [other than moral] politicall, and to take pattern by that, no Christian nation ever thought it selfe oblig'd in conscience . . .[70]

For his part, Roger Williams is sure to echo this statement in the words, "The Pattern of the Nationall Church of Israel, was . . . unimitable by any Civill State."[71] Williams and Milton thus prove to share a hermeneutic which holds the gospel as its overruling principle. Where the Old and the New Testament conflicted, the latter overrode the former. With this in mind, Israel came to be in their understanding a distinct entity in God's plan for the world. The church after Christ's coming should not directly abide by Israel's ceremonial, civil and political ordinances, as the first proved fulfilled in Christ and the following pertained to a theocratic order that was no more. In light of this, also, the state should not be bound by the Puritan vision of rebuilding the *city upon a hill*.

Williams and Milton's stance would make them in contemporary theological terms two dispensationalists, but with a difference: while Williams understood the dutiful construct of the state to be constitutionally civil—lest the civil element defile the religious—Milton envisioned the English nation as a "Christian nation." It was the Christian element which, in his mind, attributed to the state its civil nature.

In an attempt to retain Calvin's general division into spiritual liberty and liberty used in the presence of men, logical connections have been sought between the two ends of liberty, to the extent of depicting "The history of the doctrine in Puritan England" as "largely the record of its progressive transference from the theological to the ecclesiastical and political spheres, to the first through Congregationalism and the toleration controversy, to the second by the force of analogy among the Levellers."

In turning to Milton, the attempt has thus been to show how the polemist radically extends the logic of Calvin's tri-fold liberty, even one that more appropriately pertains to the spiritual dimension, to every

---

70. *CPW* 1.762.

71. Williams, *The Bloudy Tenent Yet More Bloudy*, 4.28.

challenge posed to individual liberty. In Barker's words, if "Calvin's three parts of Christian liberty find their place in his writings," the need also surfaces for them to be "radically interpreted in defense of individual liberty especially as a consequence of his argument on divorce."[72]

The need for a radical extension of the Calvinist terms of liberty, nonetheless, only comes alongside the failure to grasp the full unifying extent of Christian liberty. Such extent is potentially absolute: absolute in that it reaches from the start every dimension of life to the fullest; potentially so, for liberty operates under the direction of grace. And grace calls man to bend absolute freedom to the demands of love. Obedience, submission and restraint are themselves part of that law of love which the saint now chooses to freely pursue for his neighbor's sake and for the enhancement of collective liberties. Hence authority can only rest on others insofar as the Christian delegates them to exert it. Milton need not sacrifice truth on the altar of freedom nor grant unwarranted analogical extensions to spiritual liberty. His work is rather all about balancing liberty as a *fait accompli* and love.

If a full formulation of Christian liberty does not appear in the polemic prose prior to *De Doctrina*, I wish to insist that Milton's advocacy of public liberties plainly hinges on its principles from the very beginning. The tree is known by its fruit. Far from taking Christian liberty to its logical consequences, the reforming spirit still sweeping through England in the seventeenth century proved largely clouded by legalism, adherence to intellectual notionalism and crystallized institutions. While Calvin and Calvinist divines had kicked works of law out of the door and given the Christian man over to the rule of grace, emphasis on works as the necessary result of election and salvific grace had invited them back in through the window. Also, a formal, all too often merely intellective, consent to a set of doctrinal propositions had all too easily won acceptance as evidence of orthodoxy. Finally, the claim for objective, divinely bestowed, rights of governing offices, be they ecclesiastical or political, was to magnify the breach between individual Christianity and social and political structures.

72. Barker, "Christian Liberty," 154–55.

With Roger Williams[73] and General Baptists in the Forties, and with the latter and Quakers in the Fifties,[74] Milton takes Paul to his logi-

73. Roger Williams was apprenticed to Sir Edward Coke, the renowned jurist and champion of the subordination of the king to the common law. Under his patronage Williams was educated at Pembroke College, Cambridge. His Cambridge years at Pembroke overlap Milton's at Christ's. Cambridge was to influence Williams along Puritan lines. Although he took Holy Orders within the Church of England, it would not be long before he left the established church. Largely remembered as the founder of Rhode Island, Williams set out for the New World in 1630. By this time his separatist position was fully developed and so was his championing of freedom of conscience: if, on one hand, he regarded separation from the established church as a necessity in the pursuit of the true service of the church of Christ, on the other, he considered it not the church's or the civil magistrate's prerogative to rule in matters of belief. That which came to be known as Rhode Island was the first settlement to enjoin the separation of citizenship from religious belief and practice. Rhode Island was to become a safe haven for those who, like Baptists, Quakers and Jews, were persecuted for their belief. Williams may have become acquainted with Milton in 1643–44 upon his return to London to secure a charter for his colony, but more certainly so upon his second return to England in 1651–54. An exchange of linguistic competences occurred at this time with Milton helping Williams brush up his Hebrew and the latter introducing Milton to Dutch. Williams' libertarian and tolerationist stance largely resulted from a deterministic outlook. If the work of grace depended entirely on God's initiative, human coercion and control of truth could have no part in it. God's sovereign end was to be carried out through foreordained means irrespective of human control of events and actions (see Corns, "John Milton, Roger Williams and the Limits of Toleration"). His understanding of the separation of church and state, on the other hand, strictly resulted from his desire to preserve the church from any defilement originating in the secular element.

74. Nathaniel Paget, Milton's personal physician and, in Aubrey's words, a "familiar learned acquaintance" of his, represents a biographical liaison between Milton, Independency, Quakerism and the Baptist persuasion. A member of John Goodwin's St Stephen, Paget had an intimate friendship with prolific Quaker Isaac Penington. Penington persuaded another prominent Quaker, Thomas Ellwood, to pursue Milton's acquaintance and scholarship. It was Paget who ultimately introduced Ellwood to Milton (end of 1661–early 1662 ca.). Ellwood became one of Milton's assiduous readers, reading Latin authors to Milton every afternoon but Monday. Upon the outburst of the plague in 1665, Milton committed Ellwood to look for a house for him and his family in the area outside London where the Quaker resided. Campbell confirms that the "initiative was Milton's own, and [that] he knew the locale he had selected was an enclave of dissent and held a substantial Quaker community" (Campbell and Corns, *John Milton*, 322). Ellwood himself sheds light on the event: "Some little time before I went to *Alesbury* Prison, I was desired by my quondam Master *Milton* to take an House for him, in the Neighbourhood where I dwelt, that he may go out of the City, for the Safety of himself and his Family, the *Pestilence* then growing hot in *London*. I took a pretty box for him in *Giles-Chalfont*, a Mile from me; of which I gave him notice: and intended to have waited on him and seen him well settled in; but was prevented by that Imprisonment" (Ellwood, *Life*, 246). The imprisonment refers to Ellwood's incarceration along with Isaac Penington and other Quakers convened at a funeral in Amersham on 1 July 1665.

Trust on Milton's part and Ellwood's devotion for his quondam *Master* seem implicit in these words. Milton's desire to move to Ellwood's neighborhood, an area with so high a concentration of Quakers, may witness to no more than the poet's seeking Ellwood's particular assistance. However, it also seemingly indicates that Milton did not disdain the proximity of the Quaker community to which Ellwood himself belonged. Upon his release, Milton entrusted Ellwood with a manuscript copy of *Paradise Lost* along with a request for feed-back. Whatever we wish to make of the request, the handing of the manuscript itself seems to entail consideration, trust and cultural interaction. Ellwood's famous self-reported anecdotal claim that he persuaded Milton to write about gain (*Paradise Regained*) after writing so extensively about loss (*Paradise Lost*) is likely little more than the projection of a subjective point of view. Assuming Ellwood ever exerted an influence on Milton's thought, his transcription and posthumous edition of George Fox's *Journal*, prefaced by William Penn, is worth the notice. Other than in connection to Milton's encounter with Ellwood, Paget played a key role with respect to Milton's third marriage by recommending his aunt's granddaughter, Elizabeth Minshull, to the poet. Elizabeth was a girl of 24 from a General Baptist background. Her extended family had relations in south Cheshire, in the towns of Crewe, Wistaston, Stoke and Nantwich. A stronghold of the parliament, Nantwich largely retained Puritan as well as libertarian sentiments during the years of the Interregnum. Little is known about the dawn of the local Baptist gatherings. Evidence for the residence of its first recorded minister, Rev. Samuel Acton, in Nantwich dates back to the early 1690s, yet his status as a wealthy salt proprietor in the area in those same years argues for a well established presence. More importantly, a census conducted by Bishop Gastrell, bishop of Chester, in the early seventeenth century, records the presence of the following number of Dissenters at Nantwich: Presbyterians 157, Anabaptists 109, Quakers 13. Gastrell also mentions the presence in Wybunbury parish of an Anabaptist meeting house, whose congregation was made up of twenty-four families of Dissenters, fourteen of whom were Anabaptist (see Urwick, *Historical Sketches*, 134). The number of Anabaptists argues for a well rooted group. The years of the Commonwealth witnessed a significant expansion of the General Baptist movement in the Midlands—Lincolnshire and Leicestershire being its two main strongholds—where General Baptists far outnumbered Particular Baptists. Such expansion accounts for the General Baptist community whose significant presence was later to be recorded in neighboring south Cheshire. At the time of Elizabeth's marriage with Milton, her parish of residence was St Andrew, Holborn. After Milton's death, she returned to south Cheshire, where she lived until her death in 1727. She was buried in Nantwich reputedly at the Baptist Chapel which had been erected in Barker Street under the superintendence of Rev. Samuel Acton in 1725. One of the executors of Elizabeth's will, Rev. Samuel Acton served the Nantwich General Baptist congregation for considerable time, only to hand it over to the care of General Baptist minister and historian Isaac Kimber. It is, ultimately, significant to underscore the initial vicinity between Quakers and General Baptists. After his conversion experience in 1647, Fox's influence was first felt among General Baptists in Nottinghamshire. Soon thereafter, he was found preaching in a General Baptist church at Broughton, on the border of Leicestershire and Nottinghamshire. Quakers began to multiply in North Lancashire, Westmorland and Cumberland, a significant portion of them coming from Baptist churches. Former Baptist pastors ranked within their files as some of their most fervent proponents. While remarkable affinity of faith and practice characterized the two cal consequences as he seeks to conform all aspects of inward as well as outward life to Christian liberty. The gospel of grace is for Milton the key to true liberty. The gospel possesses a life of its own and will not be controlled and secured within the static categories of those who will have it "enacted and settled, as they call it, by the state, a statute or a state-religion."[75]

Contrary to the self-reliance and institutionalization of the dogmatic strain of Puritanism, a strong emphasis on the foundational experience of free grace is found, for one, in Dell[76] which well epitomizes General Baptist, Quaker as well as Miltonic stances:

> When men by occasion of this form [appearance of godliness] are called forth to do the great works of God, and yet are destitute of the *power* of God, their duties are above their *strength* . . . And sooner or later, meeting with *difficulties*, they faint and languish as a Snail, their works being too high for their faculties. For *nature* being strained above its power, and offering at that which is beyond its abilities, by degrees grows weary, and returns to its old *temper* again.[77]

A sharp distinction is drawn here between natural man and the man who is free by grace to live by the Spirit and by that Spirit accomplish the transcending work of love. The difference is really between doing the will of God in one's own power or in the power of God. To die to self is to dwell in the freedom of God's life. From this inward spiritual dimension, then, Christian liberty is seen as encompassing the civil, ecclesiastical and political. In Saltmarsh's words,[78] Christian liberty opens up entirely

---

movements, the Quakers' radicalization on marginal aspects and external expressions of their belief as well as their proselytizing agenda would soon be perceived as a threat by both Particular and General Baptists. Even so, Endy reports that "even Burrough, who was harsher on contemporaries than anyone but Fox, admitted that the 'free-willers' or General Baptists had correct doctrine . . ." (Endy, *William Penn*, 60).

75. *CPW* 7.256.

76. Native of Bedforshire and an undergraduate of Cambridge, William Dell (1607–1669) was a chaplain in the New Model Army. Variously charged with libertinism and antinomianism, Dell stressed the theology of free grace while opposing Ranterism. His opinions closely parallel the Quakers' as for his understanding of continuous revelation. Akin to Quaker and Separatist thought was also his criticism of the established church, his questioning of the existence of biblical ground for a national church and his opposition to tithes.

77. Dell, *Christ's Spirit*, A.

78. A native of Yorkshire, John Saltmarsh was a student at Cambridge (Magdalen

new venues for truth, as it makes the Christian an active protagonist in
every realm of public life:

> The interest of the people in Christ's kingdom is not only an
> interest of compliancy and obedience and submission, but of
> consultation, of debating, counseling, prophesying, voting, etc.
> And let us stand fast in that liberty wherewith Christ hath made
> us free.[79]

It was a similar outlook, rather than Williams' sharp distinction between
state and church as outlined in *The Bloudy Tenent*, that would define

College) in his own right. Himself a chaplain of the New Model Army under Thomas
Fairfax, Saltmarsh was parish priest at Heslerton and Brasted. Himself charged with
antinomianism, Saltmarsh, like Dell, emphasized free grace and subscribed to Bunyan's
persuasion that baptism was not of the essence with respect to Christian life and salvation. He strongly held to religious toleration and freedom of conscience and is found
bringing to task Thomas Fuller for a pamphlet called *Examinations* in which Fuller
decried Milton's *Of Reformation*.

79. Saltmarsh, *Smoke from the Temple*, cited in Bennet, *Reviving Liberty*, 101.
Bennett, among others, enlists such free Gratians as Dell and Saltmarsh in the antinomian strain. In turning away from the external demands of the Mosaic law, however,
such progressive Calvinist divines do not do away with law altogether, but they turn
to a new law. Grace as a sanctifying principle is the new rule of life, which frees from
self and gives the believer over to the life of God manifesting itself in concert with
the moral law by the Spirit of love. The broadest gap is thus manifest with the Ranter
antinomian view that all acts performed by the believer were automatically sinless.
Saltmarsh, for his part, is sure to reject easy labels, in the words, "It would be a matter
of much Peace amongst Believers, if the names of *Antinomian*, and *Legal Teacher*, and
the rest, might be laid down . . . Some hearing the *Doctrine* of *Free-grace*, think presently there will follow nothing but *looseness* and *libertinism* and the other hearing of
holiness, of *duties* and *obedience*, think there will follow nothing but *legalness* and *bondage*, and *self-righteousness*" (*Free-Grace*, A4). While pointing to antinomianism as the
common denominator in Milton, Dell and Saltmarsh, Bennett specifies that "Milton
differs importantly from Saltmarsh in that he did not accept the doctrine of predestination or "perseverance." (*Reviving Liberty*, 100). Nevertheless, if it is for those who "will
hear" God's "umpire conscience" (the Spirit) to persevere to the end (3.194–97), enthralled man is to "know how frail / His fall'n condition is and to . . . [God] owe / All his
deliv'rance, and to none but... [him]" (3.180–82). The focus in the conditional clause
appears to be on the power of God rather than on human achievement. *De Doctrina*, on
the other hand, seems to tie perseverance to human sanctification in maintaining that
the elect will "PERSEVERE TO THE END," yet only "SO LONG AS THEY DO NOT
PROVE WANTING IN THEMSELVES, AND SO LONG AS THEY CONTINUE IN
CHARITY" (*CPW* 6.505). Whereas Arminian theology (in Episcopius' formulation,
which articulates what in Arminius is but exegetical uncertainty) conceived of conversion as a dynamic process, to the extent of allowing for believers to fall away from grace,
Milton appears to rather align himself here with the Amyraldian stance and with the
view that choice is contained in his salvific design of love.

Milton's social, civil, ecclesiological and political commitment. And if the domestic microcosm was the minimal unit of society, a number of concentric circles expanded from the couple to the religious congregation and the civil community which defined the respective relations to collective and individual liberty.

The Couple

The divorce tracts reach far beyond their circumscribed and somewhat circumstantial primary objective. Both Milton's conclusions and how he gets there have more to say about Christian liberty than about divorce *per se*. Christian liberty not only affected Milton's understanding of the nature of marriage and the way in which the respective Scriptures are apprehended, but it was seen as according man freedom from the external marital bond and from the limitations posed by incompatibility within marriage. This was true of that marriage which did not match inward liberty through fit society.

In setting the boundaries for a rightful and substantial union, Christian liberty would leave with conscience the prerogative to rule in matters of divorce.[80] The role of the magistrate—bear in mind ecclesiastical courts had ceased to function in 1642[81]—can be nothing but to

---

80. *CPW* 2.343–50.

81. Before the Reformation divorce was regulated by the canon law, which regarded marriage as a sacrament. As such, marriage could not be dissolved and provision was only made for separation *a mensa et thoro*. Nullification, however, existed for impediments predating marriage (such as consanguinity, sexual incapacity, previous marriage contract, etc.). With the Reformation, the sacramental value attached to the marital bond dropped and divorce and remarriage were granted for the innocent party in cases of adultery and desertion. Favoured by Edward VI, this position was incorporated in the *Reformatio Legum Ecclesiasticarum* (1552), but was suppressed in the Commons. Even so, a commission under Cranmer had ruled the legitimacy of divorce for adultery in Northampton's case (1548). The ruling was later confirmed by Act of Parliament in 1552. All cases were ruled by ecclesiastical courts up to 1642, when ecclesiastical courts ceased to function. In 1646 authority over marriage shifted into the hands of civil authority (Stone, *Road to Divorce*, 4). Milton's writing on divorce pertinently addresses the window of opportunity which such transitional years afforded. Specifically, *The Doctrine and Discipline of Divorce* (August 1643) appeared in his first edition a month after the Westminster Assembly of Divines first convened to carry on to completion the English Reformation along Puritan lines. As the extended title of the pamphlet suggests in the words "Seasonable to be now thought on in the Reformation intended," the Assembly was manifestly Milton's ideal audience. A second edition (February 1644) would be addressed "*To the* Parliament of England, with the Assembly," thus recogniz-

"see that the condition of divorce be just and equall."[82] The limitation of individual liberty through the superimposition of the magistrate's authority therefore aims, in Williams' words, to protect "the Bodies and Goods of others."[83] In fact, the role of the magistrate is to be yet another expression of the law of love in that it aims to guarantee the preservation of mutual liberties, justice and welfare in the civil community.

As Corns notes,[84] *The Doctrine and Discipline of Divorce* would come to be associated with Roger Williams' *The Bloudy Tenent* (1644). For Ephraim Pagitt, radicals "preach, print, and practice their hereticall opinions openly: for books, *vide* the bloody Tenet, witness a tractate of divorce in which the bonds are let loose to inordinate lust."[85] If Williams' work is, in Pagitt's mind, nothing short of heretical, the charge against it is to tolerate Milton's ignominious "tractate of divorce." In that which for the Presbyterian is a battle for dogmatic orthodoxy, Milton, like Williams, never considers the subordination of truth to liberty, which would turn liberty into license.[86] His contention is that the dogmatic spirit which underlies his opponents' apprehension and apology of truth contrasts with the spirit of the gospel. The contrast is defined in terms of slavery to an external dogma which is outlined, administered and enforced by men—the Church first, then the state—and which Milton variously assimilates to the spirit of popery, and freedom resulting in truth. Truth, as it were, needed to be handled in accordance with the spirit which had produced the Reformation, the spirit of the gospel, and not by the enforced dogmas that the Reformation had produced.

ing, in Campbell's words, "that, while a constructive engagement with the latter now seemed unlikely, parliament was emerging as much more equivocal in its support for the emerging, Scottish-led Presbyterian agenda." (Campbell and Corns, *John Milton*, 169).

82. *CPW* 2.343.

83. Williams, *The Bloudy Tenent*, see the dedication.

84. Corns, "Milton, Roger Williams and the Limits of Toleration," 75.

85. Ephraim Pagitt, *Heresiography* (1645), cited in J. Milton French, ed., *The Life Records of John Milton*, 2.127.

86. It is seemingly to the Ranting sort Milton refers in Sonnet 12 as he denounces: "License they mean when they cry liberty."

The Religious Congregation

It was the service of the gospel which presented Milton with his life-
long existential paradox as that same poetic office which he envisions
as God's ultimate calling was to give way to the contingent service of
liberty.[87] The very measure of present necessity as the poet turns to the
work of the left hand is given by the paramount significance of the divine
poetical vocation which he is compelled to dismiss. By the time he begins to jot down *The Reason of Church-government*, his inward prompting has largely been repressed. More than a merely formal shift, Milton's
resort to the less congenial element of prose testifies to the passage to a
whole new existential dimension:

> Lastly, I should not chuse this manner of writing wherin know-
> ing my self inferior to my self, led by the genial power of nature

87. If Milton's return from Italy in 1639 ideally marks the end of his *Bildungsjahre*,
the antiprelatical tracts open a whole new literary season. Upon his return to London,
Milton's thoughts are gradually taken captive by the sense of a higher poetical calling.
An elegiac lamentation upon the death of Charles Diodati, his "kindred spirit" (Carey,
Complete Shorter Poems, 284), *Epitaphium Damonis* mourns the friend's dissolved
youth. In so doing, the elegy closely recalls *Lycidas*, the earlier poem commemorating
Edward King, a young Fellow of Christ's College who had lost his life in 1637. In both
works Milton transcends the occasion to reflect on death and a life falling short of its
goal. This poetic has inevitable personal ramifications for a young poet who has not
yet found his place in the world. The thought that "Ease and leasure was given thee
for thy retired thoughts out of the sweat of other men" (*CPW* 1.804) must have itself
contributed to a sense of accountability to both God and men. Hence, whereas *Lycidas*
envisions "fresh woods, and pastures new," *Epitaphium Damonis*, along with *Mansus*
(ca. 1638–39), points to the creation of a national poem (Carey and Fowler, *The Poems*,
168–71): "O, if I have any time left to live, you, my pastoral pipe, will hang far away on
the branch of some old pine tree, utterly forgotten by me, or else, transformed by my native muses, you will rasp out a British tune." Furthermore, in eight pages of manuscript
notes (Trinity ms) Milton considers topical options for an epic and a play (King Arthur
and King Alfred, for the epic, Abraham, John the Baptist, Sodom burning, Moabitides
or Phineas or Christus Patiens, for the play), while also jotting down ideas for a tragedy
bearing the title *Adam unparadiz'd* or *Paradise Lost*. It is, however, left with *The Reason
of Church-government* to project an unambiguous synthesis of the dialectic between poetry and the service of God and man. In the words of Edward Jones: "For the first time
in an unequivocal way, he [Milton] announces his poetic ambitions to write vernacular
poetry in the service of God and his country. Providing a highly selective account of
his past, Milton talks of 'an inward prompting which now grew daily' upon him that
'by labour and intent study' (which he believes to be his 'portion in this life'), he 'might
perhaps leave something so written to aftertimes, as they should not willingly let it die'"
(Jones, "Church-Outed by the Prelats," 42–58).

to another task, I have the use, as I may account it, but of my left hand . . . sitting here below in the cool element of prose . . .[88]

In due course, Milton would come to the realization that God's will for him was not divided, but was rather to be defined in temporal terms. In due time, *Paradise Lost* would rise up to be the synthesis of poetry and the service of God. In fact, the poem would come to absorb those terms of liberty which had been the prerogative of the prose. The present time yet called for a prophetic office. The poet was to divest himself of his noble robe to put on the revealing rags of the prophet. The former has a message that tends to exceed the boundaries of time, space and audience. The latter has an immanent and urgent message from God for the people:

> When God commands to take the trumpet and blow a dolorous or a jarring blast, it lies not in mans will what he shall say, or what he shall conceal. If he shall think to be silent, as Jeremiah did, because of the reproach and derision he met with daily . . . he would be forc't to confesse as he confest, *his word was in my heart as a burning fire shut up in my bones, I was weary with forbearing and could not stay.*[89]

The message the prophet-priest has to convey to the nation pertains to Christian liberty in its relation to church government.[90] In strik-

---

88. *CPW* 1.808.

89. *CPW* 1.803.

90. Milton's engagement with the debate on church government seemingly dates back to March 1641, when a distinct hand, likely Milton's, appears to have contributed "A Postscript" to *An Answer to a Book Entituled, An Humble Remonstrance*, a tract authored by the Calamy group. An expression of the Puritan persuasion within the established church, the Calamy group, which wrote under the acronymic pseudonym of "Smectymnuus," was formed by Stephen Marshall, Edmund Calamy, Thomas Young, Milton's former mentor, and William Spurstowe, and appears to have been assisted by Milton himself. The group entered a twofold controversy on church government with Laudian bishop Joseph Hall and anti-Laudian figures of moderate Episcopalian inclination. Ground for negotiation was afforded by the likes of John Williams, bishop of Lincoln, and James Ussher, archbishop of Armagh, who argued for a low-key episcopacy somewhat akin to the General Baptist. The new standard was, however, set by Hall in *Episcopacy by Divine Right Asserted* (1640). A traditional Calvinist, Hall nonetheless followed the prompting of archbishop Laud in his ecclesiological writing as he forcefully advocated the divine right of episcopacy, its linear transmission since apostolic days and the need for conspicuous wages for bishops. In *An Humble Remonstrance to the High Court of Parliament* (1641), Hall forcefully reiterated his arguments in a radically changed context. The Laudian faction was declining as Presbyterian forces in par-

ingly vivid language and imagery, *Of Reformation* places arguments for the illegitimacy of the Episcopal structure against the backdrop of the Reformation:

> When I recall to mind at last, after so many darke Ages, wherein the huge overshadowing traine of *Error* had almost swept all the Starres out of the Firmament of the *Church*; how the bright and blissful *Reformation* (by Divine Power) strook through the black and settled Night of *Ignorance* and *Antichristian Tyranny*, me thinks a soveraigne and reviving joy needs rush into the bosome of him that reads or heares; and the sweet Odour of the returning *Gospell* imbath his Soule with the fragrancy of Heaven.[91]

Milton divides Christian history into two parts: the Middle Ages were an age of darkness and tyranny which had been superseded by the light and liberty "of the returning *Gospell*." Although Milton believed that the reforming spirit had begun to manifest itself in Wycliffe and Huss' proto-reformation, the Protestant Reformation constituted the climax and watershed of history. This was not to say that with Luther the Christian reformation was complete or definitive. On the contrary, the reforming spirit was to pervade each nation, generation and individual in an ongoing process. England had been called, in Milton's mind, to fulfill this process, but was forfeiting its mission by maintaining the old vestige of slavery in the form of the Episcopal structure.[92] In the final analysis, doing away with episcopacy was tantamount to choosing the right side of history. It signified the appropriation of the liberty of the gospel in its outward ecclesiological ramifications. Indeed, all restraining factors so vividly signified by the imagery of night were aptly contrasted to the emancipation which the gospel produces.[93]

---

liament took over the scene. It is within such context, preluding to the civil war (1642), that Smectymnuus began to write of church government and freedom. Milton's foremost involvement in the diatribe was marked by five tracts in 1641–42: *Of Reformation touching Church-Discipline in England: And the Causes that hitherto hindred it*, *Of Prelatical Episcopacy, and Whether it may be deduc'd from the Apostolical times by vertue of those Testimonies which are alledg'd to that purpose in some late Treatises: One whereof goes under the Name of James Archbishop of Armagh*, *Animadversions upon The Remonstrants Defence against Smectymnuus*, *The Reason of Church-government Urg'd against Prelaty*, and *An Apology*.

91. *CPW* 1.524.

92. See Christopher, "Milton and the Reforming Spirit," 194.

93. The argument progresses in *Of Prelatical Episcopacy*, where Milton more closely addresses the issues raised by the Smectymnuuan controversy. In tackling the work of

The Reason of Church-government expands upon these arguments, by intertwining them with a more personal emphasis.[94] A clearly auto-biographical note is struck by Milton out of self-apologetic concern as he juxtaposes his poetical aspirations and cultivation to both the priestly office and the prophetic. From an early age, Milton's life had been set apart for the service of God:

> . . . the Church, to whose service by the intentions of my parents and friends I was destin'd of a child, and in mine own resolutions.[95]

One can hardly miss the Old Testament echoes of priestly consecration here. However, a tension is immediately produced by the early rise of the antagonistic element of art. From an early stage Milton works to find

moderate Episcopalian James Ussher, he does so more forcefully and uncompromisingly than his colleagues. Ussher bases his argument on early church history and the alleged endorsement of John Rainolds, Elizabethan and Jacobean theologian of mild Puritan persuasion. While at first addressing Ussher's arguments in an orderly fashion after the Smectymnuuan manner, Milton soon contravenes all dialectic rules by exposing the utter contrivance of the very tradition upon which Ussher relies. Such spurious tradition and the sophistic obscurity and adulteration it projects are again contrasted to the truth and simplicity of the gospel. *Animadversions* in turn addresses bishop Hall's defense against Smectymnuus. It does so, once again, with the ardor which comes from knowing that liberty is at stake. Milton's apprehension of the liberty deriving from the gospel is by now a ruling principle which can potentially dismantle all outward sources of restraint. Milton's language matches what is more than an ecclesiological argument. Similar to Luther's *commensalia*, his flow of speech addresses the clergy itself by portraying it as a hindrance to the gospel. His is yet no polemical vein. It is the outburst of the prophet conveyed with the authority of royal priesthood. The gospel has introduced universal priesthood, so that authority within the church ultimately falls on the individual believer and on the individual and independent congregation, as *The Reason of Church-government* would more forcefully stress.

94. A response to Milton's engagement with Hall had appeared under the title of *A Modest Confutation of A Slandrous and Scurrilous Libell, Entituled, Animadversions upon the Remonstrants Defense against Smectymnuus* (1642). The libel aimed to undermine the credibility of the author of *Animadversions*. Milton was still unknown and unpublished, a young graduate who neither held an ecclesiastical office nor a university post. Gratuitous slander overlaps sensible contentions against Milton's entitlement to inscribe his name in the controversy. A slight anachronism seems to argue against *The Reason of Church-government* (Jan-Feb 1642) being a direct response to the *Modest Confutation* (1642). Whereas *An Apology* would manifestly address the latter, the significant match between the charges raised by the confuter and the unfolding of Milton's argument in *The Reason of Church-government* may witness to the circulation of the content of the attacks prior to Milton's early engagement.

95. *CPW* 1.822.

a balance. The journey to Italy climactically symbolizes his participation in the Parnassus of poetry. This inscription in the religion of art, however, does not prevent him from being vocal about the religion of faith. Mansus' Latin distich in praise of Milton only masks his criticism of Milton's unconcealed religious stances. Upon his sojourn in Geneva, Milton would further define the terms of the dialectic in the words of his autograph dedication to Neapolitan exile Camillo Cardoini, "When I cross the sea I change my sky but not my mind." While poetry and faith would ultimately meet in *Paradise Lost*, the former proving subservient to the latter, the ministry of liberty and institutional ministry would prove mutually exclusive:

> . . . comming to maturity of years and perceiving what tyranny had invaded the Church, that he who would take Orders must subscribe slave, and take an oath withal . . . I thought it better to preferre a blamelesse silence . . . Howsoever thus Church-outed by the Prelats, hence may appear the right I have to meddle in these matters, as before, the necessity and constraint appear'd.[96]

Whatever the chronological setting for this realization may be, the passage points to the logic of tyranny and slavery pervading the church and not to art as the stumbling block ultimately preventing Milton from becoming a member of the clergy. From the obligation to sign the 39 articles (the "oath") to the structure of government, the prelates have unleashed the dynamics of tyranny, namely control, power and fear, within the church. Taking holy orders would be tantamount to submitting to those same dynamics. Milton's understanding of Christian liberty places him outside the realm of human institution and religion. Yet the liberty of universal priesthood turns the layman into a prophet-priest who can offer the sacrifices of his prose on the altar of truth and freedom. The rupture could not be more complete. Children of God under the gospel, Christians are "the heirs of liberty and grace." As such, they have also been apportioned "admirable and heavenly privileges" as a "royal priesthood."[97]

The contrast is not between two different ecclesiological views, but, ultimately, between the Old Testament and the New, the yoke of law and men and the terms of the gospel. If Milton's opponents trace episcopacy

96. *CPW* 1.822–23.
97. *CM* 3.256–62.

to Israel's priestly system, Romans 10:4 declares Christ to be the end of the law. In Milton's words, "for that the Gospell is the end and fulfilling of the Law, our Liberty also from the bondage of the Law I plainly reade."[98] The gospel is the fulfillment of the law inasmuch as it provides the substance which the priestly system and the ceremonial law foreshadowed. The gospel is the termination of the law with respect to righteousness, for it provides the righteousness which the law could never produce in man. The priestly system pointed precisely to that impotence and incompleteness, while signifying the full reality that was to come. In Christ the priestly system, with all that it entails, is superseded. Liberty from all human structures and legalistic complications is pronounced. And if church government is envisioned, it can only be out of the organic demands of love for the congregation. The entire argument, hence, implies that the legitimacy of the presbyters themselves be conditioned to their enhancing love and liberty within the congregation.

The clear anticlerical note Milton strikes in *The Reason of Church-government* is reiterated in *An Apology Against a Pamphlet Called A Modest Confutation* (1642) and foreshadows Milton's ideal drift toward congregational ecclesiology. In this respect, the close parallel between Roger Williams' and Milton's own spiritual course strictly resembles a pattern.[99] Williams' ecclesiological stances significantly unfold in four stages: from his taking holy orders in the established church to separatism, from separatism to the Baptist persuasion, and from the latter to the seeker's apprehension of all forms of Christian churches as apostate, Williams' progressive shift testifies to a linear estrangement from *the rule of men*. Milton's course is described along the same lines by John Toland in his *Life of John Milton*:

> In his early days he was a Favorer of those *Protestants* then opprobriously cal'd by the name of *Puritans*: In his middle years he was best pleas'd with the *Independents* and *Anabapstists*, as allowing of more Liberty than others, and coming nearest in his opinion to the primitive practice: but in the latter part of his Life, he was not a profest member of any particular Sect among Christians, he frequented none of their Assemblies, nor made

98. *CPW* 3.197.

99. Other notable examples of a similar pattern are Saltmarsh, Dell, and Goodwin. Parish priests at the outset of their ministry, Saltmarsh and Dell ultimately appeared to embrace Seeker positions (Dell would be buried outside the church) while Goodwin turned to Independency.

use of their particular Rites in his Family. Whether this proceeded from a dislike of their uncharitable and endless Disputes,
and that Love of Dominion, or Inclination to Persecution, which
he said, was a piece of Popery inseparable from all Churches; or
whether he thought one might be a good Man, without subscribing to any Party; and that they had all in som things corrupted
the Institutions of Jesus Christ, I will by no means adventure to
determin: for Conjectures on such occasions are very uncertain,
and I never met with any of his Acquaintance who could be positive in assigning the true Reasons of his Conduct.[100]

Toland interestingly makes Milton's ideological turn to Independency
and Anabaptism a matter of liberty. The notion itself finds further confirmation in the personal involvement which transpires from a letter
Milton addressed to a minister on behalf of a French Protestant church
of Independent leanings in 1659.[101] Toland's further unconfirmed suggestions about the latter part of Milton's life as free from any formal religious affiliation in turn present us with scenarios which seemingly match
Williams' late persuasion. That which Samuel Johnson would portray as
Milton's personal intolerance for any form of authority, whether civil or
ecclesiastical,[102] is depicted by the deist Toland as the genuine result of a
libertarian sentiment.

In the final analysis, the antiprelatical tracts envision two strands
or spirits throughout history: the spirit of the gospel of liberty and the
tyrannical spirit of man-made and self-glorifying religion. Traces of the
former could be found before the Reformation just as the dynamics of
the latter lingered on after the Reformation. Milton's ultimate prophetic
call was for men to align themselves with the spirit of the Reformation
as the vivid and visible expression of Christian liberty. Adherence to a
specific movement or theology was solely rightful insofar as that movement or theology enhanced the gospel of liberty and love. Orthodoxy
itself went far beyond formal allegiance to a set of propositions. It was to
be in tune with the gospel.

100. Toland, *The Life of John Milton*, 151–52.

101. Nuttall, "Milton's Churchmanship in 1659," 227–31. In accounting for the
document, Nuttall argues for the Independent leanings of the congregation and for
Milton's involvement in it.

102. E.g., "I know not any of the Articles [the 39 articles] which seem to thwart his
opinions: but the thoughts of obedience, whether canonical or civil, raised his indigna-
tion" (Johnson, *Lives*, 245).

To be sure, Milton's emphasis does not fall on the divine institution of "one right discipline" in the antiprelatical tracts and only "in the divorce pamphlets on 'private' liberty,"[103] as Barker argues, but it falls in both on the discipline of liberty. In initially endorsing Presbyterian ecclesiology, Milton is thus really endorsing that element in such ecclesiology which enhances freedom. In fact, Milton does not so much embrace the synodal form of church government as that libertarian principle which underlies the preservation of the local congregation from the external interference of law and men, church or state. To be sure, the Presbyterian system itself, even the most minimal form of government, could well forfeit the true purpose of church government. The Presbyterian, too, could be ranked in the human strain of religion and the word *presbyter* could in turn bespeak its detrimental etymology, for "new presbyter is but old priest writ large" (Sonnet *On the New Forcers of Conscience Under the Long Parliament*, 1646). If ecclesiology was the showcase of liberty in the antiprelatical tracts, the revolutionary principles of Christian liberty would invariably affect all other realms of life.

The Civil Community

John Milton left few wondering about his allegiance after King Charles I was executed in January 1649. *The Tenure of Kings and Magistrates* appeared in February, closely followed by Milton's appointment as Secretary for Foreign Tongues (March).[104] As Milton had previously engaged liberty within a private capacity, taking on the guise of the prophet-priest, he was now to speak as the apologist of a new law, both civil and Republican, resulting from Christian liberty. In *The Tenure of Kings and Magistrates* Milton maintains that

> No man who knows ought can be so stupid to deny that all men naturally were born free, being the image and resemblance of God himself, and were by privilege above all the creatures, born to command not to obey: and that they liv'd so. Till from the root of *Adams* transgression, falling among themselves to doe wrong and violence, and foreseeing that such courses must needs tend to the destruction of them all, they agreed by common league to

103. Barker, "Christian Liberty," 155.

104. *Articles of Peace* was published in May, followed by *Eikonoklastes* (October) and the three defenses: *Pro Populo Anglicano Defensio* (February, 1651), *Pro Populo Anglicano Defensio Secunda* (May, 1654), and *Pro Se Defensio* (August, 1655).

> bind each other from mutual injury, and jointly to defend them-
> selves against any that gave disturbance or opposition to such
> agreement.[105]

Here Milton asserts man's natural freedom, entailing authority. The fall
has subverted such creational principle, thus casting man down a destructive spiral. To prevent "mutual injury," men have joined together
on contractual grounds by binding themselves to laws. Similar rational
agreements, however, cannot possibly effect the eradication of sin and
sinful affections, but only afford an often short-lived compromise.

The cornerstone of Hobbes' own "political philosophy is the opposition between reason and emotions." While, as a model of rational construction, the "State . . . provides the only guarantee of peace and welfare
for mankind . . . , its stability is threatened not only by ignorance but also
by the disrupting influence of the passions, which operate directly or by
way of destructive doctrines or religious superstition."[106] The preservation of peace and welfare is therefore dependent on the inhibition of the
passions by the rational upholding of the state. Although Hobbes and
Milton both embrace the Renaissance *theory of the passions*, an opposite
angle informs Milton's apprehension of the role of the state. Whereas
reason is subservient to the construction of the state against passion-
induced disruptive forces in Hobbes, in Milton it is seen as preserving
freedom from the tyranny of the state. To this effect, *The Tenure of Kings
and Magistrates* argues that

> If men within themselves would be governed by reason, and not
> generally give up their understanding to a double tyranny, of cus-
> tom from without and blind affections within, they would dis-
> cern better what it is to favour and uphold the tyrant of a nation.[107]

The double tyranny of sin within and custom without impairs man's discernment of what it is "to favour and uphold the tyrant of a nation." Both
enslave his inner being. Sin obscures his mind and conscience; outward
custom exacts demands which find no correspondence within. Far from
being the projection of inner love, they inhibit both freedom and truth.
They are what the Pharisees of Jesus' day held to so dearly. By liberating both mind and conscience and engraving the law of love within,

---

105. *CPW* 3.198–99.

106. Pacchi, "Hobbes and the Passions," 79.

107. *CPW* 3.190.

the terms of Christian liberty restore reason to man and allow him to discern and reject tyranny.

In the final analysis, Hobbes believes that man is dominated by his passions to the extent that liberty is irremediably impaired on the individual level. As a consequence, he turns to the state to produce liberties by restraining the effects of the passions. Milton, on the other hand, believes in the restoration of individual liberty through grace so that the individual is free in himself and capable of projecting liberties while rejecting tyranny. The biblical perspective is superimposed to the natural as in a retrospective look at the political tracts Milton affirms that "It hath twice befaln me to assert, through Gods assistance, this most wrested and vexd place of scripture; heretofore against *Salmasius* and regal tyranie over the state."[108] Milton's biblical reference is to Romans 13:1–7,[109] namely the very passage that was construed as the foundation for arguments of unconditional submission to the king and the magistrate. The rationale underlying Milton's political stance is found no further than in the next three verses:

> Owe no man any thing, but to love one another: or he that loveth another hath fulfilled the law. For this, Thou shalt not commit adultery, Thou shalt not kill, Thou shalt not steal, Thou shalt not bear false witness, Thou shalt not covet; and if any other commandment it is briefly comprehended in this saying, namely, Thou shalt love thy neighbour as thyself. Love worketh no ill to his neighbour: therefore love is the fulfilling of the law.

After prescribing submission to authority, Paul specifies that the Christian, as a most free lord of all, owes no one submission but by the free choice of love, even love for his neighbor. As a most dutiful servant of all, however, the Christian delegates authority to the magistrate that

108. *CPW* 7.252.

109. "Let every soul be subject to the higher powers. For there is no power but from God: the powers that be are ordained by God. Whosoever therefore resisteth the power, resisteth the ordinance of God: and they that resist shall receive to themselves damnation. For rulers are not a terror to good works, but to the evil. Wilt thou then not be afraid of the power? Do that which is good, and thou shall have praise of the same: for he is the minister of God to thee for good. But if thou do that which is evil, be afraid; for he beareth not the sword in vain: for he is the minister of God, a revenger to wrath upon him that doeth evil. Wherefore must needs be subject, not only for wrath, but also for conscience sake. For this cause pay ye tribute also: for they are Gods ministers, attending continually upon this very thing. Render therefore to all their dues: tribute to whom tribute; custom to whom custom; fear to whom fear; honour to whom honour."

he may exert it in his stead as "the minister of God to thee for good" (v. 4). In his own right, Grotius, whom Milton had personally met during his trip on the continent, argued that authority comes "to the state from private individuals; and similarly, the power of the state is the result of collective agreement."[110] Even so, the Dutch jurist and philosopher did not envision limitations to the sovereignty of monarchs. In Milton's hands, as in Williams',[111] on the contrary, the principle of authority from below becomes pervasive and absolute. It becomes inherently democratic, revolutionary, subversive. Authority did come from God, but to the individual, and to kings and magistrates from individuals, for the pursuit of individual and collective liberties. In his political works, Milton extensively argues that the authority placed in the hands of the magistrates is strictly conditioned to its purpose, namely the enhancement of civil good and both individual and collective liberties. The moment that ceases, the magistrate loses his authority and the Christian resumes all direct prerogatives of freedom and love. Again epitomizing General Baptist belief and sentiment,[112] *An Orthodox Creed* reflects Milton's own apprehension by advocating submission to the *lawful* magistrate "in all lawful things."[113] The same is true of the king for Milton:

> [the king] cannot make any important decisions as to war or peace, nor even in the field of jurisdiction can he interfere with the decisions of the courts. For this reason the judges swear that in the conduct of their courts they will do nothing save in accordance with the law, not even if the king himself should by word or instructions, or even letters under his own seal, order them to do otherwise. Thus under our law the king is often termed "an infant," and is said to possess his rights and privileges only as a minor or a ward.[114]

110. Grotius, *On the Law of War and Peace*, cited in *Stanford Encyclopaedia of Philosophy*, entry Grotius.

111. "I infer that the sovereign, original, and foundation of civil power lies in the people" (Williams, *The Bloudy Tenent*, 3.249).

112. As early as 1612, Thomas Helwys' *A Short Declaration of the Mystery of Iniquity* was addressed to King James I asserting the conditional right of kings. Two of Milton's intimate theological frequentations, William Ames and Johannes Wolleb respectively subscribed to and rejected this stance. The latter argues that "we must obey, not only godly Magistrates and Masters, but also Tyrants" (Wolleb, *Abridgement*, 2.9.298–9).

113. Lumpkin, ed., *Baptist Confessions*, art. 45, 331.

114. *CPW* 4.482.

As it is implicit in these words, Milton does not initially appear to op-
pose "kingship *per se*, but tyranny" or that form of monarchy which is
not subservient to just law. It is only with the "sequence of published and
unpublished works he wrote between the autumn of 1659 and the spring
of 1660" that he begins to express "hostility not only to Stuart tyranny
in particular but to monarchy in general, and not only to monarchy but
also—adopting the republican jargon for kings, protectors, dictators and
the like—to the rule of any 'single person' whatsoever."[115]

In effect, no external rule would ultimately prove able to match
Milton's tenets of liberty and love, but the rule of God. The eschatological tension in his political works, therefore, unsurprisingly intertwines
the pursuit of perfecting the reformation with the advent of earth's last
king. In so doing, however, it merges the final reality with the present
one:

> But why do I proclaim as if performed by the people these deeds
> which . . . bear witness to the presence of God in every place? . . .
> It was by his evident will that we were unexpectedly encouraged
> to hope for that security and liberty which had been well nigh
> lost to us: We followed him as our leader . . . Who, in fact, is
> worthy of holding on earth power like that of God but . . . the Son
> of God whose coming we look for?[116]

In a very real sense, throughout Milton's pursuit of outward liberty, the
saint is seen as a subject of God's mild rule, with Christ as the king of his
soul and the sole rightful heir to the earthly throne of England. While
anticipating the eschatological realization, the spiritual, ecclesiological,
civil and political prerogatives of Christian liberty end up being assimilated under the rule of the dispenser of true liberty and Luther's two
kingdoms are conflated into one present reality. Here lies Milton's ideal
of the Christian nation. In the present reading, that is, Milton appears to
anticipate the lesson which in more recent times has found in Dietrich
Bonhoeffer its most lucid expositor.

> As long as Christ and the world are conceived as two realms
> bumping against and repelling each other, we are left with only
> the following options. Giving up on reality as a whole, either we
> place ourselves in one of the two realms, wanting Christ without
> the world or the world without Christ—and in both cases we

115. Dzelzainis, "Republicanism," 296–97.

116. *CPW* 4.305, 427–28.

deceive ourselves . . . There are not two realities, but only one
reality, and that is God's reality revealed in Christ in the reality of
the world. The reality of Christ embraces the reality of the world
itself. The world has no reality of its own independent of God's
revelation in Christ . . . [T]he theme of two realms, which has
dominated the history of the church again and again, is foreign
to the New Testament.[117]

Toleration

Another form of outward tyranny had presented itself anew in the
early years of the civil war in the guise of limitations to the freedom
of speech. The sweep of Milton's argument in *Areopagitica* witnesses
against the dogmatization of truth and the censorship of falsehood. In
fact, while Christian liberty has made the Christian free to discern truth
and choose it amidst false alternatives, that confrontation with the latter
which Christian liberty allows and urges enhances the display of true
virtue and the Christian's inward fortification in the choice of truth. Not
only so, but as John Goodwin likewise has it,[118] the free confrontation of

---

117. Bonhoeffer, *Ethics*, 58.

118. See Loewenstein, "Toleration and the Specter of Heresy," 51. Loewenstein's
portrait of Goodwin is that of a speculative personality. Though retaining Puritan
sentiments in the Thirties, Goodwin would embrace Arminian beliefs in the Forties.
An overt opponent of the divine right of kings (see *Os Ossorianum, or a Bone for a
Bishop*, 1643, against Griffith Williams, bishop of Ossory) and supporter of regicide
(*The Obstructors of Justice*, 1649), from 1642 to 1646 Goodwin primarily devoted his
efforts to battling exclusivist and dogmatic apprehensions and apologies of truth and
the authoritarian systems that enforced them. See *Imputatio Fidei, or, A Treatise of
Justification* (1642); Θεομαχία, *or the grand imprudence of fighting against God* (1644);
M.S. to A.S. with a Plea for Libertie of Conscience (1644); *Cretensis: or a Brief Answer
to An Ulcerous Treatise* (1646). From 1630–1645 he served as vicar of St. Stephen, in
Coleman Street, London, where Nathaniel Paget, Milton's personal physician, as well
as regicide and one time mayor of London Isaac Penington sr., also worshipped. In
May 1645 Goodwin was denied his living under the charge of setting up a covenanted
community within his parish. The minister would thereafter lead an Independent gath-
ering in his house in Coleman Street only to be restored to the use of St. Stephen for a
reduced revenue in 1649. In his *Imputatio Fidei, or, A Treatise of Justification*, Goodwin
argues against George Walker, a soon to be member of the Westminster Assembly, that
dogmatism was equivalent to repressing truth, whereas allowing light to shine in the
darkness of preconceived misapprehension would yield truth just as it had restored
the gospel of justification to man. Indeed Goodwin's attitude was not relativistic, but
positivistic. He did not maintain that truth was ever fluid and subjective, but that man
had to be ready to integrate the measure of light received and even discard all false

truths would work towards the genuine apprehension of *truth*.[119] Roger Williams in his own right would argue that the attitude of those in the two houses who only wish to hear what pleases them makes it "rarely possible that any other Light . . . shall ever shine on your Honours Souls, though ne're so sweet, so necessary, and though it come from God, from Heaven."[120] Fear, coercion and lack of knowledge only pervert, suffocate or numb truth. Freedom reinvigorates reason and allows it to bring truth to light. Once again the paradigmatic quality of Dietrich Bonhoeffer's thought proves compelling in the words, "truth is born only of freedom."[121]

Ultimately, the lesson of Christian liberty in *Areopagitica* is that "truth is not the property of any external form, even of a form that proclaims this very truth."[122] Truth does not need the help of man to be preserved or prevail nor will it be handled or controlled by external agents. Rather man needs truth to genuinely possess and control his inward being. It is little surprise then if in these gospel times Christ is to be the "only Lord of Conscience,"[123] and tares are to be allowed to grow alongside wheat. Along these lines, The Standard Confession of General Baptists (1660) maintains:

> . . . it is the will, and mind of God (*in these Gospel times*) [my italics] that all men should have the free liberty of their own Consciences in matters of Religion, or Worship, without the least oppression, or persecution, as simply upon that account; and that for any in Authority otherwise to act, we confidently believe is expressly contrary to the mind of Christ, who requires . . . that the

though long-entertained opinions once truth was disclosed. A process of confrontation of diverging truths was thus not only tolerable, but desirable for the enhancement of ultimate truth. Hence Goodwin could resort consistently to Calvin and yet go beyond predestinarian soteriology to endorse general atonement. As the offer of grace was free, so was the reception. In his mind, the gospel extended an invitation that man was free to accept or reject. Ultimately, Goodwin's Arminian understanding of free will, alongside his participative apprehension of truth, formed the basis for the breadth of his tolerationist outlook.

119. See Norton, "The Praxis of Milton's Truth." Cf. *CPW* 6.122–3.

120. Williams, *Queries*, in *The Complete Writings*, 2.253.

121. Cited in Metaxas, *Bonhoeffer*, 95.

122. Fish, "Driving from the Letter," in Nyquist and Ferguson, eds., *Re-Membering Milton*, 243.

123. Lumpkin, ed., *The Baptist Confessions*, art. 46, 331–32.

> Tares, and the Wheat should grow together in the field, (which is
> the world) until the harvest (which is the end of the world) . . .[124]

Milton's adherence to such tenets is foreign to the urge for self-preservation often felt by General Baptists. Even so, a common rationale underlies both. For both Milton and General Baptists Christian liberty stands as the ultimate foundation of toleration in matters of conscience and belief in that it frees truth from the constraint of human categories and legal rulings and hands it over to the individual apprehension of God in Christ by the Spirit of truth.

Paradise Lost was already under way when a renewed sense of prophetic urgency called the poet to set aside, one last time, his ultimate poetical vocation to write *A Treatise of Civil Power in Ecclesiastical Causes: Shewing That it is not lawfull for any power on earth to compel in matter of Religion* (1959) and *Considerations touching The likeliest means to remove hirelings out of the church. Wherein is also discourc'd Of Tithes, Church-fees, Church-revenues; And whether any maintenance of ministers can be settl'd by law* (1959). Once more, in addressing "The Parlament of the Commonwealth of England with the Dominions thereof," Milton was speaking as a Christian to Christians. Here, more than ever before, the polemist appears to place himself in the strain of that "substantial number of Baptists, radical Independents, and Levellers" who, in the words

---

124. Lumpkin, ed., *The Baptist Confessions*, arts. 24, 232–33. The Standard Confession (1660) epitomizes General Baptist doctrine in the second half of the seventeenth century. More specifically, it largely reflects General Baptist doctrine in the years prior to and ushering in the Restoration. The Confession held to the extent of atonement as general, individual unbelief being the sole ground for eternal damnation and Christ the only foundation of election of "such as believe, and so are in Christ," apart "from foreseen faith" or works of human righteousness. Far from specifying its origin, faith was in turn defined as "assent to gospel truth" and trust in the "remission of sins and eternal life to be had in Christ." Children were given assurance of salvation along with all those who would persevere in the faith (Lumpkin, *Baptist Confessions of Faith*, arts. IV, VI, VIII, X, XVIII, 225–28, 230). Visible churches were defined by the preaching of the gospel message, the baptism of repentant believers, prayer, the laying on of hands for the bestowal of the Holy Spirit, fellowship and godly living (arts. XI–XIV; 228–29). In distinguishing between the spiritual and the civil realms, the Confession vigorously stressed liberty of conscience in religious matters based on the golden rule and the parable of the wheat and the tares (art. XXIV, 232–33). Also, it stressed the *conditional* duty on the part of Christians to obey the civil magistrates (art. XXV, 233). Along with the general resurrection and general judgment, the eschatology of the Confession included a reference to the second coming and Christ's reign with his children over the nations of the earth, yielding premillennial overtones (arts. XX–XXII, 231–32).

of John Coffey, "insisted that the New Testament paradigm required the church to be a purely voluntary, non-coercive community in the midst of a pluralistic society governed by a 'merely civil' state. Although their position was not without its ambiguities, it constituted a startling break with the Constantinian assumptions of magisterial Protestantism."[125]

By 1659 Milton fully shared with Williams the distinction between the voluntary religious community and the civil state identified in these words. However, while Williams regarded the source of power behind the civil state as "not religious, Christian &c. but naturall, humane and civill,"[126] Milton traces the source of all authority to the very New Testament paradigm calling for a voluntary, non-coercive religious community and a merely civil state.

In the pamphlets above, Milton also shows peculiar adherence to contemporary Quaker concerns.[127] His arguments, unlike the Quaker's, however, do not hinge on the intrinsic illegitimacy of all earthly authority,[128] but around the illegitimacy of the coalescence of religious

125. Coffey, "Puritanism and Liberty Revisited," 961.

126. Williams, *The Bloudy Tenent*, 3.398.

127. After the fall of the Protectorate in 1659, George Fox pleaded with the reconvened Purged Parliament to replace the established church with the Society of Friends as the leading religious element in the nation. At the time, the Quaker stance on issues of toleration, the corruption of the state church and the illegitimacy of tithes found a notable advocate in none other than Milton. The Restoration shattered all Quaker hopes in 1660, when the Friends came to be associated with radical groups as the virtual nemesis of the newly established order and Fox was imprisoned at Lancaster for five months under charges of conspiracy. The suppression of the Fifth Monarchist upheaval led by Thomas Venner in January 1661 accounts for Fox's *The Peace Testimony*, in which the Quaker committed the Society of Friends to unconditional pacifism. During the reigns of Charles II and James II, Fox confronted external persecution as well as internal dissension. If the Quaker Act of 1662 forbade refusal to take oaths, a distinctive Quakers shared with Mennonites, the Conventicle Act of 1664 included the prohibition to attend Quaker gatherings and deportation to the tropical colonies for seven years (Campbell and Corns, *John Milton*, 326). Ronald Hutton has it that by the end of that year "every surviving member of the movement had been gaoled" (Hutton, *Restoration*, 211). Henceforth, we find Fox in Ireland, continental Europe (Germany and Holland), the American colonies and the West Indies. Back in England, Fox contravened the Test Act of 1673 by refusing to take an oath and suffered a long imprisonment at Worcester, which cost him his health. While at Worcester, he began dictating his autobiographical *Journal*, which was published posthumously in 1694.

128. Upon his conversion experience in 1647, Fox became convinced that all earthly authority, be it secular or ecclesiastical, was spiritually impotent and bereft of the righteousness which formed the sole basis for legitimate authority. A direct experience of God was to replace man-made religion. God's message was to come to individuals di-

and civil authority in ruling against the individual conscience. While *Considerations touching The likeliest means* strictly appropriated both general and particular Quaker conclusions, *A Treatise of Civil Power* polished the arguments of *Areopagitica* only to draw, with Williams, a clear line between civil matters and matters of conscience. In distinguishing between the two, Milton came to conceive of heresy as punishable by the magistrate only insofar as it amounted to a visible breach of the civil law.[129] Personal belief, much like divorce and speech, was to fall under the jurisdiction of conscience, "for beleef or practice in religion according to this conscientious perswasion no man ought to be punishd or molested by any outward force on earth whatsoever."[130]

If in the political tracts Milton had directed his focus to Christian liberty as freedom from oppressive and unlawful governments, he now felt inwardly persuaded to discharge his duty before God by advocating Christian liberty as freedom from the rule of men in matters of conscience.[131] However, while extending freedom of conscience to Bible-abiding Protestants and Jews alike—the latter's freedom of conscience proving all the more consequential in view of Israel's conversion to Christ at the second coming[132]—Milton, unlike Williams, excludes Catholicism from the scope of toleration inasmuch as the latter is less a conscience-seated religion than "a Roman principalitie . . . endevouring to keep up her old universal dominion under a new name."[133]

---

rectly through the inner light of God. The saints, those who would allow themselves to be vivified by the inner light, were placed above human hierarchies. This understanding was reflected in specific courses of action, such as omitting signs of deference. One such instance occurred when Thomas Ellwood encountered some old acquaintances of his in Oxford. Ellwood writes: "A Knot of my old Acquaintances . . . saluted me after the usual manner, putting off their Hats and Bowing, and saying 'Your Humble Servant, Sir,' expecting, no doubt, the like from me. But when they saw me standing still . . . they were amazed: 'What? Tom, a Quaker?' To which I readily and cheerfully answered, 'Yes, a Quaker.' And as the words passed out of my Mouth I felt joy spring in my Heart . . . that I had strength and boldness given me, to Confess myself to be one of that despised People" (Ellwood, *History of the Life*, 63–64).

129. *CPW* 7.252.

130. *CPW* 7.242.

131. *CPW* 7.240.

132. *CPW* 2.561–68. Also see *Of True Religion*, where Milton plainly echoes Amyraut in calling for the toleration of all Protestants based on their common adherence to the Word of God.

133. *CPW* 7.255.

The rejection of Augustinian replacement theology appears to underlie Milton's understanding here. As the kingdom of God on earth, the church had replaced Israel as both a temporal and spiritual kingdom bound to exert, by divine right, control over all social, political as well as religious structures.[134] Whereas the established church of England and the Puritan establishment would have maintained respectively that civil and political authority rested in the hands of the king and the parliament, they would argue in unison that God's moral law was to be enforced in its entirety by both religious and civil power. This was not only true of that which for Calvinists was the second table of the Decalogue, namely those commandments which related to social relationships, but also of those commandments which pertained to man's relationship to God, the first table.

Milton speaks of the same spirit of popery associating both the established church and mainstream Puritans to the Roman church. For Milton neither church nor state are ever to rule over the individual conscience. Rather, they ought to be the extension of a free conscience. Along these lines, in sanctioning the freedom of conscience from inward as well as outward restraint, Milton's terms of Christian liberty appear to envision an inward haven of freedom—its own state and its own church—which is to unfold outwardly in both a religious and a civil fashion. The resulting religious and civil institutions must needs abstain from self-assertion, self-preservation as well as from the enforcement of their aspirations, as their very existence is inextricably dependent on and bound to individual freedom. The liberal benefits of this outlook will naturally invest both the Christian and the non-Christian in a society that will comprise both Christian and secular elements under the rule of Christian liberty.

Much like early Friends, Milton "worked to change the world as . . ." he "had been changed."[135] In the libertarian struggle to affirm the principles of Christian liberty in England during the years of the Interregnum, he was yet confronted with the dire reality of the progressive disruption of liberty which culminated in the Restoration. To recover an expres-

---

134. See Diprose, *Israel and the Church*, 87–89. See also Ryrie, *Basic Theology*, 460–63, 520, 592; idem, *Dispensationalism*, 64, 127–31.

135. These words are referred by Barbour to early Quakers. See Barbour, *The Quakers in Puritan England*, 160.

sion coined by Steven Marx, Milton was now a prophet disarmed.[136] The weapons of war and law had failed. Conversion, as opposed to social reform, was now to become the primary focus of his testimony. If outward restoration could only begin with the personal restoration of Adam and Eve, restored individual liberty alone would yield reconciliation as the firstfruits of all outward liberties.

136. See Marx, "The Prophet Disarmed."

2

Christian Liberty and *Paradise Lost*

I f Milton's prose reflects his attempt to see Christian liberty realized in the outward realm, *Paradise Lost* is a return to its constitutive elements as a fully accomplished inward reality. It is the poetical creation of the new man.[1]

Whereas at a first glance the poem appears to expand on the ramifications of the fall and its relation to man's faculties and liberty in a way that closely parallels Augustinianism and Thomist Scholasticism, a broader analysis shows a shift from Scholastic to Scriptural and Reformed categories in book 12 which goes alongside a shift in Milton's focus from externals to internals. But first things first:

> . . . Justly thou abhorr'st
> That son, who on the quiet state of men
> Such trouble brought, affecting to subdue
> Rational liberty; yet know withal,
> Since thy original lapse, true liberty
> Is lost, which always with right reason dwells

1. Continuity with the prose can be appreciated in the poem, where Milton proves to align himself with Calvin's tri-fold division of the Mosaic law as civil/political, ceremonial and moral (see *PL* 12.230–5; 297–99): while the first "is but the arme of the moral lawe" (*CPW* 2.322), Christ is both the substance to which the shadows of the ceremonial law pointed, and the passive fulfillment of the moral law in man. The outward principle of works of law is thus supplanted by the inward Spirit-driven principle of faith working through love (*PL* 12.487–89). For the poem to bring up the most distinctive category of the "moral law" is to set it *lexically* in the company of the mainstream theologies, not least William Ames' (Ames, *Marrow*, 111, 139, 269, 287, 291, 318), as opposed to *De Doctrina*, where explicit references to the "moral law" are nowhere to be found. In fact, the Latin treatise consistently regards the law as a unity and, as such, as abolished in its entirety with the advent of Christ.

Twinned, and from her hath no dividual being:
Reason in man obscured, or not obeyed,
Immediately inordinate desires
And upstart passions catch the government
From reason, and to servitude reduce
Man till then free . . . (12.79–90)

"That son" refers here to Nimrod. While Genesis is quite cryptic about this figure, Milton appears to draw from the Augustinian tradition, which finds in Josephus its fountainhead. According to this tradition, Nimrod embodies the principle of prideful ambition and rebellious opposition to God.[2] It is quite unsurprising that Milton chooses this Satanic mimesis to epitomize the slavery of sin and, by contrast, shed light on the twofold nature of liberty.

Liberty is both inward and outward, the full unfolding of the latter resting on the foundation of the former. Outward liberty had attracted Milton's every effort for little less than two decades. To see liberty reflected in the laws and institutions of his country he had given up poetry. True liberty was yet to be sought within.

In the lines above, inward liberty is defined as "rational liberty" or the complement of "right reason," its inseparable twin. Reason stands at the threshold and reaches inward as well as outward. Its role is to govern man and yield obedience to God. Nevertheless, man's first disobedience has divorced reason from liberty by affecting pervasively, if not absolutely, both reason and will. Postlapsarian Adam himself exemplifies this truth as he fails to will, let alone do, what he should:

. . . But from mee what can proceed,
But all corrupt, both Mind and Will deprav'd,
Not to do onely, but to will the same
With mee? (10.824–7)[3]

This reality has been variously reflected in human experience ever since Adam's original lapse. If the fall has "obscured" reason, thus preventing it from properly informing the will, the choice of not obeying the truthful dictates of reason originates in the will. The twofold detrimental dynamic has opened the door to "inordinate desires" and "upstart passions" which have darkened the mind and taken over the control of

2. See Hardin, "Milton's Nimrod."
3. Cf. 30–31.

man from reason. He who was "till then free" has thus been reduced to inward slavery.

The early modern *theory of the passions* appears to generally inform the passage. Man's mental steadfastness before the fall was defined in terms that closely parallel Augustine by J. F. Senault: "In this happy estate the soul commanded with mildness, the body obeyed with delight, and whatsoever object presented itself, these two parties did alwaies agree."[4] The positive balance was yet disrupted by sinful affections. In reviewing the soul's condition in light of Adam's fall, Edward Reynolds envisioned the eclipse of reason as the essential result of the introduction of unruly passions and affections. Deriving his authority from Augustine, Reynolds depicted Adam as free from all distempers and inward turmoil, with his passions as naturally subordinated to reason. The fallen condition was, on the contrary, characterized by the impairment of right reason resulting in the inability to discern things "according to their naked and naturall truth, but according as it finds them beare in the Fancie those impressions of Pleasure, which are most agreeable to corrupted nature."[5] Both Milton and Reynolds envision fancy as a new channel replacing reason and paving the way for the unrestrained display of sinful affections. All in all, Milton would have commended John Donne's figurative portrayal of will's capitulation under reason's captivity:

> I, like an usurpt town, to another due,
> Labour to admit you, but oh, to no end,
> Reason your viceroy in mee, mee should defend,
> But is captiv'd, and proves weake or untrue[6]

The slavery of sin thus depicted called for the dispensation of the law as a teacher. Although the law proceeded from God and would produce partial outward restraint of evil and thus relative freedom,[7] the slavery

4. Senault, *The Use of Passions*, 54–59.

5. Reynolds, *A Treatise of the Passions*, 65. The position outlined by Reynolds is essentially the one adopted by Richard Hooker and endorsed by the majority of seventeenth-century divines, both Anglican and Puritan.

6. Donne, "Batter My Heart" in Serpieri and Bigliazzi, eds., *Poesie*, 600.

7. Pervasive though the subjugation of enthralled man to the rule of men is, human self-exposure to tyranny would vary in degree. The law, as noticed, would still be able to inform collective liberties in terms of expediency, in terms, that is, of those limitations which mitigate sinful affections and thus enhance outward liberties. Some nations, however, would decline from reason to the extent that restraint of their outward liberty would only occur as a rightful remedy: Yet sometimes nations will decline

of sin would be to the observance of the law what the law of gravity is to flight. The law would relentlessly exact its demands without according man the ability to break free from sin. A slave to sin, man would come to conceive of the law as tyranny, his desperate condition being thereby laid bare and his impotence further amplified:

> . . . Doubt not but that sin
> Will reign among them, as of thee begot;
> And therefore was law given them to evince
> Their natural pravity, by stirring up
> Sin against law to fight (12.285–89)

Not only is loss of inward liberty behind the magnification of the law as tyranny, but, echoing *The Tenure of Kings and Magistrates*, the loss of inward liberty, occasioned by the slavery of sin and amplified by the rule of the law, is also invariably behind man's subjection to outward tyranny or the rule of men. While man is no longer able to discern and thereby withstand outward oppression, his condition of slavery proves ultimately sanctioned by God himself as he allows for "violent lords" to carry out his judgment. The judgment itself is dictated by individual defiance of liberty for sinful affections. It is necessitated by what is tantamount to the choice of self over God. Even so, those who carry out the judgment by restraining outward freedom bear full responsibility for their tyranny:

> . . . since he permits
> Within himself unworthy powers to reign
> Over free reason, God in judgment just
> Subjects him from without to violent lords;
> Who oft as undeservedly enthral
> His outward freedom: tyranny must be,
> Though to the tyrant thereby no excuse. (12.90–96)

Far from merely involving the civil and political realms, tyranny would come to define the religious as well. To this effect, in the unfolding of his theology of history in book 12, the poet purposely accounts for the period which would succeed the descent of the Spirit and the dispensation of the New Testament through the apostles, the time, that is, when

---

so low / From virtue, which is reason, that no wrong, / But justice, and some fatal curse annexed / Deprives them of their outward liberty, / Their inward lost . . . (12.97–101).

> Their ministry performed, and race well run,
> Their doctrine and their story written left,
> They die; but in their room, as they forewarn,
> Wolves shall succeed for teachers, grievous wolves,
> Who all the sacred mysteries of Heav'n
> To their own vile advantages shall turn
> Of lucre and ambition, and the truth
> With superstitions and traditions taint,
> Left only in those written records pure,
> Though not but by the Spirit understood.
> Then shall they seek to avail themselves of names,
> Places and titles, and with these to join
> Secular power, though feigning still to act
> By spiritual, to themselves appropriating
> The Spirit of God, promised alike and giv'n
> To all believers; and from that pretense,
> Spiritual laws by carnal power shall force
> On every conscience; laws which none shall find
> Left them enrolled, or what the Spirit within
> Shall on the heart engrave. What will they then
> But force the Spirit of Grace itself, and bind
> His consort Liberty ... (12.505–26)

Michael here foretells what the New Testament would also overshadow,[8] that is, the coming of false shepherds who would seek personal glory and power. To this very end, they would mar that truth which alone is found in the New Testament with self-crafted superstitions and traditions and hold to truth as their sole prerogative. Truth, however, while accessible, cannot be claimed as a human possession, but is for the Spirit to disclose. Not content, the false shepherds would further pursue secular power through the appropriation of titles and names while screening themselves behind the charter of spiritual authority and, by making distinctive claims to the Spirit of God, they would avail themselves of superior, if self-arrogated, authority to force man-made laws on consciences.

The echo of *Areopagitica* and *A Treatise of Civil Power* is apparent here. Two sources of spiritual laws are contrasted as well as the respective ways in which they have been communicated and by which they are appropriated. On one hand, the source is God. He has communicated his spiritual laws through Scripture (laws left "enrolled") and through the Spirit's inward autograph. The written record and the law the Spirit

---

8. See John 10:1–10.

engraves on the heart of those who believe are thus both upheld and complementary. The second source is men. Their laws are not to be found either in Scripture or within. The laws of God are appropriated by grace. The laws of men are imposed by force. God frees consciences. Men control them. Liberty is wedded to that Spirit who manifests his life in man on the basis of the true freedom God has provided by his grace. Slavery is to deny the "Spirit of Grace" for selfish advancement. The history of mankind proves defined by this denial and, therefore, by the fall:

> Since thy [Adam's] original lapse, true liberty
> Is lost . . .

The *enjambement* works here to the effect of emphasizing both the distinctiveness of this kind of liberty and the loss thereof. It doesn't matter what degree of relative liberty laws can produce through restraint of sin. That liberty, let alone any form of human rule, is not true liberty, Milton seems to be saying. In fact, the very liberties procured by laws as well as freedom from the tyranny of men are closely dependent on true liberty. Yet true liberty is lost.

Where can it be found? If loss of true liberty has come as a result of the captivity of right reason produced by the introduction of sinful affections within man, inward liberty can only be born anew through freedom from the slavery of sin. Book 12 now abandons all terminology relating to man's inner faculties to turn to Johannine and Pauline discourse. Here the governmental function of regenerated reason is derivative, as it is indicated to stem from pre-existing unconditional liberty. The words of Jesus in John's Gospel match Milton's in pointing to sin as the enslaving factor, while drawing to the Son as the key to true liberty:

> Verily, verily, I say unto you, Whosoever committeth sin is the servant of sin. And the servant abideth not in the house for ever: *but* the Son abideth ever. If the Son therefore shall make you free, ye shall be free indeed.[9]

Whereas the rehabilitation of the inner faculties of man yields the restoration of true freedom in Augustine, the principle of the *knowledge of God* introduces us to a reversed perspective in Milton. Inward liberty must first be established for the inner faculties to be restored to the fullness of their function. In other words, right reason can only be born of

---

9. John 8:34–36.

freedom. Or else, reason only truly frees if it is free. In the evangelical words, freedom is a synonym for sonship and no sonship can subsist where there is sin. To think that man's pre-emptively restored abilities may effect the eradication of sin is tantamount to tying man's freedom to his performance, thus turning Christian liberty into a dynamic process. Yet the Son resolves to make man free apart from his works by doing away with sin and its ramifications in his own flesh:

> . . . to the cross he nails thy enemies,
> The law that is against thee, and the sins
> Of all mankind, with him there crucified,
> Never to hurt them more who rightly trust
> In this his satisfaction . . . (12.415–9)

Sin and the law being thus nailed to the cross, inward liberty no longer coincides with a free ability and its positive enactment for those "who rightly trust / In this his satisfaction," but with an unchanging position with respect to God. Sin can no longer harm and law no longer constrain, but the mind and conscience thus cleared from what obscured reason and conscience are free under the rule of grace:

> Some blood more precious must be paid for man,
> Just for the unjust, that in such righteousness
> To them by faith imputed, they may find
> Justification towards God, and peace
> Of conscience, which the law by ceremonies
> Cannot appease, nor the moral part
> Perform, and not performing cannot live.
> So law appears imperfect, and but giv'n
> With purpose to resign man in full time
> Up to a better cov'nant, disciplined
> From shadowy types to truth, from flesh to spirit,
> From imposition of strict laws to free
> Acceptance of large grace, from servile fear
> To filial, works of law to works of faith. (12.293–306)

Unlike the Medieval tradition, yet much like Paul and the Reformed strain, Milton here indicates that "justification towards God, and peace

/ Of conscience" are found in the Son's imputed righteousness. A shift is marked from liberty based on performance to inward liberty based on grace, from true liberty, that is, based on what man is and does to true liberty based on what the Son is and would do. In articulate theological language, the General Baptist *An Orthodox Creed* argues to the same effect that God,

> out of his free grace and love to fallen man, in order to his recovery out of this sinful and deplorable state, hath freely offered him a second, or a new covenant of grace, which new covenant of grace *is* Jesus Christ [my italics], in remission of sins, through faith in his blood . . . for by faith we receive that righteousness that the law, or the first covenant, required of the first Adam; which righteousness Christ hath fulfilled in our nature which he took of the virgin Mary, by his active obedience, and is, by God's free donation, made over to us by imputation; for he hath made him to us wisdom, righteousness and sanctification . . . Christ hath not only fulfilled the sanction of the law . . . but hath also voluntarily suffered the curse of the law, being made a curse for us, that we might receive the blessing of Abraham, and the promise of the spirit thro' faith in his blood.[10]

Christ is here said to be the new covenant of grace inasmuch as he embodies grace and provides the ground upon which the new covenant can be established through both his active and passive righteousness. The lexis of *imputation* in *Paradise Lost*[11] and the confession contrasts Grotius' concept of rectoral or governmental atonement, while it plainly reflects the Reformed and Pauline theology of substitutionary atonement.[12] Milton further argues that to place one's faith in the Son's righteousness is tantamount to turning from slavery to the ritualism of shadows and one's impotence to fulfill the moral law to the substance of grace and the filial status in the Spirit. A matching synthesis of the dispensational shift from law to grace is manifestly found in Ames' *Marrow of Theology*:

> The testament is new with relation to what existed from the time of Moses and in relation to the promise made to the fathers

10. Lumpkin, ed., *The Baptist Confessions*, art. XVI, 307.

11. E.g., 3.290–91; 12.409.

12. Cf. 2 Cor 5:21. See Campbell, *John Milton and the Manuscript of De Doctrina Christiana*, 112–13. See also Poole, "Theology," 478–79; Falcone, "More Challenges," 234–36.

... Its difference in quality is in clarity and freedom ... Clarity occurs, first in the more distinct expression than heretofore of the doctrine of grace and salvation through Christ and through faith in him ... Second, it is expressed not in types and shadows, but in a most manifest fashion ... Freedom comes, first, in doing away with government by law, or the intermixture of government of works, which held the ancient people in a certain bondage. The spirit of adoption, though never fully denied to believers, is also most properly said to be communicated under the New Testament ...[13]

In his own right, Fox points to the new Spirit-empowered filial state ushered in by the covenant of grace. In resorting to the biblical type of "Rest," however, he sheds further light on the constitution of the son's new inward microcosm of liberty:

Christ arose from the dead on the First-day of the week; and they that believe on him are entered into Christ, their Rest; the Christians meet together to worship God on the First-day of the week; and on the First-day of the week it was that God said, "Let there be light, and there was light." The Jews' rest was on the seventh-day of the week, which was given to them as a sign of the eternal rest of the Lord, sanctifying them, after they came out of the land of Egypt; for before that time the Lord had not given to man and woman his outward Sabbath-day to keep, neither in the old world, nor after in Abraham's time, nor in Isaac's, nor in Jacob's time; until the Jews came out of Egypt to Mount Sinai in the wilderness. Then the Lord gave the law and his Sabbath, as a sign in the old covenant, of Christ the Eternal Rest in the new covenant; and they that believe do enter into Christ, their Rest.[14]

Like Milton, Ames and the General Baptist creedal formulation, here Fox contrasts the old covenant with the new, the outward rest of the Sabbath with the inward. The law could only afford the outward as a sign of true inward rest; Christ *is* the eternal inward rest and he who believes on him enters "into Christ," his rest. Once again, a position is entailed with Christ as both the way and the final Canaan of liberty. As it is for Milton, in both Fox and the Baptist confession the passage from the old covenant to the new marks a passage from signs to their signified, from

13. Ames, *Marrow*, 205–6.
14. Fox, *A Journal of the Life*, 307.

outward to inward, from liberty through dynamic achievements to positional rest, through faith in the Son.

This shift entails a new kind of inward liberty, which differs from prelapsarian freedom. If prelapsarian Adam and Eve were free insofar as their free intellect and will complied with God's good will, in the words of Thomas Pierce[15] "Alia etiam *Arbitrii libertas* est in Statu hominis Regenerati, Conversique. Nam ex Statu depravationis in Statum Gratiae [Quenam in tercio hominis Statu] conversus, ab errore in Veritatem, ab incredulitate ad Fidem, à tenebris ad Lucem, à peccatis ad Deum." Most notably, grace is a state resulting from having been transferred from darkness to light, from sin to God. In turn, this new position determines a condition whereby "Novam arbitrii libertatem, non ab ipso sane Peccato, sed *a Peccati Servitute*, evestigio consequitor. Nova luce accensus, novis viribus munitus per Spiritum Sanctum."[16] In other words, freedom from the slavery of sin results in a new freedom of the will, which amounts to, as it were, Christian liberty's first efficiency.

Fulfilled in man's place and its wages paid, the law loses its prerogative to condemn, constrain and stir man's enslaving affections. It no longer serves the child as an external set of rules and prescriptions, but its moral essence can be discerned and observed by the free and adult subject through works of faith. The latter supplant works of law as deeds which are built upon man's reliance (faith) on his pre-established inward liberty by the new light of the indwelling Spirit. Indeed all factors which held reason captive appear to dissipate as man is pronounced free at the beginning of his walk and given over to "the Spirit of truth":

> The promise of his Father, who shall dwell
> His Spirit within them and the Law of Faith,
> Working through love, upon their hearts shall write
> To guide them in all truth . . . (12.487–90)

15. A Calvinist to the end of 1644, Thomas Pierce turned to a mild Arminianism, on which he then expanded in 1655. A graduate of Magdalen College, Oxford, he would be appointed Dean at the Restoration.

16. Pierce, *Corpuscolum pacificatorium*, 131–32. Translation: "Different is the freedom of the will for the man who is in a state of regeneration and transformation. For he has been transferred from a state of depravation to a state of grace (i.e., to the third state of man), from error to truth, from incredulity to faith, from darkness to light, from sin to God . . . A new freedom of the will results [from this state], not to be sure a freedom from the very presence of sin, but from the slavery of sin. Illumined by new light, [the believer] is endowed with new strength through the Holy Spirit" (my translation).

After Jesus' departure from earth, his disciples are promised not to be left orphans. A comforter, the Paraclete, will come from heaven to dwell within man. God's perpetual law of truth will no longer be encompassed in external formulaic prescriptions, but will become part of man's inward essence. By engraving the law on the heart of man, the Spirit will thus fulfill the prophecy of Jeremiah and provide the inward counterpart and synthesis of that truth which is only found in the "written records pure," in fact, those same records which are "but by . . . [that] same Spirit understood." The new law will no longer be a law of works, but a law of faith, as the Spirit will solely pursue it in man on the basis of faith in the Son's imputed righteousness. Such faith in turn will not be void of works (12.427), for the distinctive expression of faith shall be love.

The reader will immediately recall the words of Paul in Romans 3:28, "Therefore we conclude that a man is justified by faith without the deeds of the law." *De Doctrina* finds in the specification "of the law" the key to overcoming the alleged discrepancy between Paul and James in the New Testament: if for James "by works a man is justified, and not by faith only,"[17] it is because he is referring to "works of faith."[18] "Paul does not say that man is justified simply through faith, without works, but *without the works of the law*."[19] As a result, *De Doctrina* goes so far as to argue, in Thomistic terms, that "if to believe is to act," as the examples show which the treatise draws from the Old Testament, "then faith is an action, or rather a habit acquired by frequent actions . . . Actions, however, are usually said to be effects rather than instruments; or perhaps they might better be called causes, though of less moment than principal causes."[20]

The Latin treatise here yet fails to account for something *Paradise Lost* seemingly underscores: faith has a very definite object under the full manifestation of the covenant of grace and its revelation to Adam. If the object is Jesus and his work on the cross, and if faith is "trust" (12.418), it follows that works of faith cannot be causes, if secondary.[21]

17. Jas 2:24.

18. *CPW* 6.490.

19. *CPW* 6.490.

20. *CPW* 489. In arguing for *De Doctrina's sola fide* justification, Campbell does not acknowledge the reference to works as secondary causes of justification (Campbell, *John Milton and the Manuscript of De Doctrina Christiana*, 111).

21. Rom 4 is exemplary of this point in that the prototypical faith of Abraham is

The benefit of Christ is, on the contrary, embraced by that quality of faith in the Son which produces works as effects.[22] While the likes of Ames get lost in defining internal-external dynamics,[23] Calvin has it best, "No faith, or only a dead faith, is without works."[24] That Milton is referring to true faith as opposed to dead faith without yielding ground to works of faith as a cause of justification is conclusively indicated by the assurance given to Adam that "This godlike act / Annuls thy doom" (427–8), a *single* internal act of living faith delivering him from "the death" he "should have died / In sin for ever lost from life" (12.428–9).[25]

Final though the gap from Scholastic categories to Evangelical may appear to be, we read that true liberty "from [right reason] hath no dividual being." In other words, there cannot be one without the other. Both William Ames' *Marrow* and *De Doctrina Christiana* speak of "right reason"[26] as the ability to "discern the chief good"[27] leading to "absolute rectitude"[28] or "self-government and self-control."[29] The latter include "both the control of one's own inner affections, and the pursuit of external good and resistance or endurance of external evil"[30] or "outward as well as inward obedience" to God's will.[31] Hence both works appear to match the understanding of freedom as restored through the rational control of sinful passions.

It has been argued, however, that in Milton right reason is only revived by true liberty. In other words, the freedom reason provides proves

---

trust that God will give him a progeny regardless of human impotence.

22. *CM* 17.9: "It is faith that justifies, not agreement with the Decalogue; and that which justifies can alone render any work good; none therefore of our works can be good, but by faith; hence faith is the essential form of good works, the definition of form being, that through which a thing is what it is."

23. Ames, *Marrow*, 234–36.

24. Calvin, *Commentaries: James*, 22.2.314.

25. While the arrangement of the lines directly associates "this Godlike act" with the act of embracing the benefit of the cross by faith not void of works, the entire motion of the passage maintains a connection between "this Godlike act" and "His death for man" (425) which points to the other side of one and the same coin.

26. Cp. Ames, *Marrow*, 225; *CPW* 6.720.

27. *CPW* 6.395.

28. Ames, *Marrow*, 225.

29. *CPW* 6.720.

30. *CPW* 6.720.

31. Ames, *Marrow*, 226.

in Milton an effect, as opposed to a cause, of the inward liberty produced by grace. In fact, reason can only be *right* if it is born of freedom.

What comes first then? The answer comes to us by exploring the relationship between right reason and faith. Milton appears to do away with the Thomist vision of faith as intellect-based obedience perfected by will-driven charity[32] only to embrace Luther's equation of *recta ratio* with *fides*.[33] In the Reformer, right reason is assimilated to faith,[34] provided the latter amounts to right thinking about God[35] and trust in his faithfulness and truthfulness.[36] Insofar as it coincides with faith, right reason (initially upheld by prevenient grace) is informed by that true liberty (initially in the form of the Son's clothing Adam and Eve's nudity) which is for faith to appropriate and which has the power to hold the principle of sin at bay. Right reason and true liberty therefore appear to transpire simultaneously.

Although early Reformers would themselves subscribe to Milton's stances, a more manifest common denominator among Milton, General Baptists and Quakers is found in Moyse Amyraut and Saumur[37] which

32. See *Summa*, 22ae. q. 4, art. 3. Myers, *Milton's Theology of Freedom*, 119.

33. Christopher, *Milton and the Science of the Saints*, 98–99.

34. Luther, *Luther's Works*, 2.262.

35. Ibid., 2.238, cited in Christopher, *Milton and the Science of the Saints*, 98–99.

36. Luther, *Luther's Works*, 2.295, cited in Christopher, *Milton and the Science of the Saints*, 98–99.

37. The Academy of Saumur inextricably binds its name to the personality and work of the French Protestant divine Moyse Amyraut, (1596–1664). Born at Bourgueil the son of a lawyer, Amyraut was directed to the forensic profession by his father. After earning the degree of licentiate of laws at the University of Poitiers, he turned to the study of divinity. We next find him in Saumur, a pupil of the Calvinist John Cameron, and a licensed minister of the French Protestant Church. As such, he was first appointed to the church of Saint Aignan and, two years later, Saumur. After the publication of his *Traité des religions* in 1631, Amyraut was chosen to represent the provincial synod of Anjou, Touraine and Maine at the national synod of Charenton. Here he was committed to address the king with *The Copy of their Complaints and Grievances for the Infractions and Violations of the Edict of Nantes*. Whereas Catholic representatives had been accorded the right to stand, Protestant delegates had addressed the king on their knees. Amyraut displayed his strong sense of liberty and entitlement by refusing to kneel down and, his resolution remaining unmitigated even after Richelieu's personal address, he was ultimately granted the same right as the Catholic deputies. The Quakers would themselves come to be known as somewhat less than deferential in their demonstrative acts. Over thirty works are attributed to his pen. His generally Calvinistic background does not altogether obliterate his distinctive approach. In his *Traité de la predestination* (1634), Amyraut expounded his one-way predestinarian view of *univer-*

contributes to the definition of Milton's drift from the rationalism of mainstream post-Reformed Scholasticism to the spiritualism informing Independency, Quakerism and General Baptists. In writing to Richard Jones, a former pupil based in Saumur, on 1 August 1657, Milton emphatically manifested his approval of the Saumur Academy which Jones was attending:

> a place where you can enjoy cultured leisure and the society of learned men . . . So long as you remain there, you will be in har-

salismus hypoteticus. Calvin's limited extent of atonement was replaced by the view of atonement as universal yet hypothetical. The sufficiency of Christ's satisfaction for all sinners was in fact juxtaposed to its limited efficacy. Whereas grace could be offered to everyone, only individual faith could appropriate its salvific efficacy. To be sure, "Amyraut maintained the Calvinistic premises of an eternal foreordination and foreknowledge of God, whereby he caused all things inevitably to pass: the good efficiently, the bad permissively . . . But in addition to this he taught that God foreordained a universal salvation through the universal sacrifice of Christ offered to all alike (*également pour tous*), on condition of faith, so that with respect to God's will and desire (*voluntas, velleitas, affectus*) grace was universal, but as regards the condition it was particular, or only for those who would not reject it and thereby make it ineffective . . . " He reasoned from the standpoint of God's love towards his creatures; Calvinism reasoned "from the result, and made actual facts interpret the decrees." "Amyraut also made a distinction between natural ability and moral ability, or the power to believe and the willingness to believe: due to intrinsic depravity man possessed the former, but not the latter" (Schaff, *Creeds of Christendom*, 1.483). A charge of heresy would not fail to rise which was addressed at the consecutive synods of Alençon (1637), Charenton (1644) and Loudun (1659). In all three instances Amyraut was acquitted of all charges. Far from suffering from these attacks, the renown of the Academy of Saumur soared alongside Amyraut's lectures. One of Amyraut's notable pupils, the Quaker William Penn entertained views on religious freedom and toleration variously reflective of Amyraut's own. Notable is also Amyraut's advocacy of fellowship among all Christian churches holding to the main tenets of the Reformation. For all the dogmatic controversies, Amyraut's theology was largely regarded as in line with the Reformed tradition. In expressing his disagreement with the Saumur divines, François Turrettin consistently identified them as "our ministers" (*Institutiones theologiae elencticae*, 4.17.4; 12.6.3; 14.14.6) on the ground of shared fundamentals. John Owen himself praised both Cameron and Amyraut's understanding of divine justice and the Trinity (Muller, *Post-Reformation Reformed Dogmatics*, 1:79–80. On Amyraut's view of the Trinity, see Moyse Amyraut, *De mysterio trinitatis*, part 1, 3–5). The main promoter of Amyraldian hypothetical universalism in England and himself a pupil of John Cameron was William Davenant. Davenant held to a general atonement in terms of intention and sufficiency. God's universal desire for the salvation of all men formed the basis for conditional salvation. "In the floor debate on redemption at the Westminster Assembly, Edmund Calamy of the Davenant School attempted to insert Amyraldism into the Catechism" (Blunt, "Debate of Redemption at the Westminster Assembly," 5–10).

bor; elsewhere you will have to beware the Syrtes, the Rocks and
the Song of the Syrens.

Saumur is unreservedly described here as a haven, a safe refuge of truth
being contrasted to the beguiling appearance of truth against which
Jones should guard himself "elsewhere." Amyraut's progressive reaction
against post-Reformed Protestant Scholasticism constitutes a significant
trait d'union between Calvinism and Independent, General Baptist and
Quaker theology. In fact, his shift from a theology centered on intellective faculties to logocentric spiritualism[38] finds a notable counterpart
in both Quakers and General Baptists and, though largely accounted
for in terms of purpose and genre, it is ideally reflected in the ultimate
spiritualism of Milton's poetry.

In *De l'élévation de la foy et de l'abaissement de la raison* (1641),
Amyraut argues for the limited or relative potential of natural reason,
yet the unlimited reach of faith opening the eyes of natural reason. Faith
(right reason) he thus regards as far surpassing natural reason, though
encompassing its functions, a dying to self to be built up by the grace
and light of Christ.[39] Along the same lines, with regard to salvation and
the Christian life, Milton understands God's prevenient grace as shedding light on man's frail condition that he may fully trust in the deliverance provided at the cross:

> . . . once more I will renew
> His lapsed powers, though forfeit and enthralled
> By sin to foul exorbitant desires;
> Upheld by me . . .
> . . .
> By me upheld, that he may know how frail
> His fall'n condition is, and to me owe
> All his deliv'rance, and to none but me. (3.175–82)

---

38. Endy argues for Amyraut as a rationalist based on his assessment of his earliest
treatise (1631), while siding with B. G. Armstrong (*Calvinism and the Amyraut Heresy*)
in considering the French divine as substantially though not formally Calvinist (Endy,
William Penn, 100). Amyraut's early rationalism granted, a drift towards spiritualism
appears to inform his treatise *De l'elevation de la foy* (1641) and his different visual angle
on predestination in his *Traité de la predestination* marks a decided step in the direction
of conceiving of God's love as personally pursuing all individuals.

39. Likewise Penington maintains that man "is to be wholly broken down and
brought to nothing, even in the very Naturals, that he may be new made and built up in
the newness of the Spirit" (*Some Questions and Answers*, in *Works*, 1.363).

That divine act of upholding man's natural faculties which for Myers is to result in true liberty in terms of freedom of choice[40] is in fact defined by the recurrence of the object pronoun "me." The circular motion of the chiasmus "Upheld by me . . . By me upheld" contrasts the person on whom the delivering initiative rests with man's enthralled and impotent self. The result of the quickening of grace is not to enable man's faculties to achieve true freedom, but to allow man to perceive his condition and rely on the one who alone is the true source of deliverance.

In the final analysis, *Paradise Lost* breaks away from Scholastic tenets in its understanding of faith as right reason's selfless pursuit of God and in the concomitant assimilation of Christian liberty to the principle of grace and its Spirit-empowered ramifications. If *Paradise Lost* is about how to make man free in the first place, the answer is found in its soteriological message.

In seeking an embryonic introduction to the poetical unfolding of the latter in the poem, no more defining sketch is found than in Isaac Penington's witness to the manifestation of God

> By the voice of his Son, by the arm of his Son, by the virtue of his Son's light and life inwardly revealed and working in our hearts. This loosed us inwardly from the darkness, from the bonds of sin and iniquity, from the power of the captive and destroyer, and turned our minds inwardly towards our Lord and Saviour, to mind his inward appearance, his inward shinings, his inward quickening; all which were fresh from God and full of virtue.[41]

---

40. Myers, *Milton's Theology of Freedom*, 152. See pp. 154–55, n. 64.

41. Penington, "The Testimony of Thomas Ellwood Concerning Isaac Penington," x.

3

Inner Light and Christian Liberty

If Christian liberty is to the public Milton what the imagery of light is to the embedded poet, inner light is indeed to the poem what the concept of Christian liberty is to the prose. If so, the imagery of light is best read as the poetical translation of Christian liberty with respect to the poet, with the latter as the poetical transposition of the prophet-priest of the prose.

In *Milton and Scriptural Tradition* Leland Ryken argues for "a study of the reliance of texts upon texts" to be "built around the concepts of a pre-text [the biblical tradition] and an intertext. The pre-text is any previous work that a writer [Milton] assumes as a necessary framework for his work [*Paradise Lost*]. The real meaning of the new work is not self-contained but consists of what lies *between* the texts."[1]

Regina Schwartz, for her part, underscores how for Milton "biblical theology was inseparable from biblical poetics," even so much so that the poet wrote "his own theology most forcefully in his poetry."[2]

---

1. Ryken, "Introduction," in *Milton and the Scriptural Tradition*, 19. It was C. S. Lewis who first envisioned the distinction between the Bible as a source and a literary influence: "A source gives us things to write about; an influence prompts us to write in a certain way" (Lewis, *The Literary Influence of the Authorized Version*, 15). Ryken suggests that the impact of the Bible on Milton extends beyond what Lewis' use of the term *influence* indicates, for it entails the bearing of a number of literary models which Milton knew and imitated. In Ryken's reckoning, the Bible also "provides a context within which Milton's poetry reveals its fullest meanings to a reader." These apprehensions constitute the platform upon which intertextual criticism builds shedding light on what Frye defines as the archetypal imagery which from the Bible is translated into the literary imagination (see Ryken, *Milton and the Scriptural Tradition*, 4–27).

2. Schwartz, "Milton on the Bible," 37.

The ensuing discussion on the poet, the imagery of light and its relation to Christian liberty in *Paradise Lost* acknowledges the writings of
John, Paul's epistles and the Reformed, Independent, General Baptist
and early Quaker traditions as Milton's primary pre-text. In so doing,
it endeavors to isolate the intertext by making the pre-text interact with
Milton's biblical and theological poetics.

Ryken himself identifies light as "a complex biblical symbol. It
stands for God and, by extension, his heavenly dwelling. It implies moral
goodness or holiness, and is contrasted to darkness. It pictures salvation
and is linked especially with the redemptive activity of Christ. It symbolizes truth and understanding, as opposed to error or ignorance. And it
represents joy, God's favour, and life, in contrast to sorrow and death."[3]
The scholar further contends that "the fact that Merritt Hughes could
conduct a comprehensive survey of criticism on Milton's light imagery[4]
without touching upon these complex biblical meanings is an index to
how much remains to be done on the biblical imagination in Milton's
poetry."[5] This chapter aims to address that vacuum. In so doing, it seeks
to show how the imagery of *inner light* in *Paradise Lost* points to inward
liberty as the sole ground out of which the poem may rise to convey the
substance of true liberty.

In commenting on the words of the Gospel of John referring to the
Logos as "true light,"[6] both Luther and Calvin take it to describe Jesus as
both the essence of light and as the conveyor of light to the world. In so
doing, they distinguish him from any derived source of light and truth.
So Calvin:

> . . . whatever is luminous in heaven and in earth borrows its
> splendour from some other object; but Christ is *the light*, shining
> from itself and by itself, and enlightening the whole world by its
> radiance; so that no other source or cause of splendour is any-
> where to be found. He gave the name of *the true light*, therefore,
> to that which has by nature the power of giving *light*.[7]

Luther, after his pastoral outlook, is careful to stress the latter part of
Calvin's portrayal of Christ as light:

3. Ibid., 23.

4. Hughes, "Milton and the Symbol of Light," 63–103.

5. Ibid., 23.

6. John 1:9–10.

7. Calvin, *Commentaries: John*, 17.2.132.

> this Light, Christ, is not merely a light for itself; but with this
> light He illumines men, so that all reason, wisdom, and dexterity
> that are not false or devilish emanate from this Light, who is the
> Wisdom of the eternal Father.[8]

The imagery of light was widely shared by the entire Protestant community, orthodox and heterodox alike, and recourse to it would have raised a number of associations in readers with respect to the identification of light, light as a medium and light as revelation and source of interpretation. For all the fluidity of the imagery, however, no one would have failed to look past a materialistic and mechanist reference to light as a physical medium to its biblical/theological significance and to the ramifications of the theological as well as moral dichotomy between darkness and light.

Oftentimes overstated or misunderstood, Fox's a-systematic teaching on the nature of inner light explores all such signified. In his *Journal*, Fox addresses the alleged statement of a fellow inmate at Lancaster, one Major Wiggan, a Baptist preacher, who contended that "the true light, which enlighteneth every man that cometh into the world, is but natural":

> I answered, "that the true light, which enlighteneth every man
> that cometh into the world, was the life in the Word, and that
> was divine and eternal, and not natural; and he might as well
> say that the Word was natural, as that the life in the world was
> natural . . . Besides, that light could not be the Scriptures of the
> New Testament, for it was testified of before any part of the New
> Testament was written; so it must be the divine light, which is the
> life in Christ, the Word, before the Scriptures were. And the grace
> of God, which brought salvation, had appeared unto all men, and
> taught the saints; but they that turned it into wantonness, and
> walked despitefully against the Spirit of grace, were the wicked.[9]

Fox is here addressing a rationalizing attitude which commonly led to the identification of light as the natural faculty of reason or the Scriptures. While the former's function was limited to things visible, the latter alone could make man wise unto salvation. Fox turns the tables and points to the very reality of light to which the New Testament itself testified. Like Luther and Calvin, Fox related the imagery of light to Christ the Word,

---

8. Luther, *Sermons on the Gospel of St. John*, cps. 1–4, in *Luther's Works* 22.30.

9. Fox, *A Journal of the Life*, 22–23.

the prologue of the Gospel of John being their shared source. The light was divine, as it was "the life in the Word," namely "the life in Christ, the Word." The preposition *in* retains here both an indication of state and purpose. That is to say, the life is experienced through Christ, and the life is found in Christ, the latter being the essence of true life. This is tantamount to saying that Christ is and communicates the true light. Not only so, but the light ultimately comes to coincide with "the grace of God, which brought salvation," for the latter is the divine light which "appeared unto all men" before the Scriptures of the New Testament were dispensed.

A consistent Quaker emphasis is recognizable here in that the light of heaven is said to be communicated prior to and apart from the Scriptures of the New Testament. While early Quakers, alongside Milton, would consistently resort to the Scriptures as the essence of and witness to the light of Christ and his grace, they would also point to the non-circumscribed experience of that which the Scriptures signified.

Orthodoxy rejected immediate inspiration and illumination, while testifying to the inward guidance of the indwelling Spirit. Milton himself does much to restore ultimate authority to the Bible as in *A Treatise of Civil Power* he warns against anyone claiming "the illumination of the Holy Spirit . . . to be in himself, much less to be at any time for certain in any other." For this very reason, for Milton the Scriptures must remain "the main foundation of our Protestant religion."

This is not to say, however, that the illumination of the indwelling Spirit is excluded altogether. On the contrary, in John 16 "God hath promised by his Spirit to teach all things," as long as by all things one intends all things that are "absolutely necessary to salvation."[10] The law of faith working through love is itself a Spirit-driven impulse that overrules the letter of Scripture, and yet finds an apt outward counterpart in the truth of Scripture as it is apprehended by the Spirit.[11]

True spiritual guidance is therefore limited to soteriology and the experiential fulfillment of God's moral will in concert with the spirit of scriptural teaching, yet in opposition to "all assertion without pertinent

10. *CPW* 7.242.

11. *De Doctrina Christiana* apparently contradicts both prose and poem. While, in Regina Schwartz's words ("Milton on the Bible," 49), the theological treatise, much like *Paradise Lost*, envisions "a double scripture," unlike the poem the Latin work subordinates the written external word to the internal "unwritten word" (*CPW* 6.587–90).

scripture" or additions dictated "for the Teachers sake, whom they [followers of such teachers as make Scripture subservient to direct inspiration] think almost infallible." All such things resulting from "affections" and "private interest" must prove "through Infirmity, implicit Faith."[12]

In regarding Milton's position as incompatible with that of Quakers and Baptists, Martin[13] fails to identify the respective orthodoxy of the latter and the varying emphases within early Quakerism. The idea that the inner light may diverge from or add substantial truth to Scriptural teaching surfaces in Restoration Quaker Robert Barclay, yet finds no substantial support in the writings of early Friends George Fox and Isaac Penington. For Fox and Penington direct spiritual guidance consistently complies with Scripture in a unique marriage of freedom and authority which identifies the inner Word with the spirit of the written word.

The apprehension of light as an inner principle of liberty and authority in the poet draws us immediately to the incipit of book 3 of *Paradise Lost*. It is not to *Paradise Lost*, however, that the germs of the poet's existential meddling with the imagery of light are to be traced, but to sonnet 19, possibly as early as 1652 or 1655:[14]

> If I consider how my light is spent
> Ere half my days in this dark world and wide,
> And that one talent which is death to hide
> Lodged with me useless, though my soul more bent
> To serve therewith my maker, and present
> My true account, lest he returning chide,
> "Doth God exact day-labour, light denied?"
> I fondly ask. But patience, to prevent
> That murmur, soon replies, "God doth not need
> Either man's work or his own gifts; who best
> Bear his mild yoke, they serve him best: his state
> Is kingly. Thousands at his bidding speed,
> And post o'er land and ocean without rest;
> They also serve who only stand and wait."

12. *CPW* 7.293; 8.422.

13. Martin, *Milton among the Puritans*, 74.

14. Campbell, ed., *Complete English Poems*, 106. The date of composition is unknown, but the sonnet may have been written shortly after Milton completely lost his sight early in 1652. The fact that the poem follows the sonnet on the massacre of the Waldenses in Piedmont may, on the other hand, suggest a later date, possibly 1655, when the persecution occurred.

As he jots down his existential manifesto, Milton questions providence and the ways of God to his servant. It is not yet time for him to serve his maker through the talent of poetry, for the very light the poet needs to put his talent to use is denied by the one who gave the talent in the first place. No doubt, in considering how his "light is spent," Milton is mindful of his physical condition. In the context of the parable of the talents and of his long-envisioned poetical commission, however, eyesight manifestly stands as an objective correlative for the spiritual condition from which all service for God stems. And if Milton's talent is suited to his calling, as it need be, then the spiritual condition produced by the bestowal of light will yield poetical inspiration.

The denial of light, however, casts the poet down the spiral of paradox, "Doth God exact day-labour, light denied?" A lesson in humility is entailed: God does not need man's work nor his talents, not even our poet's! The whole argument seems yet to undermine the parabolic teaching around which the sonnet revolves. The Gospel of Matthew indicates that the master expects the talents to be multiplied. And Milton knows this very well as he envisions the master chiding his servant at his return.

The apparent contradiction is superseded when Christian liberty, rather than inertia, is intended as underlying Milton's realization that "God doth not need / Either man's work or his own gifts." While being aware of the master's demand for his "true account," Milton comes to the realization that service is not about what or how much, but about how, "who best / Bear his mild yoke, they serve him best."[15] The yoke presently takes on the form of longsuffering, which humbly to bear is Milton's true service.

The yoke is "mild," for grace informs its nature. Grace alone may call for the present shift from the necessity of personal performance ("My true account") to faith in God's power ("his state / Is kingly. Thousands at his bidding speed"). Grace alone elevates standing and waiting to the status of service ("They also serve who only stand and wait"). As the spiritual condition for service, light demands to be assimilated to such grace, even that light which is bestowed, in Fox's words, in "the life of Christ, the Word," or "the grace of God, which . . . had appeared to all men."

15. On the static service of God, see Barton, "They also Perform the Duties of a Servant."

If so, Sonnet 19 is really about the appropriation of light as the inward dimension of Christian liberty underlying all service against the yet external demands of the poet's ultimate divine commission. That very light would have to be appropriated again and again, and once more when the service of God would come to coincide with Milton's life-long vision and true account. The latter would transpire in 1658, as the poet reckoned it no longer time to stand and wait, but to turn to the Spirit to support his higher calling:

> . . . what in me is dark
> Illumine, what is low raise and support (1.22–23)

The adjectives "dark" and "low" here point to Milton's sensing his falling short of the high task that is set before him. The moral connotation of the terms is far from elusive, and even more so as the agent of illumination and elevation is identified as the Spirit. The contrasting image of darkness and light apparently points to Johannine symbolism. The very light of heaven is needed to sing of providence, that is, to sing both of God's ways and of the righteousness of his dealings with men. Even so, more than the height of the poet's argument is behind the need for light. The source of all darkness is sin. Light may either dispel sin or expose it and make it known. The general movement of book 1 points to the latter function: no sooner does the invocation end than the Spirit resolves to drag Milton through the kingdoms of darkness and chaos for the length of two books.

Light is ultimately to shine on the poet's inward condition against the inward as well as outward darkness of the infernal world. As the poet receives that measure of light which enables him to illumine both Satan's inward hell and outward obscurity, the light of the Spirit also allows him to sound the darkness of his own moral slavery. The paradox of "darkness visible" (1.63)[16] is thus made possible in that the commensurate portion of light which the poet receives enables him to see, in fact, to observe, both outward (hell's) and inward (Satan's and his own) darkness.

> Escaped the Stygian pool, though long detained
> In that obscure sojourn, while in my flight
> Through utter and through middle darkness borne
> With other notes than to th'Orphean lyre

---

16. Regarded as "difficult to imagine" by T. S. Eliot. See respective note in eds. Kerrigan, Rumrich, and Fallon, *Paradise Lost*, 15.

> I sung of chaos and eternal Night,
> Taught by the Heav'nly Muse to venture down
> The dark descent, and up to reascend (3.14–20)

Having re-emerged from the sojourn of obscurity, the poet revisits light, but is not in turn visited by light's "piercing ray," which alone brings the dawn. A *gutta serena* (serene drop) has extinguished all sight. While the Spirit has illumined the nature of darkness, the poet is not yet partaking in inner light. A veil remains before his eyes as he wanders through the night. Lack of full sight and the obscurity of night again point to the poet's inward condition and, secondarily, to his alienation from the ultimate object of his poetical contemplation. Far and removed from light and liberty, the poet fails not to attend the places of inspiration, where

> . . . the Muses haunt
> Clear spring, or shady grove, or sunny hill,
> Smit with the love of sacred song; but chief
> Thee Sion and the flow'ry brooks beneath
> That wash thy hallowed feet, and warbling flow (3.27–31)

The superimposition of Urania to the Spirit of the invocation in book 1 is matched here by the juxtaposition of the classical source to the biblical, with the former as subservient to the latter. More than the Muses' shady grove and sunny hill, Sion is the poetical place of sacred inspiration. As the biblical equivalent of Helicon, Sion stands as a metonym of both Hebrew poetry and salvation. The poetry of salvation is itself Milton's portion, the synthesis of his conflicting callings and aspirations. While underscoring such synthesis, Sion also stands for an inward dimension of liberty. With its subterranean brooks, it symbolizes the effluence of grace and the life of the Spirit producing the ultimate place of inspiration. Even so, Milton is still a stranger in Sion. While he physically shares the favorable fate of blind poets and prophets of old, all poetical syntax remains obscure to his inward eyes for want of light.

> . . . Thus with the year
> Seasons return, but not to me returns
> Day, or the sweet approach of ev'n or morn,
> Or sight of vernal bloom, or summer's rose,
> Or flocks, or herds, or human face divine;
> But cloud instead, and ever-during dark
> Surrounds me . . . (3.40–46)

Time goes by and seasons return, but the cycle of day and night fails to reproduce itself. The perpetual night of the poet is one of slavery to his poetical impotence, which closely parallels Satan's slavery to his inner self. The source of impotence for both is not to be sought in outward or physical restraint, but in inward enthrallment. Similarly Lady in *Comus* (1634) declares:

> He that hath light within his own clear breast
> May sit i' the centre, and enjoy bright day;
> But he that hides a dark soul and foul thought . . .
> Himself is his own dungeon (350, 356–58)

The germs of Milton's theology of inner light are all present here, thirteen years before Fox's conversion experience. While Lady may enjoy the freedom of day-light even in the midst of outward darkness, the poet, like Satan, proves "his own dungeon," for the darkness of night lies within him. Such inward darkness in turn makes the poet blind to what of creation can be absorbed through the senses and to what of God is reflected in the creature—in fact in his reason ("human face divine").

As perpetual darkness and cloud surround the seer spiritually, he is bereft of both true (heavenly) and natural light. If he seeks the latter he will find neither. If he seeks the former he will find both. The poet is yet caught in a paradox for the appropriation of true light is beyond the reach of human endeavor. All flights to heaven are bound to prove an Icarus-like ascension as Light is pronounced "unapproachèd" (3.4). God, in fact, dwells in the very light which "no man can approach unto":[17]

> Thee Father first they sung omnipotent,
> Eternal King; thee author of all being,
> Fountain of light, thyself invisible
> Amidst the glorious brightness where thou sitt'st
> Throned inaccessible, but when thou shad'st
> The full blaze of thy beams, and through a cloud
> Drawn round about thee like a radiant shrine,
> Dark with excessive bright thy skirts appear,
> Yet dazzle Heav'n, that brightest Seraphim
> Approach not, but with both wings veil their eyes. (3.372–82)

The gesture of the seraphim manifestly replicates Moses' act of covering his face in order not to expose the Israelites to the fading yet consuming

17. See 1 Tim 6:16.

reflection of God's glory.[18] God's inaccessibility is not merely the result of sin, but an absolute fact, for even the spotless seraphim are subject to its limitation. The radiance of God conceals his countenance (3.375–77) and it bespeaks the impossibility for his creatures to know him. Yet the opposite is also true, for God can be known in the Son:

> Thee next they sang of all creation first,
> Begotten Son, divine similitude,
> In whose conspicuous count'nance, without cloud
> Made visible, th'Almighty Father shines,
> Whom else no creature can behold; on thee
> Impressed the effulgence of his glory abides (3.383–88)

Unmistakable Johannine and Pauline overtones pervade these words and define the poem's Christology. The poem insistently depicts the Son as the exact representation of God and effulgence of his light. Albeit God is "invisible" (3.375), he is made "visible" in the Son (3.386). Though no creature can draw near God's light (3.381–82), the Son reaches out to the creature as the effulgence of the Father (3.386). And if a "cloud" and "ever during dark" surround the poet (3.45–46), he is given to "behold" God "without cloud" in the Son's "conspicuous count'nance" (3.385). The Gospel of John best affords a synthesis here in the words:

> No man hath seen God at any time, the only begotten Son, which is in the bosom of the Father, he hath declared him.[19]

The Son's countenance is similarly portrayed in Milton in terms of the declarative image of God, his verbal expression or his μορφή. In a detailed study of the latter term in Greek philosophy, Philo and the New Testament, J. B. Lightfoot comes to the conclusion that, far from pointing to the external involucres or appearance, μορφή indicates what is intrinsic and essential.[20] Nothing less can be read into the poet's possibility to see God "without cloud" in the Son, as the limitation that is seen as superseded in these lines is that which prevents even the seraphim

18. See Exod 34:29–35.

19. John 1.18. Cf. *PL* 3.279.

20. Lightfoot, *Philippians*, 127–33. The entire argument is regarded as an utter impossibility in *De Doctrina*. For the Latin treatise, the Son cannot share the Father's essence since the former can be seen while the latter is invisible (*CPW* 6.237, 297). Also, the Latin treatise has it that if possessing the form of God meant possessing his own essence, the Son's kenosis would entail the emptying of God's very essence, a contradiction in terms for the antitrinitarian (*CPW* 6.275). Cf. n. 37.

from accessing God's *unapproachable* light. In other words, Milton is not referring to an ultimately veiled vision. His words rather work to the same effect as Jesus' claim, "he that hath seen me hath seen the Father."[21]

Ultimately, the exceptive clause "Whom else no creature can behold" looks forward to the removal of the poet's own veil (3.25–26) and cloud (3.45), which is only effected by the act of turning one's eyes on the Son. Scripture graphically underlines the same movement:

> And not as Moses, which put a veil over his face, that the children of Israel could not stedfastly look to the end of that which is abolished: But their minds were blinded: for until this day remaineth the same vail untaken away in the reading of the old testament; which vail is done away in Christ. But even unto this day, when Moses is read, the vail is upon their heart. Nevertheless when it shall turn to the Lord, the vail shall be taken away. Now the Lord is that Spirit: and where the Spirit of the Lord is, there is liberty.[22]

The words of Paul compare the veil covering Moses' face to the Israelites' inability to read that which was intrinsically transitory. In F. F. Bruce's words, "The Israelites' inability to see the glory shining from Moses' face, fading though that glory was, is treated as a parable of their descendants' present inability to realize the transitory character of the Mosaic order and to recognize the unfading glory of the gospel dispensation."[23] The veil solely drops when man reads the transitory nature of the Old Testament as pointing to the New. It drops when he turns away from Moses' face to look to Christ and the unfading glory of the gospel.

If the poet has so far found himself in the company of them to whom "the god of this world has blinded the *minds . . .* to keep them from seeing *the light of the gospel of the glory of Christ, who is the image of God*" [my italics],[24] ultimate vision and authority may only come alongside exposure to that same light.

> So much the rather thou celestial light
> Shine inward, and the mind through all her powers
> Irradiate, there plant eyes, all mist from thence
> Purge and disperse, that I may see and tell
> Of things invisible to mortal sight. (3.51–55)

21. John 14:9.

22. 2 Cor 3:13–17.

23. Bruce, *1 & 2 Corinthians*, 192.

24. 2 Cor 4:4.

In Johannine and Pauline fashion, the poet expands on the imagery of sight-giving light by calling on the celestial light to shine inward. In shining within, light is to irradiate the seat of obscurity or that which Paul identifies as man's *inner being* (Rom 7:21), in fact the *mind* (Rom 7:25). Here light is called to plant eyes.

While English Puritans and Anglicans alike conceded Luther's argument that the vision of God was limited in this life to his back side, Milton seems to embrace the Friends' confidence that "they could, by means of the inner light, observe the Word as it came from the very mouth of God."[25] With early Friends, he appears to indicate "that the light brought . . . a special immediate knowledge of God and spiritual realities through a 'spiritual eye' that gave them the kind of direct knowledge or vision of God that man's faculties, operating with the phantasms arising from sense experience, could not provide."[26]

In that early Quaker thought can be consistently traced back to Johannine and Pauline theology, Penington is right as he labors to stress its identity with orthodox belief. To this effect, the nature of the inner light is best assimilated to the life in the Word or the redeeming grace of God. In freeing man's inner being, the latter yields an immediate vision of God and spiritual realities which far surpasses the mere reach of man's natural faculties. In fact, the poet has come to the realization that the knowledge of God and of spiritual realities is beyond the apprehension of reason or sensible experience. He knows, with Bacon, that "if any man shall think by view and inquiry into these sensible and material things to attain that light, whereby he may reveal unto himself the nature or will of God, then, indeed, is he spoiled by vain philosophy."

In order to attain to the light of God, whereby he may reveal his nature or will, light itself must reach down and make God known. As the center of all spiritual faculties, the Pauline mind is to function as a receptacle and seat of a whole new microcosm of liberty. Far from merely identifying light as an infused divine virtue yielding power to ascend to God, in calling on light to free the mind the poet is rather pointing to the gospel as that descending ray which frees man from all internal darkness and turns his natural and corrupt (blind) intellect into the seat of true light.[27] This reading is confirmed by the fact that the function of light

25. Endy, *William Penn*, 183.

26. Ibid., 75.

27. See Endy on Barclay, in *William Penn*, 151.

is no longer that of making sin manifest, but one of *purging*. The verb attaches to "all mist" a moral connotation as the result of sin and, once again, ties Milton's poetics to Pauline theology:

> . . . the Father, which hath made us meet to be partakers of the inheritance of the saints in light: who hath delivered us from the power of darkness, and hath translated us into the kingdom of his dear Son: in whom we have redemption through his blood, even the forgiveness of sins.[28]

The inheritance the Colossians share with the saints is "in light" and the kingdom of light into which they have been transferred is the realm of God's "dear Son: in whom we have redemption through his blood, even the forgiveness of sin." Participation in light is therefore closely related to the forgiveness of sin through the blood of the Son. As the latter's atoning work "hath delivered us from the power of darkness," that same light of redemption is to permeate the poet and deliver him from all obscurity. The resulting domain of freedom in turn forms the ground for *higher* vision (the vision of God in Christ through his gospel) and poetical inspiration, as the poet is given to "see and tell / Of things invisible to mortal sight."

While the fall—it is sin that has brought about mortality—has impaired man's vision of things that are known through inward sight, the ineffable is manifestly included in the poet's expectations.[29] The expectation of the reader who seeks a successful poetical representation of that which is ineffable in the poem is, on the contrary, frustrated. Reisner correctly underscores the gap which separates fallen speech from the implications of ineffability. The vision of God is ultimately lost in this gap, but it is this loss which yields, in Reisner's words, the poem's central metaphor "about the unbridgeable gulf between what the poem actually says on the level of words and what the poetry shows on the level of poetic effect 'about' that which is unknowable, ineffable, and finally lost."[30] In other words, Milton is saying, "This is that." His poetic impotence is there to illustrate that very loss for which the poem is to account.

At the beginning of book 3, however, the poet is found cherishing the genuine possibility for the receptacle of light not only to see, but

---

28. Col 1:12–14.

29. Cf. Reisner, *Milton and the Ineffable*, 171–233.

30. Ibid., 172.

also to tell of things ineffable. If a fulfillment of such claim exists, it does not transpire in poetical terms. Fallen language can only succeed spiritually where the poet has failed poetically insofar as something like a sacrament occurs. In this respect, the meaning of words can never frame God, but God can make himself known in the words. Effluence of the celestial light through the poet, the words of the poem communicate the Son and *are*, as it were, the Son, namely the Word who gives life to lifeless and impotent signs just as it created the cosmos and restores the poet to spiritual life.

While a similar function was regarded by orthodox divines as the sole portion of Scripture and virtually exposes Milton to the charge of blasphemy, the poet makes no mystery of the height of his calling as he calls for that same Spirit which inspired the shepherd of Oreb to carry him along.[31] He can do so inasmuch as "God hath promised by his Spirit to teach all things," as long as by "all things" one intends all things "absolutely necessary to salvation" and spiritual life. In other words, Milton entreats the conveyance of the light of salvation and liberty through the words of the poem of that same Spirit which inspired the Scriptures of Moses. The poem thus concurs with Scripture, being ascribed that same role which Luther envisioned for the preaching of the Word. Finally, in intertwining conspicuously Scripture with poetry, Milton is able to achieve a significant synthesis of the soteriological function of the Spirit and the very words of the Bible.

It is to the light conveyed by the particular revelation of God's Word through the Spirit, rather than to the relative achievements of man's discursive reason, that *Paradise Regained* itself points:

> . . . he who receives
> Light from above, from the fountain of light,
> No other doctrine needs, though granted true;
> But these are false, or little else but dreams,
> Conjectures, fancies, built on nothing firm. (*PR* 4.288–92)

Shawcross urges us to appreciate "the point that Milton is making in rejecting human hypotheses about life or how to live life, as well as the oratory of Greece and Rome and its overview of authoritatively governing writers. Jesus is rejecting, in this second of three temptations by Satan, the excessive, the unnecessary, what falls in Milton's way of thinking into

---

31. See 1.6–10. Cf. 2 Pet 1:21.

the avaricious, since it becomes materialistic and not concerned with man's essential life needs. The only *necessary* knowledge for man is God's Word, Milton is saying."[32]

For all the merit of this contention, it must be noted that Milton extends his apprehension of light beyond the static content of Scripture to the very dynamic and personal experience of that content. Its limitless functions granted, the life-giving light of the Word must be individually allowed to shine inward. Far from retaining forms of sacramental idolatry, Milton, with Fox, is sure to emphasize the experiential, relational, and personal aspect whereby the light which descends from heaven is appropriated.

Once "Light from above" is received, "from the fountain of light," the divine absolute is embraced alongside God's vision and guidance in all truth pertaining to salvation and spiritual life.[33] If even angelic reason and senses fall short of the divine light—let alone the poet's fallen faculties—the only way to experience light is to receive it as a gift from heaven. The invocation of the weak and blind poet does just that and it teaches the lesson that to come to the light of the gospel (see John 3:21) is, in the words of Augustine, "to acknowledge that we are miserable and destitute of all power of doing [any spiritual] good."[34] To this same effect, the invocation may be ostensibly associated with Paul's claim and exhortation to the Corinthians to "walk by faith, not by sight,"[35] as well as to Augustine's maxim, *Credo ut intelligam*.

Here lies the key to understanding Milton's falling short of poetical compression for the sacrament of the Word. While failure to achieve a true and consistent association of sensibility with respect to God's nature and will seems to amount to final loss for a poet who has waited all his life to fulfill his poetical calling, this very loss bears in itself all the quality of evangelical paradox: the blind see, the weak are strong and not powerful poetical images but bare words are clothed in the Son.

For all the consistent early Quaker identification of the Son and the gospel of grace as the essence of inner light, both the Son and the Spirit

32. Shawcross, *Rethinking Milton Studies*, 152.

33. Endy argues that in "Fox's thought the primary function of the light was to bring a strong sense of the presence of Christ. The light was a metaphor for this encounter between the divine and the human" (Endy, *William Penn*, 151).

34. Quoted in Calvin, *Commentaries: John*, 17.2.129.

35. 2 Cor 5:7.

were interchangeably referred to as its agents. Accordingly, in pointing to the Son as he who is and conveys the light of heaven, Milton intertwines his functions with those of the Spirit in the creation of the world, the spiritual re-creation of the poet and the resulting creation of the poem:

> Hail holy light, offspring of Heav'n first-born,
> Or of th'Eternal coeternal beam
> May I express thee unblamed? Since God is light,
> And never but in unapproachèd light
> Dwelt from eternity, dwelt then in thee,
> Bright effluence of bright essence increate.
> Or hear'st thou rather pure ethereal stream,
> Whose fountain who shall tell? Before the sun,
> Before the heavens thou wert, and at the voice
> Of God, as with a mantle didst invest
> The rising world of waters dark and deep,
> Won from the void and formless infinite.
> . . . On his right
> The radiant image of his glory sat,
> His only Son . . . (3.1–12, 61–63)

While those reading the anti-Trinitarianism of *De Doctrina* into *Paradise Lost* are ready to dismiss the invocation to light as variously pointing to the personification of an attribute of God or to physical light,[36] the incipit of the *Book of the Son* (book 3) yields a clear-cut portrait of the latter's nature[37] to those who acknowledge Genesis 1:1–3 and the prologue of

36. See Kelley, *This Great Argument*, 92. Not so Hunter et al., who view light in the passage as a reference to the Son (*Bright Essence*, 149–56).

37. Kelley's *This Great Argument* (1941), Hunter, Patrides, and Adamson's *Bright Essence* (1971), and Campbell, Corns, Hale and Tweedie's *Milton and the Manuscript of De Doctrina Christiana* (2007) have set the boundaries for the mainstream attitudes toward the relationship between *De Doctrina* and *Paradise Lost* over the past decades. Kelley's reading of the Latin treatise as a theological gloss upon the poem, along with his masterful notes to book 6 of the Yale edition of Milton's prose works, laid the foundations of critical orthodoxy. A stern reaction to Kelley's work would have to wait until the Sixties, when Patrides made his case for the alignment of Milton's theology with traditional Christian orthodoxy (*Milton and the Christian Tradition*, 1966). A new critical standard was only provided a few years later by Patrides, Hunter and Adamson's revisiting of the theology of both treatise and poem. If throughout the Seventies and Eighties *Bright Essence*'s often recondite subordinationist attempt at disjoining or variously reconciling *Paradise Lost* and *De Doctrina* under the banner of orthodoxy was generally maintained, it would not be long before the treatise's heterodoxy took over the scene again (Bauman, *Milton's Arianism*, 1987). All attempts at sorting out the relationship between treatise and poem came to a sudden halt in 1992, when Hunter

the Gospel of John as its primary pre-text. In it the same creating *Logos*[38] who by the word of his mouth,[39] "the [very] voice / Of God,"[40] "didst

first questioned Milton's authorship of *De Doctrina* ("The Provenance of the *Christian Doctrine*," 1992; see also *Visitation unimplor'd*, 1998). The ensuing vibrant debate ultimately resulted in Campbell, Corns, Hale and Tweedie's recent effort. The latter is hailed by many as conclusive today, but finds, in our understanding, in arguments of continuity and in close theological comparison a stumbling block. Arguments of continuity trace a most natural backdrop for the poem's theology proper to the words of *Of Reformation*'s invocation: "Thou therefore that sit'st in light & glory unapproachable, *Parent of Angels* and *Men!* Next thee I implore omnipotent King, Redeemer of that lost remnant whose nature thou didst assume, ineffable and everlasting *Love!* And thou the third subsistence of Divine infinitude, *illumining Spirit*, the joy and solace of created *Things!* One *Tri-personall* GODHEAD!" (*CPW* 1.613–14). Far from holding to a tri-personal Godhead, it has been noted how *De Doctrina* maintains a strongly anti-trinitarian stance (*CPW* 6.218). The Son is therein depicted as the recipient of the substance of God, yet as not sharing his very essence (*CPW* 6.211), and as perpetual, yet not eternal (*CPW* 6.211). On the contrary, the light of heaven in the poem is said to be "of th'Eternal coeternal beam," the dwelling of God "from eternity" and "Bright effluence of bright essence increate." To view the light so portrayed as anything other than God himself is tantamount to creating an irreconcilable dualism between God and light: both are said to exist from eternity and light is pronounced uncreated—as is assumed God alone is—as well as streaming from God's own essence. In other words, light is everything *De Doctrina* states only God can be. Even so, the light of heaven is significantly identified as "offspring of Heav'n first-born," thus marking its otherness from God. In its hymn on the Son, Colossians 1:15–17 reads: "[He] is the image of the invisible God, the *firstborn* [my italics] of every creature: for by him were all things created, that are in heaven, and that are in earth, visible and invisible, whether they be thrones, or dominions, or principalities, or powers: all things were created by him, and for him: and he is before all things, and by him all things consist." The Son is, in fact, heaven's firstborn throughout the New Testament. If the celestial light is the same as the "of all creation first / Begotten Son" (3.83–4), generation, contrary to *De Doctrina*, must be so interpreted as to signify the Son's position as pre-eminent life-giving αρχέ as well as his relationship of divine love with the Father (cf. *CPW* 6.205–6, 302–3). The "image of the invisible God" (cf. 3.374) and light (cf. 3.3), the Son is only rightfully identified with the holy light of heaven as the "radiant image of his [the Father's] glory" (3.62) in whom "th'Almighty Father" is "made visible" and "shines" (3.386; the possibility of the Father being made visible in the Son sharply contrasts with *CPW* 6.237, 297). In the final analysis, the Son in the poem appears as nothing short of the "ineffable and everlasting *Love*" of the prose. The effluence of God's very essence whose piercing ray descends to man in his darkness and saturates him with the gospel, the Son is the light of the knowledge of the unknowable God communicated by the prevenient, concomitant and subservient agency of the "third subsistence of divine Infinitude, [the] *illumining Spirit*." Like Augustine, Milton must resort to the term *person* (cf. "*Tri-personall* GODHEAD") to not remain silent.

38. *PL* 3.708; 7.163.

39. Ibid., 7.164

40. Ibid., 3.9–10

invest / The rising world of waters dark and deep"—even that which the
Spirit "won from the void and formless infinite" or "vast abyss"[41]—is the
true light that is coming into the world to make a new *spiritual* creation.[42]
The theological synthesis of the two Scriptural passages is ultimately afforded by Paul in what amounts to an all-encompassing backdrop for
the Son's poetic role as *Logos*, wisdom and light in the two threshold
moments of history:

> For God, who commanded the light to shine out of darkness,
> hath shined in our hearts, to give the light of the knowledge of
> the glory of God in the face of Jesus Christ (2 Cor 4:6).

Just as light flowed from the command, in fact, from the Word of God
at creation, so did the light the poet invokes at the beginning of book
3 stream forth "at the voice / Of God" and "as with a mantle didst invest / The rising world of water dark and deep." In the same way as the
God who is light has shone "in our hearts," the poet calls on the light of
heaven to shine inward. With light comes the knowledge of the glory
of God, just as the inner light is to enable the poet to "see . . . things
invisible to mortal sight." And if for Paul the knowledge of the glory of
God shines in the face of Christ, in Milton the Son is "the radiant image
of his [God's] glory" in whose countenance alone is the poet to see God
without cloud.

To be sure, the overlapping of the Spirit and the Word at creation
and in the work of illumination may sensibly lead to the conclusion that
the light Milton revisits is identical with the Spirit of God in the initial
invocation in book 1. So the invocation:

> And chiefly thou, O Spirit, that dost prefer
> Before all temples th' upright heart and pure,
> Instruct me, for thou know'st; thou from the first
> Wast present, and with mighty wings outspread
> Dove-like sat'st brooding on the vast abyss
> And mad'st it pregnant . . . (1.17–22)

Mindful of De Doctrina's warning not to call upon the Spirit,[43] Maurice
Kelley, and a plethora of critics after him, regards the Spirit here as "a

---

41. Ibid., 1.21–22; 7.234–37.

42. John 1:9; 1:13.

43. CPW 6.295.

personification of the various attributes of God the Father."[44] Even so, in commenting on the presence of the Spirit at creation, *De Doctrina* refers to it as "the *spirit* of God," "a reference to the Son, through whom, as we are constantly told, the Father created all things."[45] W. B. Hunter comes to this same conclusion by way of theological reasoning,[46] so that in his reading the Spirit and the holy light of heaven end up being assimilated to the Son. While the solution offered by *De Doctrina* (and Hunter), if unsatisfying from a dramatic point of view, may seem to settle the discussion from a theoretical one, the problem of identification materializes again when, in turning to book 7, the reader is faced with the simultaneous presence and involvement of both Son and Spirit in creation:

> My overshadowing Spirit and might with Thee [the Son]
> I [the Father] send along . . . (7.165–66)

The reference to the gospel narrative of the Annunciation would have proven inescapable to the seventeenth-century Scripture-saturated mind in light of its definition of the Spirit as "overshadowing" and "might": "The Holy Ghost shall come upon thee, and the power of the Highest shall overshadow thee" (Luke 1:35). Milton was thus associating the Spirit active in the first creation with the Spirit active in the new creation inaugurated by the coming of Jesus in the flesh. This same Spirit, as opposed to the Son, plainly matches the Spirit of the invocation in book 1. The identification occurs as Raphael's language in book 7 echoes 1.20–21 as well as the pre-text of Genesis 1:2:

> . . . on the wat'ry calm
> His brooding wings the Spirit of God outspread
> And vital virtue infused (7.234–36)

Granted the identity of the Spirit in books 1 and 7, in the latter the Spirit appears to be conversant with one "*eternal* Wisdom" [my italics] (7.9–10). Book 3 in turn identifies the latter as the "Son of my [the Father's] bosom," who "alone" is his "Word, [his] wisdom" (169–70), namely the light that streams forth "at the voice of God."

Although the Spirit is itself called to "illumine" what in the poet is "dark," he is only able to inspire the poetical creation, just as he infused

---

44. Kelley, *This Great Argument*, 106–18.

45. *CPW* 6.282.

46. Hunter et al., *Bright Essence*, 149–56.

his virtue in the creation of the world, insofar as he sheds light on the poet's darkness and directs him to the source of light. In the words of John, the Spirit will guide you in all truth for he ". . . shall receive of mine [the Son's], and shall shew it unto you."[47] No less is signified by the Spirit being called "the Spirit of Grace" (12.525). In fact, if the light of the knowledge of the glory of God is in the gospel of the Son alone, it is given to the Spirit to reveal one's spiritual darkness and communicate the Son alongside his transforming life and vision on the grounds of grace. If right reason is twinned with liberty, it is given to the "Spirit of Grace" to be joined in indissoluble marriage with it, its "consort" (12.526).

All such poetical and theological inferences point to a twofold dynamic with respect to the soteriology of light. What is entailed is respectively a translation from darkness to light and the ensuing actualization of salvific grace in one's life. One and the other pertain to the benefits of the same gospel of grace. It is too much to think of Milton as picturing the outpouring of light in a parabolic sense as the experience of conversion informing inspiration. Milton's involvement is far too personal and dramatic to attach to it a merely didactic purpose, nor should we understand his invocation as envisioning his personal need for salvation. While, contrary to Fallon's Arminian argument,[48] Milton's tri-fold soteriological division (3.183–201) more appropriately falls under the Amyraldian framework,[49] we can reasonably agree with the critic that the poet ranks himself amongst the beneficiaries of peculiar grace. To this effect, Milton rather envisions the ministry of inner light as the *actualization* of all that the dispensation of the gospel entails that he may *appropriate* liberty—lest he continue to wallow in the old slavery and darkness—and out of that liberty fulfill the service of God through the talent of poetry. Second Corinthians 3:18 affords a conclusive theological counterpart to this reading in the words:

> But we all, with open face beholding as in a glass the glory of the Lord, are changed into the same image from glory to glory, even as by the Spirit of the Lord.

---

47. John 16.14.

48. Fallon, *Milton's Peculiar Grace*, 197. Also see, by the same author, "Elect above the Rest," 93–116.

49. See Keeble, "Milton and Puritanism," 135–36.

μεταμορφούμεθα, the Greek term used in this verse to indicate transformation, points to the effect of the direct contemplation of the glory of God as it shines in the gospel of grace, namely the metamorphosis of the individual after the image of God the Son by the agency of the Spirit of liberty. The ultimate condition of the poet visited by the light of heaven is to surpass that of the seraphim, "unto whom it was revealed, that not unto themselves, but unto us they did minister the things, which are now reported unto you by them that have preached the gospel unto you with the Holy Ghost sent down from heaven; which things the angels desire to look into."[50] Grace ultimately opens the door to greater sight and knowledge than was first accorded Adam in the garden. It opens the door to liberty from sin, and thus from external constraint and the limitation of derivation. If sinless prelapsarian Adam, in the perfectibility of his knowledge, could have attained to the limited vision of the seraphim, heaven can now meet the poet where he is in the fullness of its radiance and glory. Supreme refraction of such light, *Paradise Lost* amounts to no less than the ultimate poetical unfolding of the poet's realization of Christian liberty and immanent vehicle of light.

---

50. 1 Pet 1:12.

4

Satan's Inward Prison

In his essay "Milton's Satan" in *The Cambridge Companion to Milton*,[1] John Carey rightly refers to the atavistic antithesis between anti-Satanists (e.g., Charles Williams, C. S. Lewis, S. Musgrove and Stanley Fish) and pro-Satanists (A. J. A. Waldock, E. E. Stoll, G. R. Hamilton, William Empson, William Bryson and Neil Forsyth) as something insoluble. More than that, Carey points to the critical contrast as the measure of ambivalence in Satan's character. This ambivalence cannot be done away with by siding with either of the two fronts without at the same time losing half the truth. In fact, the ambivalence of Satan is intrinsic to his character and projects unique depth.

For all the merit of his contention, however, Carey only takes a picture of Satan's symptoms, without telling us what the disease is. He steers clear of the vital questions: what accounts for Satan's ambivalence? What determines it? Is there a unifying rationale behind Satan's inward dialectic? The present chapter aims to provide a diagnosis of the condition behind Satan's ambivalence by pointing to his inward slavery to sin and thus to the rule of law and of God. In so doing, the following pages identify Satan as the negative counterpart to the reality of Christian liberty and the backdrop against which both the poet's and Adam and Eve's actualization of liberty acquires its proper significance.

In their attempt at defining Satan, critics on both ends of the debate have largely exploited categories of good and evil, foolishness and heroism, deceitfulness and truthfulness, law and energy. Carey himself seems to move from much the same premises as he states that

---

1. Carey, "Milton's Satan," 160–74.

"Milton's effort to encapsulate evil in Satan was not successful,"[2] hence
Satan's ambivalence. Ambivalence granted, Carey's premises are flawed.
Milton was never trying to encapsulate evil in Satan, nor was he trying
to portray him as a heroic personification of freedom. In fact, we should
not ask ourselves whether Satan is good or evil only to conclude that
he is caught in a tension between the two, nor should we ask ourselves
whether he stands for absolute liberty against conventional order or for
merely disruptive antinomianism. We should ask ourselves whether or
not Satan is free. Satan is not free. As such, his character is not positive
or negative, but tragic.

Along the same lines, Burden rightfully reads into *Paradise Lost*
a twofold epic: a Satanic sub-epic of heroic virtue and tragic fall is juxtaposed and contrasted to a human epic of freedom.[3] Satan's good is
hidden in God. The tragedy rests in his failure to choose true liberty
(inward filial fellowship with God) over self. It rests in the surrender
of free reason to enslaving self-seeking affections. In turn the source of
his enslavement is not external. It is not God or hell, but his inner being, with evil (his opposition to God) as but a consequence of his inner
slavery to self. An "example of self-deception and the deception of others which are incident to the surrender of reason to passion,"[4] evil is an
obliged path, the only form of atonement in a downward spiral which
knows no redemption.

Satan's laceration is evident from his initial dialogical exchange
with Beelzebub. His tone is defiant and undaunted in his opposition to
God, but his words are uttered "in pain" and "racked with deep despair"
(1.125–6). While in a doxological epiphany of grace (Sonnet 19) the
poet is enabled to see love and freedom ("his mild yoke") in the high
sovereignty of God ("his state / Is kingly"), Satan can only know heaven
as a "tyranny" (1.124). The source of his oppression, however, is not
found without, but within:

> Is this the region, this the soil, the clime,
> Said the lost Archangel, this the seat
> That we must change for Heav'n, this mournful gloom
> For that celestial light? Be it so, since he
> Who now is sov'reign can dispose and bid

2. Ibid., 161.
3. Cf. Burden, *The Logical Epic*.
4. Hughes, *Ten Perspectives on Milton*, 177.

> What shall be right: farthest from him is best
> Whom reason hath equaled, force hath made supreme
> Above his equals. Farewell happy fields
> Where joy for ever dwells: hail horrors, hail
> Infernal world, and thou profoundest Hell
> Receive thy new possessor: one who brings
> A mind not to be changed by place or time.
> The mind is its own place, and in itself
> Can make a Heav'n of Hell, a Hell of Heav'n. (1.242–55)

Satan here contrasts heaven with hell in terms of darkness and light. The progress of the poet from the realm of darkness to the celestial light is inversely matched by Satan's course from the latter to "this mournful gloom." So has God's sovereign will disposed. And if the poet's progress is from spiritual darkness and a defiled sense to the liberating vision of God in the Son, Satan bids farewell to joy only to embrace the horrors of the infernal world. Even so, the outward reality of heaven and hell, light and darkness, liberty and slavery is not what dictates true bliss or damnation, vision or blindness, freedom or thralldom. In fact, just as the mind of the poet is to be irradiated for him to gain sight, so for Satan the mind stands as the seat of an inward microcosm ("its own place") projecting heaven or hell.

As in his dedicatory note to a Protestant Italian exile to Diodati's Geneva, here again Milton echoes Horace's maxim "the sky not the mind changes in one who crosses the sea" (*Epistulae.* 1.2.27). The intellect is not only seen in Cartesian terms as the region of Satan's essence (*Cogito ergo sum*), but as that which defines the nature of his essence regardless of outward changes. The mind which has been pervaded by light is a heaven irrespective of external circumstances. The mind which has embraced darkness is hell irrespective of external light. The creature can thus be free even in the infernal confinement, if it is free within. Lucifer, accordingly, was free in heaven not because his celestial dwelling created the conditions for freedom, but because his mind was heaven. Space or time indeed do not change the mind. However, sin has. The spoiling of the mind produced by sin has ushered in hell within. In saying that "place or time" have not changed his mind, then, Satan is really pronouncing his own sentence, for his mind is its own hell. Just as hell could never affect the heaven within, Satan's microcosm of destitution and slavery could never be mended by outward bliss. Much to the contrary, it caused for part of that bliss (other angelic beings) to fall with it. If it is thus true that the mind "Can make a Heav'n of Hell," since the inception of sin Satan's mind has only been capable of making "a Hell of Heav'n." The following lines shed light on the nature of the sin which enslaves Satan:[5]

> What matter where, if I be still the same,
> And what I should be, all but less than he
> Whom thunder hath made greater? . . . (1.256–58)

Satan envisions force, as opposed to reason (248) or elevation of mind, as that element which makes God greater than him. In hell now as in heaven, therefore, Satan depicts his mind, his inner being, as equal to God's. His slavery to self is thus the result of that unfillable gap which, on the contrary, separates his derived nature from the divine. The freedom God, with Milton, accords Satan in hell can never be true liberty, but mere absence of an external rule:

> . . . Here at least
> We shall be free; th'Almighty hath not built
> Here for his envy, will not drive us hence:
> Here we may reign secure, and in my choice
> To reign is worth ambition though in Hell:
> Better to reign in Hell, than serve in Heav'n. (1.258–63)

Hell is conceived of here as a place of freedom, yet only insofar as freedom is defined as lack of external restraint and tyranny as submission and service. It has yet been noted that the freedom "place or time" grant cannot, in Satan's own words, change the mind. It cannot yield true liberty. In the inward realm of the mind, true liberty is only found in the free service of love ("serve in Heav'n"). It follows the terms of outward freedom in hell ("to reign in Hell") are the very terms of the tyranny of the mind. Hell's king is therefore a slave. His kingdom rests on the foundation of pain and deep despair, which sin renews and which outward freedom feeds. Where inward freedom is suppressed, necessity and desperation alone ensue. Necessity and desperation in turn underlie Satan's harangues as well as his abortive attempt to "grieve" and "disturb" God and to "resist" and "pervert" his gracious will (1.160–68).

The council of hell has deliberated that they should no longer wage war against the Omnipotent, but perversely undertake to thwart his plan for a new race. Hence at the outset of book 4, after a long journey

---

5. For the literary sources of Milton's portrait of the generation of Sin, see Martin, "The Sources of Milton's Sin Reconsidered."

through hell and chaos, Satan finally approaches the earth. In carrying out his freedom as hell's sole king, Satan embodies slavery: the scenario changes for him, but not so his inner torment. In a bout of dramatic irony, Satan's prideful words come to haunt him: as "one who brings / A mind not to be changed by place or time," he is far from free. Rather,

> . . . like a devilish engine back recoils
> Upon himself; horror and doubt distract
> His troubled thoughts, and from the bottom stir
> The Hell within him, for within him Hell
> One step no more than from himself can fly
> By change of place: now conscience wakes despair
> That slumbered, wakes the bitter memory
> Of what he was, what is, and what must be
> Worse; of worse deeds worse sufferings must ensue.
> Sometimes towards Eden which now is in his view
> Lay pleasant, his grieved look he fixes sad,
> Sometimes towards heav'n and the full blazing sun,
> Which now sat high in his meridian tow'r (1.17–30)

The chiasmic structure of "The Hell within him, for within him Hell" reflects the entrapment of "a devilish engine" which "back recoils / Upon himself." Horror and doubt haunt Satan's thoughts and stir the hell within in a circular motion which finds no end. Satan is lost in a maze of the mind. That which he carries within is an infernal microcosm.

"now conscience wakes despair." "That slumbered" may refer to either or both conscience and despair. The awoken conscience renews the obliterated thoughts of what he could be and what he used to be. It makes him sensitive to repressed feelings and imagination. Having noted how the change of place does not affect Satan's mind, now Milton shows how time likewise cannot change it. Conscience stirs the reminiscence of Satan's loss in time: past, present and future are all equally infernal dwellings. The past brings with it bitter regret for all that he has lost; the present yields the infernal chains of the mind, and the future elides all hope.

The vision of the earthly paradise as well as of heaven adds to the awakening of conscience. Sad, Satan fixes his "grieved look" on Eden, heaven and the full blazing sun. He is captured for a time by what he sees. His eyes become fixed on their object, that is, he contemplates. He is not indifferent to beauty, life and light. In fact, such sight brings sadness upon him, as his mind is enraptured for a time by that which it strongly desires but can no longer have.

Carey sees Satan's ambivalence in passages which, like the present one, reveal the conscience's recognition of beauty and which are yet promptly rebuffed by the fiend's recollection of his condition and determination.[6] The critic concludes that "Beauty and delight are his natural element. Hatred is an effort of his will."[7] A distinction between Satan and his conscience is, however, in order. Beauty and delight are indeed Satan's natural element, insofar as Satan is identified with the eternal conscience God has implanted in him (as in all his rational creatures). Nevertheless, inasmuch as Satan's conscience is dormant for the vast majority of the poem, beauty and delight cannot be regarded as his natural element. It is rather only when his conscience awakes that it may yield temporary epiphanies of long-forgotten beauty and delight.

Milton now appears to point to the light which, not received, ultimately sanctions Satan's self-judgment. The "full blazing sun, / Which now sat high in his meridian tow'r" has a notable homophone in "The radiant image of his [God's] glory [who also] sat [on God's right] / His only Son":

> O thou that with surpassing glory crowned,
> Look'st from thy sole dominion like the God
> Of this new world; at whose sight all the stars
> Hide their diminished heads; to thee I call,
> But with no friendly voice, and add thy name
> O Sun, to tell thee how I hate thy beams
> That bring to my remembrance from what state
> I fell, how glorious once above thy sphere. (4.32–39)[8]

The juxtaposition of the Christological reference to the astronomic works to the effect of stressing Satan's physical and outward fall as well as his spiritual and inward. The caesura after "to thee I call" leaves the reader suspended. Is Satan going to echo the poet and call on the celestial light to shine inward and irradiate the mind?[9] The unit of meaning

6. Carey identifies 1.619–20 vs. ff.; 9.464–66 vs. 9.473–75; 4.362–64 vs. ff. as such passages ("Milton's Satan," 166–69).

7. Carey, "Milton's Satan," 168.

8. Milton's nephew Edward Phillips reports that these lines date back to 1640–42. See Forsyth, *The Satanic Epic*, 60.

9. For the suggestion of an asymmetric parallelism in the poet and Satan's invoca-

promptly affords a negative answer. Satan calls on the Sun/Son to tell him how he hates its beams. His hatred is hardly an effort of the will, but a necessity. His choice of self-elevation and conscience with all its fruits are mutually exclusive. If conscience makes the creature sensitive to light again, hatred amounts to a form of self-defense in one who longs for that light which he has chosen to reject.[10] It puts an end to the sorrow and laceration which the renewing exposition to the sun has produced, by repressing conscience. Satan is his own gaoler and his prison "pride and worse ambition" (40).

A theodical intent is undoubtedly behind the lines that immediately follow. The same, however, also testify to the inward conflict between conscience and sin, namely a battle which reflects Satan's inner being falling short of Christian liberty:

> Ah wherefore! He deserved no such return
> From me, whom he created what I was
> In that bright eminence, and with his good
> Upbraided none; nor was his service hard.
> What could be less than to afford him praise,
> The easiest recompense, and pay him thanks,
> How due! Yet all good proved ill in me,
> And wrought but malice; lifted up so high
> I 'sdained subjection, and thought one step higher
> Would set me highest, and in a moment quit
> The debt immense of endless gratitude,
> So burdensome still paying, still to owe;
> Forgetful what from him I still received,
> And understood not that a grateful mind
> By owing owes not, but still pays, at once
> Indebted and discharged; what burden then? (4.42–57)

The flame of conscience still flickering, the veil of pride is partially lifted only to be recovered again and again. All the reality of the injustice of Satan's course suddenly becomes vivid before his eyes. The reader can feel the pain and he can feel the despair produced by the gap between what Satan's conscience perceives as right and good and his choice. "Ah wherefore!" There was nothing in God nor in the blissful condition God had apportioned him which could account for his rebellion. On the con-

---

tions to light in the openings of books 3 and 4, see Wigler, "The Poet and Satan Before the Light."

10. See Forsyth, *Milton's Satanic Epic*, 341.

trary, his creational "bright eminence" called for gratitude and praise, "The easiest recompense." "How due!"

In emphasizing the elevation of his original position, however, Satan is pointing to the very reason for his fall. All "this good" brought forth "ill." His primacy as an angelic creature "wrought but malice." The status God freely accorded him in his goodness provided the ground for evil. Whereas at a superficial glance Satan's words seem to trace the origin of evil to good, a closer look bespeaks the quality of paradox. By contrasting Satan's fall with God's goodness, his words in fact work to the effect of magnifying his guilt. The very grammar Satan resorts to ultimately causes for all blame to fall on him, "I 'sdained subjection, and thought one step higher / Would set me highest." The first person active verb form points to responsible action. The echo of Isaiah 14:12–15 is anything but elusive:

> How art thou fallen from heaven, O Lucifer, son of the morning! How art thou cut down to the ground, which didst weaken the nations! For thou hast said in thine heart, I will ascend into heaven, I will exalt my throne above the stars of God: I will sit also upon the mount of the congregation, in the sides of the north: I will ascend above the heights of the cloud; I will be like the most High.

As in the biblical passage Lucifer's sin consisted of five *I wills* against the will of God, so the principle of prideful rebellion must not be traced to the cherub's bliss, but to his choice. "Lifted up so high," he could have chosen to rejoice in his position as a gift of God's love and "pay him thanks" as a reflection of that same love. On the other hand, he could have chosen to turn his eyes on the intrinsic eminence of self and separate it from the one who gives it meaning. His mind saw his own self as the very end of existence and, pride being thus ushered in, it pursued its absolute elevation.

While tracing "Satan's sin from its inception to its fully blown expression as self-authoring pride," Anderson argues that "the essential negation belonging to envy is his ethical core."[11] Be it so, the circular motion whereby envy and pride chase and inform one another points to self-assertion as Satan's ultimate end. The very principle of inward slavery, envious pride supplanted grace, namely the principle of inward

---

11. Anderson, "Satanic Ethos and Envy," 138.

liberty. Hooker similarly points to self-assertion as the only direction in which such a being could sin:

> It seemeth therefore that there was no other way for angels to sin, but by reflex of their understanding upon themselves; when being held with admiration of their own sublimity and honor, the memory of their subordination unto God and their dependency on Him was drowned in this conceit; whereupon their adoration, love and imitation of God could not choose but be also interrupted.[12]

Criticism has strongly objected to a God who expects gratitude from his creature. Unmindful of the possibility that the dramatic dialogue between Father and Son in book 3 actually portray the dialectic of righteousness and love within the Godhead—one that finds its synthesis at the cross[13]—Empson has portrayed Milton's God as an "egocentric, legalistic and self-justifying" bully.[14] C. S. Lewis, for his part, while tracing God's expressions to Milton's magnification of a hierarchical order, has invariably read such lines as "Ingrate, he had of me / All he could have" (3.97–98) as amplifying God's remoteness from the things of man. Both have failed to read the negation of the principle of gratitude into the definition of Satan's inward enslavement. Thomas Erskine points to this same principle in the maxim, "in the new Testament, religion is grace, and ethics is gratitude."[15] F. F. Bruce expands on these words by stressing that if

> . . . this dictum were turned into Greek, one word, *charis*, would serve as the equivalent of both "grace" and "gratitude"; for the gratitude which divine grace calls forth from its recipient is also the expression of that grace . . .[16]

The philological relation is seemingly behind Satan's expansion on the lost dynamics of gratitude. The burden of paradox drives the point home. Satan pictures gratitude as a "debt immense." The benefit received is such that there is nothing the creature can do to repay it. As he turned his eyes on himself, Satan could only perceive gratitude in legalistic terms, in

---

12. Hooker, *Of the Laws of Ecclesiastical Polity*, 1.4.2.

13. See Falcone, "More Challenges," 235–36.

14. Ostriker, "Dancing at the Devil's Party," 400.

15. Erskine, *Letters*, 16.

16. Bruce, *Paul*, 19.

terms, that is, of never-ending restitution. Like an external law, gratitude was regarded as continually demanding satisfaction, "So burdensome still paying, still to owe." The archangel failed to understand the very nature of gratitude. He failed to understand that gratitude stems from grace. If gratitude was to be perpetual, it was because grace was also perpetual ("what from him I still received"). True gratitude is the portion of the mind which understands that "By owing [it] owes not, but still pays, at once / Indebted and discharged." True gratitude is never-ending response to never-ending favor. If it is then true that the inward apprehension of grace called forth the ethics of gratitude whereby God's rule was perceived as mild, it is as true that the inward denial of grace turns grateful subjection into legalistic oppression and God into the oppressor.

Satan next envisions the alternative scenario of an inferior creational status. Had not God made him what he was, had he ordained him some inferior creature, ambition would have found no harbor in him. We know by now that Milton's strategy is to build a straw man only to knock it down. His is no mere rhetorical strategy, though, nor is he barely trying to involve the reader in a didactic or cathartic process, as Fish would argue. The circular movement of the language rather reflects the dialectic of the tormented soul, which seeks an escape from its prison never to find one. Like the engine that recoils upon himself and like the demons who "reasoned high / Of providence, foreknowledge, will and fate, / Fixed fate, free will, Foreknowledge absolute, / And found no end, in wand'ring mazes lost" (2.558–61), Satan's mind is caught in the circular motion of endless speculative torment. The different scenarios Satan's mind tentatively projects serve as a backdrop amplifying the ultimate responsibility of the individual will:

> . . . Some other power
> As great might have aspired, and me though mean
> Drawn to his part; but other powers as great
> Fell not, but stand unshaken, from within
> Or from without, to all temptations armed.
> Hadst thou the same free will and power to stand?
> Thou hadst: whom hast thou then or what to accuse,
> But Heav'n's free love dealt equally to all? (4.61–70)

A different creational premise would not have changed the conclusion, since the latter was not dependent on the former. Other creatures sharing Satan's creational status had not fallen. Had he not "the same free will and power to stand" as they? He had. He had the freedom and strength sufficient to discard his own image and choose God. He did not. The common denominator in all Satan's projections is not found either in the internal or external conditions set by God, but in his own free will. Over and over, Satan is brought back to his free choice as the ultimate cause of his enthrallment. Over and over, he is reminded that, due to his choice, there is no shelter, no haven of liberty, for the mind.

One more paradox is now sure to surface: if it was his free will that caused him to fall, even that free will which God accorded him in his love, God's very love is then to blame. Far from it, the act of charging love with the fall again testifies to nothing but Satan's inner grief. Again, Satan is not so much trying to discharge himself by blaming God as he is looking for a way out for his mind. Satan's inward dialectic ultimately provides none, other than the renunciation of self:

> Be then his love accursed, since love or hate,
> To me alike, it deals eternal woe (4.69–70)

The oxymoron "love accursed" witnesses to the freedom of the will as that which has brought forth "eternal woe." In cursing love, in fact, Satan is really cursing himself:

> Nay cursed be thou; since against his thy will
> Chose freely what it now so justly rues.
> Me miserable! Which way shall I fly
> Infinite wrath, and infinite despair?
> Which way I fly is Hell; myself am Hell (4.71–75)

This passage adds conclusive emphasis to the idea that in choosing self instead of allowing *charis*, namely love, to bear its natural fruit of gratitude, Satan has become his own prison. His choice has ultimately attracted both inward and outward restraint in the form of "Infinite wrath, and infinite despair." From either he cannot flee. And if for Satan "Which way I fly is Hell," it is not because he is circumscribed within hell's bounds. After all, he is now in sight of the earthly paradise. Satan rather embodies hell, for his choice, that is, his rational essence, is what generates it. In the final analysis, the microcosm within is as much a fully defined reality as the hell without. It is a place of the mind. There,

> . . . in the lowest deep a lower deep
> Still threat'ning to devour me opens wide,
> To which the Hell I suffer seems a Heav'n. (4.76–78)

One last paradox presents itself as the superlative "lowest" is threatened to be superseded by the comparative "lower." The passage is reminiscent of the fact that the mind can make a hell of heaven. Even more so, here Satan tells us that the mind can make a worse hell of the infernal world that he harbors. Is there no salvation, no room for liberty?

> . . . is there no place
> Left for repentance, none for pardon left?
> None but by submission . . . (4.79–81)

The chiasmus "Left for repentance, none for pardon left" plainly ties pardon to repentance. If negation of grateful submission is what has introduced all hell within, indeed restoration can only come through death to self. Like the fall, Satan's rehabilitation does not depend on God's willingness to forgive, but on his free choice. The circular motion exploited thus far in the soliloquy continues to inform the progress of Satan's dialectic search for relief. Satan's questioning of God's gracious nature now backfires to indicate, once more, that God's love will not be found wanting, yet its appropriation falls on individual choice. The word submission, nevertheless, brings disdain and the mere thought thereof shame. The oxymoronic boast that he could "subdue / Th' Omnipotent" (4.85–86) has placed him highest among "the spirits beneath" (4.83), yet lower he sinks:

> . . . Ay me, they little know
> How dearly I abide that boast so vain,
> Under what torment inwardly I groan;
> While they adore me on the throne of Hell,
> With diadem and scepter high advanced
> The lower still I fall, only supreme
> In misery; such joy ambition finds (4.86–92)

The outward visible reality is here meaningfully contrasted to the inward and invisible. As for Adam and Eve after the fall, the slavery of sin progressively disrupts the original identity and harmony of inward and outward. The more Satan receives adoration on the throne of hell "with diadem and scepter high advanced," the lower within he falls. The spirits beneath see his infernal elevation, but they do not see "Under what torment inwardly" he groans. They see him supreme, yet he is "only supreme / In misery" within.

The outward reality is thus inversely proportional to the inward as Satan is caught in a tension between outward glory and inward misery which only intensifies his sense of solitude. He is alone in his slavery, because he alone inhabits the microcosm within. It is here, in the solitude of the inward microcosm as it surfaces in the soliloquies, that the true Satan appears, without the mask of outward heroism and glory, stripped of true liberty. The external freedom Satan enjoys in hell as hell's supreme king cannot change him, nor can it restore true liberty. Far from it, the contrast between the inward and the outward reality only serves to amplify the distinctive trait of his loss of inward liberty, even his lack of love. Satan does not love anyone but himself. He does not love God, but he does not love his hosts of infernal angels either. His public speeches rather testify to demagogy and manipulation. Satan is only bound to turn to the fallen angels to enhance his pride and selfish schemes. He can only be a tyrant in hell.

To be sure, as his conscience awakes for a time and alerts him to beauty in the contemplation of two of far nobler shape, Satan realizes that the proper response to beauty is love. Nevertheless, he cannot help relating the novel creatures to their creator and, as a result, to the enmity between himself and God. Envy, jealousy and hatred must take the place of love in his conscience and mind for his inner self to be fed. Satan now hypothetically makes room in his dialectic for the very pardon and repentance the thought of which he had previously entertained and questioned:

> But say I could repent and could obtain
> By act of grace my former state; how soon
> Would highth recall high thoughts, how soon unsay
> What feigned submission swore: ease would recant
> Vows made in pain, as violent and void.
> For never can true reconcilement grow
> Where wounds of deadly hate have pierced so deep:
> Which would but lead me to a worse relapse
> And heavier fall: so should I purchase dear
> Short intermission bought with double smart.
> This knows my punisher; therefore as far
> From granting he, as I from begging peace (4.93–104)

Origen had argued that Satan would ultimately be forgiven. Milton discards this conclusion while making every effort to ascribe unlimited graciousness to God's nature.[17] In so doing, he appears not to fully align himself with the magisterial Reformation, which generally held that no provision had been made for angelic redemption. William Ames epitomizes this position as follows:

> In the angels there was no *anastasis*, or restoration, because, first, they fell from the highest excellence; and, second, the angelic nature did not completely perish. But in the sin of the first man all mankind perished.[18]

In the lines of book 4, we are made to approach the issue of whether or not there is still room for redemption for Satan from the fiend's point of view. Because God's eternal decree accords and contains free choice, Milton can allow Satan to choose the destiny of damnation that is already written for him in heaven. This means that the possibility to find redemption is there all along, but it also means that Satan will not choose it. While envisioning the alternative to his condition, Satan knows that his vows of submission would be dictated by pain. Hate has pierced through his essence too deeply for inward reconciliation to prove pervasive and real. No sooner were rehabilitation provided than his pride and hatred would once again reveal his true and unvaried nature. God knows this, "therefore as far / From granting he, as I from begging peace." In other words, God's choice does nothing but sanction Satan's own. Tackling the issue from a different angle, in book 3 God declares that

> The first sort by their own suggestion fell,
> Self-tempted, self-depraved: man falls deceived
> By the other first: man therefore shall find grace,
> The other none . . . (3.129–31)

Satan and his host of fallen angels fell without facing external temptation. For this reason, Satan will not find grace. Again, God's decree must be regarded as containing Satan's ultimate choice. Whereas Stavely traces Satan's ultimate condition to the same Arminian pattern which, in his mind, informs all the characters in Milton's rational universe,[19] Milton rather appears to reason, in the Amyraldian fashion, from the benevolence of God, and not, as Calvin, from the standpoint of God's decree. In testifying to Satan's fall being conceived within, apart from

---

17. See Robins, *If This Be Heresy*; Patrides, "The Salvation of Satan," 467–78.

18. Ames, *Marrow*, 114.

19. Stavely, "Satan and Arminianism in *Paradise Lost*," 125–39.

external compulsion or temptation and as the result of free choice, the fiend's soliloquy in book 4 closely parallels the divine angle. God knows that the principle which yielded Satan's unconstrained fall would reproduce itself over and over. The nature of the initial fall encompasses all future potential falls, hence preventing God from granting grace and Satan from seeking it.

Determining the nature of Satan's ultimate punishment is beside the point here,[20] for Satan *is* his own ultimate punishment. Here lies the emphasis of the poem with respect to the true character of hell. Just as the eschatology of liberty will be inaugurated within Adam and Eve, so does Satan presently embody the final hell.

Turning down the path to Christian liberty, Satan only seals his destiny as one of self-enhancement. Grace not received and inward liberty forfeited, all love is denied towards God and God's creatures. The way of Christian liberty brings forth hope and good (love). The way of self results in the loss of all hope and all good (love). From now on, Satan's sustenance will only be found in evil as the only way to exorcise fear and regret:

> All hope excluded thus, behold instead
> Of us outcast, exiled, his new delight,
> Mankind created, and for him this world.
> So farewell hope, and with hope farewell fear,
> Farewell remorse; all good to me is lost;
> Evil be thou my good . . . (4.105–10)

Our reductionist approach must ultimately lead us to the conclusion that Satan is much more than a character. He personifies a whole theology. He in fact stands for that principle of inward enthrallment and outward tyranny which Milton had extensively countered through the work of the left hand and which he now committed poetry to destroy in the life of Adam and Eve.

---

20. Brodwin has detected a discrepancy between *De Doctrina* and *PL* with respect to Satan's ultimate doom. For Brodwin, the orthodox view of Satan's eternal torment expressed in the treatise is replaced by a mortalist stance ably disguised in the poem, which assimilates the fiend's destiny to that of mankind against a Socinian and pseudepigraphal backdrop (see Brodwin, "The Dissolution of Satan in *Paradise Lost*," 165–207).

5

Eschatology Inaugurated

Christian Liberty and Adam and Eve

Prelapsarian Liberty

When Adam and Eve are introduced in book 4, we see them through Satan's eyes, that is to say, we see them through the eyes of Satan's fall. Although the fiend sees "undelighted all delight," we feel that his perspective, unlike that of his public speeches, yet much like that of his soliloquies, is reliable and truthfully insightful. He sees

> Two of far nobler shape erect and tall,
> Godlike erect, with native honor clad
> In naked majesty seemed lords of all,
> And worthy seemed, for in their looks divine
> The image of their glorious Maker shone,
> Truth, wisdom, sanctitude severe and pure,
> Severe but in true filial freedom placed;
> Whence true authority in men . . . (4.288–95)

In these lines we find a clear depiction of prelapsarian liberty.[1] Being made in the image of God, Adam and Eve are not merely "Godlike

---

1. In "Scripture's Constraint and Adam's Self-Authoring Freedom," Di Benedetto focuses on the dialectic between Adam's freedom and the narrative constraints of Scripture. There is a sense in which Adam can only choose that which he has already chosen in the biblical narrative. Accordingly, Adam's freedom in *Paradise Lost* is limited to that space of Scriptural silence which Milton can fill with his imagination. While Milton is there all along preventing Adam's narrative freedom from changing the

erect," but endowed with "Truth, wisdom, sanctitude severe and pure." Their holiness, like God's, is characterized by purity and severity, as it is steadfast and righteous, not subject to shades of compromise. However, Milton hastens to counterbalance severity with "filial freedom." Even more so, the severity of their sanctity is "in true filial freedom placed." In other words, the milieu of their sanctity is filial freedom. If then no weakness transpires from the holiness of their countenance, their strict compliance with divine righteousness is that of the son and daughter who are free to obey their Father. In this respect they can be said to dwell in Augustinian *libertas*. The latter is supported by that elevation of mind and conscience which manifests itself in sufficiency of truth and wisdom. All in all, they are "just and right, / Sufficient to have stood, though free to fall" (3.98–99). That is to say, while enjoying full freedom to do what they will, they are supplied with all they need to do what they should. Absolute negative liberty, that is, is matched by positive liberty. While negative liberty makes man the ultimate *faber fortunae suae*, positive liberty alone is and preserves true filial freedom, namely the source of "true authority."

Milton thus marks a gap between Augustinian theology, which he embraces in the words above, and the assumption, epitomized in Penington's statement hereafter, which saw in Adam's constitutional weakness the reason for the fall:

> Nothing can act above its nature. *Adam*, when he fell, shewed the weakness of his nature, *The Prince of this World* came and found somewhat in him to fasten upon. Frailty is a property of the flesh. Weakness is proper to the earthly image, as strength to the heavenly.[2]

In Penington's understanding, Satan had identified frailty in the human flesh, thus casting shadows over God's perfect creation, while also undermining Adam's freedom of choice. The sufficiency of Milton's Adam argues to much the opposite effect. In fact, it argues for free will and it frees God from the most immediate allegation of being the author of an imperfect creation. What is more, it stands in sharp contrast with

---

course of history, Adam's freedom, both positive and negative, need be affirmed as that which determined the course of history.

2. Penington, *Divine Essays*, 65. Cited in Poole, *Milton and the Idea of the Fall*, 19.

the idea hereafter expressed that Adam's mind is a blank slate on which external solicitations may write their own story:

> A Childe . . . Is a Man in a small Letter, yet the best Copie of *Adam* before hee tasted of *Eue* or the Apple . . . His Soule is yet a white paper vnscribled with obseruations of the world, where-with it becomes a blurr'd Note-booke.[3]

Milton's Adam is no *tabula rasa* and environmental influence is not invincible in him. Like Locke after him, Milton regards the filter of reason as decisive. Ever-perfectible knowledge of good, intelligence and the ability to control both the realm of conscience, mind and visible reality are ingrained in human nature. More than spontaneous choice, God therefore accords man the freedom which Hobbes, in his mechanist worldview, denies him, namely the freedom resulting from the genuine possibility to choose amongst alternatives.[4]

Such freedom is not only available potentially, but it is given to express itself efficaciously through the single prohibition to eat from the tree of the knowledge of good and evil. If, in Corns' words, "God's interdiction of the fruit of one tree has a logic-defying arbitrariness," it is only because "what is significant is the interdiction itself, not the interdicted object."[5] A first external law, which we may call the Adamic code, the prohibition ultimately amounts to the possibility to choose against the Maker and know experientially all that is contrary to God. Liberty in turn results both from natural sufficiency to obey the command and

---

3. John Earle, *Micro-cosmography*, sg. Bir-v, cited in Poole, *Milton and the Idea of the Fall*, 17.

4. In Pacchi's words, "Hobbes' emphasis on the mechanically necessary determinism which directs human actions is reinterpreted on the theological plane—as, for instance, during the discussions on free-will with Bishop Bramhall—by stressing the role God plays in determining human behaviour, using words which bring to mind the doctrine of predestination. Of course, it should not be forgotten that the description of the hard power relationship between God and Man is strongly influenced by the political model of the relationship between civil ruler and subject" (Pacchi, "*Leviathan* and Spinoza's *Tractatus*," 130). On Hobbes' treatment of free-will, in particular in its connections with the doctrine of predestination, see Pacchi's introduction to Hobbes' *Of Liberty and Necessity* (1972); Hobbes' *The Questions Concerning Liberty, Necessity and Chance*, vol. 5, esp. 138–47, 208–21, 298–300, the latter work encompassing noteworthy references to Luther, Zanchi, Bucer, Calvin and the Synod of Dort; and Fallon, *Milton among the Philosophers*.

5. Corns, *Regaining Paradise Lost*, 75. Cf. CPW 6.352.

from the alternative to transgress it. *An Orthodox Creed* shares Milton's rationale in the words:

> God hath endued the will of man with that natural liberty and power of acting upon choice, that it's neither forced, nor by any necessity of nature determined, to do good or evil: but man, in the state of innocency, had such power and liberty of will to chuse and perform that which was acceptable and well pleasing to God, according to the requirement of the first covenant.[6]

For the Baptist statement, as for the poem, "in the state of innocency" Adam was sufficient to stand, as he possessed both the "power and liberty of will" to do so, yet free to fall, inasmuch as choice was "neither forced, nor by any necessity of nature determined, to do good or evil." In other words, although he was endowed with everything he needed to "chuse and perform that which was acceptable and well pleasing to God," no intrinsic or extrinsic necessity acted on his choice to keep or to break the "requirement of the first covenant."

Adam's creational freedom similarly proves in Milton characterized in theodical terms, which, much like the Baptist statement, point to the omission of sovereign necessity. God's righteous course is justified insofar as man's utter freedom is affirmed. Accordingly, it is in the apology of divine perfections that the full extent of human prelapsarian freedom is defined:

> They therefore as to right belonged,
> So were created, nor can justly accuse
> Their Maker, or their making, or their fate,
> As if predestination overruled
> Their will, disposed by high decree
> Or high foreknowledge; they themselves decreed
> Their own revolt, not I: if I foreknew,
> Foreknowledge had no influence on their fault,
> Which had no less proved certain unforeknown.
> So without least impulse or shadow of fate,
> Or aught by me immutably foreseen,
> They trespass, authors to themselves in all
> Both what they judge and what they choose; for so
> I formed them free, and free they must remain,
> Till they enthrall themselves: I else must change
> Their nature, and revoke the high decree

---

6. Lumpkin, ed., *Baptist Confessions of Faith*, art. XX, 312. Cf. *CPW* 6.351–3.

Unchangeable, eternal, which ordained
Their freedom; they themselves ordained their fall. (3.111–28)

In what is a sharp and unmistakable statement of faith, Milton here nails down his belief with regard to the relationship between God's decrees and man's prelapsarian liberty. The poet apparently departs from both supralapsarianism[7] and a deterministic idea of foreknowledge, as he causes responsibility to fall entirely on Adam and Eve. The two progenitors of mankind cannot blame their Creator as either the direct or indirect author of the fall: God did not cause them to fall, he did not give them a nature that could not withstand the test, nor was the necessity of a higher plan pressed upon their choice. On the contrary, their free will was pre-ordained by a high decree, unchangeable, eternal, which could not be overturned by a conflicting design or foreknowledge, but which was to allow for and indeed contained the fall. And if man's fall "had no less proved certain unforeknown," it is because, as Danielson has it, Milton bore in mind the clear-cut seventeenth-century theological distinction between "certainty," based on non-deterministic foreknowledge, and "necessity."[8] Danielson turns to Thomas Pierce as one who would in the late Fifties prove anything but shy of this differentiation, "What God decreed to effect will come to pass unavoidably, and by necessitation . . . But what he only decreed to permit, will contingently come to pass; yet . . . with a certainty of event, because his foreknowledge is infallible."[9] In light of such distinction, *An Orthodox Creed*, in its own right, could state that God "foresaw Adam's fall, but did not decree it." Foundational to a similar understanding, in turn, was the creed's belief "that known unto God are all his works from all eternity."[10] Hence the concept of foreknowledge as "certainty of event" came to be defined as a theological contrivance or accommodation of the idea of divine knowledge of event and creature irrespective of time. At the outset of the Middle Ages, Boethius, whom Lorenzo Valla regards as the first of Scholastic philoso-

7. Supralapsarianism is the doctrine that places election to salvation before the decrees inherent to creation and the fall, an idea that would apparently trace the origin of the fall to God himself. Cf. *CPW* 6.162.

8. Danielson, "The Fall and Milton's Theodicy," 150–51. For an informed defense of Milton's theodicy, see Danielson, *Milton's Good God*.

9. Pierce, *Self-Condemnation*, cited by Danielson, "The Fall and Milton's Theodicy," 151.

10. Lumpkin, ed., *Baptist Confessions of Faith*, art. X, 304.

phers, in his *De Consolatione Philosophiae* (524ca) had equated the entirety of God's knowledge, even his *prescientia*, to man's present *scientia*. Milton, in his own right, is sure to depict God as "beholding from his prospect high, / Wherein past, present, future he beholds" (*PL* 3.77–78). God's ever-present knowledge, to be sure, does not work to the effect of determining what must *certainly* come to pass, but acknowledges reality as the decree ordaining freedom allows it to be. The decree, as it were, necessitates man's freedom of choice, which in turn shapes man's destiny as it is encompassed by God's benevolent plan.

By its very nature, too, the decree leaves it with man to put an end to his freedom, "free they must remain / Till they enthrall themselves." A fundamental theoretical passage is entailed here. To break the requirement of the first covenant is to choose against God, it is to choose for the slavery of sin, for true freedom results from choosing for God. True liberty, in fact, appears to amount to more than mere freedom of choice. True liberty is inextricably related to fellowship with the object of choice. Even more so, both negative and positive freedom only serve to define the true substance of liberty as relational:

> Not free, what proof could they have giv'n sincere
> Of true allegiance, constant faith or love,
> Where only what they needs must do, appeared,
> Not what they would? What praise could they receive?
> What pleasure I from such obedience paid,
> When will and reason (reason also is choice)
> Useless and vain, of freedom both despoiled,
> Made passive both, had served necessity,
> Not me. (3.103–11)

Virtue is only displayed when faced with a test. The test is provided by the prohibition. Choice makes the dichotomies efficient: the contrast between "what they needs must do" and "what they would" is one between necessity ("needs"), coercion ("must"), and will ("would"). In endowing man with free will, God effectually gave allegiance, constant faith and love their being. Ultimately, though, the contrast between necessity and choice is one between subservience and fellowship. Milton turns from the intrinsic value of moral virtues as the reflection and counterpart of God's moral essence to the very relationship they are to inform ("What praise could they receive? / What pleasure I").

Any genuine relationship with God must be grounded on the freedom of reason to choose against God. Both will and reason prove "Useless and vain" when despoiled of freedom and made passive. Without negative freedom, that is, Adam and Eve are nothing but automata who only serve necessity, as opposed to the true God. Milton's argument here bears the long echo of *Areopagitica*:

> Many there be that complain of divine Providence for suffering Adam to transgress. Foolish tongues! When God gave him reason, he gave him freedom to choose, for reason is but choosing; he had been else a mere artificial Adam, such an Adam as he is in the motions. We ourselves esteem not of that obedience, or love, or gift, which is of force; God therefore left him free.[11]

The veracity of obedience and love is inextricably bound to the freedom of the choice thereof. God necessitates the freedom of this choice, as opposed to the choice itself, because to freely choose obedience and love is to genuinely choose him. True liberty can thus be traced to one's free relationship with God, and not directly to freedom of choice. The latter freedom rather proves instrumental in that it yields the conditions in which filial freedom is enjoyed.

In the final analysis, Adam and Eve reflect divine truth, wisdom, holiness severe and pure, couched in filial freedom, being sufficient to stand yet free to fall. Only in such state could their actions prove genuine and meaningful. Only given such state could God be acquitted and man elevated, as well as their personal relationship enhanced. In turn dodging the supralapsarian shadows cast on theodicy by his system of divinity and stressing the relational significance of unnecessitated obedience, Calvin points to the principle whereby the first man in his creational perfection was able to choose to enthrall himself:

> Adam, therefore, could have stood if he would, since he fell merely by his own will; but because his will was flexible to either side, and he was not endued with constancy to persevere, therefore he so easily fell. Yet his choice of good and evil was free; and not only so, but his mind and will were possessed of consummate rectitude, and all his organic parts were rightly disposed to obedience, till, destroying himself, he corrupted all his excellencies.[12]

11. *CPW* 2.527. Cf. *CPW* 6.352–3.
12. Calvin, *Institutes*, 1.15.215.

Adam and Eve's Perfectibility

The contrast between creational perfection and the fall was to pose not only a theological but also a poetical problem for Milton. On one hand, Milton had to justify how the perfect creation of a perfect God could be subject to the fall.[13] On the other, he had to credibly balance absolute rectitude in the characters and the free choice of evil. Calvin's words pave the way for Milton's own confrontation with one and the other. Albeit Adam and Eve, while effectively free to choose good or evil, had a "mind and will . . . possessed of consummate rectitude" and "were [both] rightly disposed to obedience," they were "not endued with constancy to persevere." In other words, they were not complete. Here lies the ultimate synthesis of theodicy and the fall. Constancy comes in the form of fortification in the truth through the testing of faith.[14] In *Areopagitica* we read that proof of virtue as well as fortification in the choice of truth cannot come to pass apart from consciousness of all that lies before man. Such consciousness, or rather knowledge, both positive and negative, is precisely that with which the consummate rectitude of Adam and Eve's reason is not fully supplied. Positive knowledge encompasses the knowledge of God and his will. Negative knowledge encompasses the knowledge of evil.

Adam possesses a measure of innate knowledge. For one thing, he can name created things (8.271–73). However, he does not know the nature of the inanimate things he names (8.280–82). He senses personal identity, yet he knows not how he came into being nor can he describe his birth other than in terms of his present experience (8.253–56, 287–91). Likewise, he does not know either his origin or purpose (8.270–71).[15] And if God has "put eternity into man's heart,"[16] to the extent that Adam knows a Creator is behind creation and possesses an inward prompting to pursue, love and adore God, he is still unaware of the nature of the Godhead and of the terms which are to inform his relationship with it (8.280–82). Raphael will be instrumental in relaying that portion of

13. In *Fallible Perfection*, Musacchio shows to what extent Milton's theological context, particularly that of Reformed and post-Reformed theology, affords sufficient justification of how perfection may allow for the fall.

14. Cf. Jas 1:3. "Patience" in the King James Version and Geneva Bible is better rendered as "constancy" or "perseverance."

15. See Corns, *Regaining Paradise Lost*, 57–58.

16. Eccl 3:11 (*ESV*).

knowledge which Adam will be able to process: the free state of his being in book 5, elements of theology proper in book 6, creation in book 7 as well as elements of cosmology in book 8[17] and a survey of things to come with the full manifestation of the covenant of grace are all part of such revelation. Through all this, divine instruction is substantially integrated with Adam's own investigation. In fact, discursive reason is the active counterpart of revelation and education in the process of perfecting knowledge.

Even so, the positive end of perfectibility bespeaks limitations. In *Of Education* Milton underscores the necessity to envision education as a gradual process that goes from the elementary and tangible to the far-fetched and abstract, for this is how man apprehends. He best understands that which he can know through or relate to the senses. God and things invisible, therefore, must be approached through a process of accommodation. The latter understanding is largely shared and variously stressed throughout *Paradise Lost* as Adam seeks knowledge and is accorded that portion of knowledge which he can progressively contain:

> . . . for thy good
> This is dispensed, and what surmounts the reach
> Of human sense, I shall delineate so,
> By lik'ning spiritual to corporal forms,
> As may express them best . . . (5.570–74)

Milton's postlapsarian world is called upon to share the same learning method that informs Adam's prelapsarian reality. While Scholastic reason plays a key-role in filtering the impulses provided by the senses, Milton does not shy away from emphasizing the role of the senses in the process of learning. On the contrary, the senses are seen here as instrumental to the scrutiny of nature, the cosmos and man, after the fashion of the Baconian process of observation and experimentation.

That which is apprehended by means of the senses in turn acquires significance as a sign pointing to a reality beyond the senses. The pos-

17. As Andrew Mattison underscores ("'Thine Own Inventions,'" 41), criticism, following in Fish's and Schwartz's footsteps, has largely assumed that the conversation between Adam and Raphael is governed by Raphael's warning about a possible fall. For Mattison, "Fish's 1967 book *Surprised by Sin* provides a reading of the passage clarified and further developed, but essentially unchanged, in his recent *How Milton Works*. Schwartz's focuses more on Raphael's discussion of heavenly actions in which Adam can participate, such as praise, but still regards the warning as the interpretive center of the conversation."

sibility of likening "spiritual to corporal forms," that is, seems to point to Platonic shades of meaning, suggesting, in Emerson's words, that "every natural fact is a symbol of some spiritual fact."[18] All that is beyond the apprehension of the senses must be related by association to that which is learnt sensibly. Revelation, in other words, must address man's sense-bound faculties by pointing them to the natural symbols of supernatural realities. This learning process leaves room for indefinite progress. To this very effect, Adam's perfection does not cause his knowledge to be static, for "God made [him] perfect, not immutable" (5.524). In other words, a dynamic process is to enhance Adam and Eve's knowledge of God and his universe. So Adam to Raphael:

> O favorable spirit, propitious guest,
> Well hast thou taught the way that might direct
> Our knowledge, and the scale of nature set
> From center to circumference, whereon
> In contemplation of created things
> By steps we may ascend to God. (5.507–12)

Once again, the same learning method is purported in the poem which is envisioned in *Of Education*. However, the objective apparently differs. In the prose work the ultimate goal is to achieve as clear a knowledge of God as the contemplation of derived objects may afford. In the poem prelapsarian Adam and Eve may progressively *ascend* to God. Given this possibility, the definition of the terms of Adam and Eve's vertical progress is also sure to appear in the poem as Adam projects his gaze into outer space and inquires into the heavenly spheres:

> God to remove his ways from human sense,
> Placed heav'n from Earth so far, that earthly sight,
> If it presume, might err in things too high,
> And no advantage gain. (8.119–22)

If understanding in *Of Education* "cannot in this body found itself but on sensible things," in a way that closely parallels Bacon's own stance the poem understands God to have removed "his ways from human sense" and "Placed heav'n from Earth" too far for "earthly sight" to see. To be sure, the prose tract does not say that postlapsarian man can know God's ways through his senses more than the poem says that prelapsarian Adam can see what is invisible through his earthly sight. What both

18. Emerson, *Nature*, 1081.

works say is that man's ascension to God before the fall is limited just as the measure of man's understanding of the invisible after the fall is. The emphasis is more on the absolute otherness of God than on the scope of the human faculties either before or after the fall.

If there seems to be little or no difference between prelapsarian Adam and postlapsarian man's rational potential, this is only so inasmuch as the divine standard makes the earthly relative. In light of this, Milton is not underestimating the effects of the fall nor is he equating the human condition before and after his lapse. What Milton is doing is noting how the knowledge man can attain to through education, reason and the senses, much as it expands, is *always* relative and confined within the boundaries of derivation. What the scrutiny of God through the senses may yield is nothing but object lessons of that which is unattainable. To speculate and venture further into knowledge than what concerns his life on earth is purposeless, vain, prideful and, ultimately, enhancing a kind of knowledge which does not result in godliness:

> Solicit not thy thoughts with matters hid,
> Leave them to God above, him serve and fear;
> . . . joy thou
> In what he gives thee, this Paradise
> And thy fair Eve; heav'n is for thee too high
> To know what passes there; be lowly wise:
> Think only of what concerns thee and thy being; (8.167–68, 170–74)

While arguing for the angelic status as the limit to Adam and Eve's progress, Augustine had, in his own right, envisioned obedience and submission, rather than self-indulgent speculation, as the way to true wisdom:

> For he created man's nature to be midway, so to speak, between
> the angels and the beasts in such a way that, if he should remain
> in subjection to his creator as his true Lord and with dutiful obe-
> dience keep his commandment, he was to pass into the company
> of the angels . . .[19]

Adam likewise acknowledges the prime wisdom of Raphael's admonition and, in contrasting it to the speculative nature of human fancy, hints at the negative implication of "unchecked" mutability:

---

19. Augustine, *The City of God*, 12.22.

> . . . apt the mind or fancy is to rove
> Unchecked, and of her roving is no end;
> Till warned, or by experience taught, she learn,
> That not to know at large of things remote
> From use, obscure and subtle, but to know
> That which before us lies in daily life,
> Is the prime wisdom . . . (8.188–94)

For all the positive, albeit limited, course of perfectibility and dynamic creational perfection, it is here, in this same dynamic gap afforded by mutable knowledge, that evil can insinuate itself. For the General Baptist's *An Orthodox Creed*, Adam had been made "after the image of God, in knowledge, righteousness, and true holiness, having the law written on his heart, and power and liberty of will to fulfill it, yet mutable, or under the possibility of transgressing, being left to the liberty of their own will, which was subject to change."[20] In book 5, Eve is troubled by an "uncouth dream, of evil sprung" (5.98). Adam rightfully wonders, "Yet evil whence? In thee can harbor none, / Created pure." The poem points to both an internal receptacle and an external source of evil which in turn shed light on the potentially detrimental nature of perfectible knowledge: the former is found in man's

> . . . lesser faculties that serve
> Reason as chief; among these Fancy next
> Her office holds; of all external things,
> Which the five watchful senses represent,
> She forms imaginations, airy shapes,
> Which reason joining or disjoining, frames
> All what we affirm or what deny, and call
> Our knowledge or opinion; then retires
> Into her private cell when nature rests,
> Oft in her absence mimic Fancy wakes
> To imitate her; but misjoining shapes,
> Wild works produces oft, and most in dreams,
> Ill matching words and deeds long past or late.
> Some such resemblances methinks I find
> Of our last evening's talk, in this thy dream,
> But with addition strange . . . (5.101–16)

Fancy can be roughly defined as imagination. "She forms imaginations" and "airy shapes," which are yet assembled, made sense of and controlled by reason. It is when reason "retires / into her private cell,"

20. Lumpkin, ed., *The Baptist Confessions*, art. XI, 305.

in sleep, that "mimic Fancy wakes," unrestrained, "To imitate her." In so doing, it reveals its disruptive potential and its incapability to organize its projections according to clarity and truth. On the contrary, "misjoining shapes, / Wild work produces oft, and most in dreams, / Ill matching words and deeds."

An objective correlative for this state of things is found in the garden. Adam and Eve are called to tend Eden, lest it grow wild and out of the control of rational care. Like Adam and Eve, the garden is the result of a perfect creation. Like Adam and Eve, however, the garden is susceptible to change.[21] Prelapsarian reason will yield positive change, provided it is not misled or restrained by an external source.

Adam acknowledges in Eve's account of her dream elements of the conversation occurred the evening before, "But with addition strange." If it is possible, "most in dreams," for fancy to scramble thoughts, words and images, Adam identifies elements in Eve's dream that do not pertain to their past experience. Eve herself tells Adam that she has "dreamed, / If dreamed, not as I oft am wont, of thee" (5.31–32). These additions can be nothing but external suggestions. Her fancy takes her, for instance, "on a sudden to the tree / Of interdicted knowledge" beside which stands "One shaped and winged like one of those from Heav'n / By us oft seen" (5.51–52, 55–56), who addresses the forbidden tree and in a series of three rhetorical questions rationalizes the desirability and indeed the rightfulness of eating of the fruit of the tree, "Forbidden here, it seems, as only fit / For gods, yet able to make gods of men" (5.69–70). The source of the evil oneiric projections is indeed external. It is Satan. As the final part of the Argument to book 4 indicates, "two strong angels . . . find him [Satan] at the ear of Eve, tempting her in a dream."[22]

Although, as Adam has it, no evil can harbor in Eve, the fiend identifies ground for mutability in her. Impotent though he is against right reason, he proves eager to wait for her guard to be low and reason retired "into her private cell." Only then will he be able to stir helpless fancy, thus guiding, as it were, Eve through the rationalizing motions that will be hers at the hour of trial, the hour, that is, when his plucking and tasting will turn into her plucking and eating. By exploiting unguarded fancy, Satan can thus address mutable knowledge and introduce notions of relativism where the prohibition admits none. Although Adam is able,

21. See Diekhoff, "Eve's Dream and the Paradox of Fallible Perfection."
22. Petty, "The Voice at Eve's Ear in *Paradise Lost*."

through reason, to explain the dream away and persuade Eve to let go of it, the mind has stored the resulting, if bewildering, information. The latter has become knowledge upon which Satan will be able to build. If knowledge is the ground of perfectibility, and if, as such, it informs reason, which in turn processes that knowledge and informs the will, an external source of negative information has the disruptive potential to misguide reason and obscure the will.

God knows this, so from the outset he works to supply Adam and Eve with sufficient information as to rightly inform reason, yet not so much as to forfeit the ultimate test.[23] In order for the first objective to be achieved and render man inexcusable, the Argument to book 5 reads that God "sends Raphael to admonish him of his obedience, of his free estate, of his enemy near at hand; who he is, and why his enemy, and whatever else may avail Adam to *know* [my italics]." While it is true that distorted information can only come from an external source, such external source does exist. Created in utter rectitude though Adam and Eve are, Satan constitutes a real threat to their filial freedom. Book 6 thus expands on the nature of the threat by portraying the war in heaven and providing historical perspective to Satan's insidiousness. Even so, as noted, God knows not to provide so much information as to prevent the test from taking place. In fact, God himself has carefully "prepared," in Corns' words, "the test which they are to undergo. He has permitted Satan to leave hell (1.212), he has watched his progress without intervening to hinder it (3.69–79), and he has in effect restrained the angelic guards which he had placed in Eden so they neither arrest nor assault Satan when they find him (4.1010–15)."[24]

The Separation Scene

The poet has long worked to set the stage for the ultimate test. In book 9 he brings the work to completion. It is morning and Satan has of late entered the serpent as Adam and Eve set out to their daily labor. Eve, like Adam, is the recipient of that divine instruction which is sufficient

23. Bear in mind, to this effect, that full freedom is only afforded where choice is not merely spontaneous, but the result of exposure to alternatives; secondly, true obedience to the person of God can only be shown where negative alternatives are provided; thirdly, the constancy to persevere is only produced by the overcoming of tests and trials.

24. Corns, *Regaining Paradise Lost*, 73.

to uphold reason in the hour of trial. Unlike Adam, though, Eve has received heavenly knowledge to a large extent indirectly. If Adam has been instructed by Raphael, Eve has only apprehended significant divine truth from Adam. Not only so, but in making both Adam and Eve free, creation has endowed both with equal authority, yet diverse purposes. They prove

> . . . in true filial freedom placed;
> Whence true authority in men; though both
> Not equal, as their sex not equal seemed;
> For contemplation he and valor formed,
> For softness she and sweet attractive grace,
> He for God only, she for God in him (4.294–9)

Inequality between Adam and Eve here does not pertain to natural essence, but to purpose (note four "for" in lines 97–99). Whereas Milton's differentiation, rooted as it is in the writings of Paul, is evident in the poem, Milton, with Paul, ascribes to Eve such independent dignity and rational virtue before God and man as only finds the literary equal in *Comus'* Lady.[25] An anaphor in lines 97–98 ("For"—"For") introduces us to Adam and Eve's individual yet parallel purposes, whereas the chiasmus of line 299 intertwines them in God.

In the definition of Eve's purpose, the indication is found of a diversity which can enhance the efficacy of the final test. Delicacy, beauty and grace are Eve's natural finality, as opposed to Adam's "contemplation" and "valor." Not only so, but Eve's purpose to glorify God is inextricably bound to her unity with Adam, "she for God in him." All these dispositions are in turn poetically matched by the physical description of the respective hair:

> . . . hyacinthine locks
> Round from his parted forelock manly hung
> Clust'ring, but not beneath his shoulders broad:
> She as a veil down to the slender waist
> Her unadornèd golden tresses wore
> Disheveled, but in wanton ringlets waved
> As the vine curls her tendrils, which implied
> Subjection . . . (4.301–8)[26]

25. Along these lines, McColley's *Milton's Eve* ransoms Eve's freedom and mutuality with Adam from the tradition of misogyny. Juhnke argues for residual misogyny in Milton in "Remnants of Misogyny in *Paradise Lost*." For Eve as embodying the qualities of poetry, see McColley, "Subsequent or Precedent?"

26. 1 Cor 11:1–16 is the primary backdrop for this passage. "Doth not even nature

Two (301–3) and four (304–8) run-on lines inform the respective representations of Adam and Eve's hair and nature, the former proving rich
yet limited and controlled, a symbol of reason and forceful stability,
the latter entailing profluent and natural beauty as well as unrestrained
spontaneity. The natural and uncontrolled fall yet comes to a sudden stop
upon the implication of gently required and freely yielded "Subjection."[27]
While Eve's hair, more closely than Adam's, matches the degenerating
potential of Eden's vegetation and, not tended, its inclination to irratio-
nal and conspicuous overgrowth, Eve's ringlets testify to her free choice
to repose herself under Adam's rational authority, thus controlling her
own "tending to wild." While the image of the vine tendrils curling
around an elm, a topos of marital union in classical literature,[28] speaks of
Eve's willing adherence to Adam's guidance, the image of an ivy clinging
to a tree overshadows the potential disruption of conjugal unity through
independent and self-seeking assertion.[29] Sammons maintains that "before the Fall, the vine/elm and ivy/tree images coalesce to suggest both
the special nature of prelapsarian marriage and the possibility of Adam
and Eve's sinning."[30] Brown correctly identifies the parallel between
these images and the illustration of the vine and the branches in John
15, while envisioning the anticipation of "the disastrous effects of the
branch becoming independent of the vine through his descriptions of
other trees in the garden, the ones Adam and Eve attend to."[31] Just as the
branches need pruning to bear fruit, so do Adam and Eve; each in its
own order, though, for "the head of every man is Christ: and the head
of the woman *is* the man."[32] The effect of Eve forfeiting Adam's pruning,
as Adam Christ's, would bring barrenness and alienation from the vine.
Not only so, but independence and separation would prove detrimental
for "neither is the man without the woman, neither the woman without

---

itself teach you, that, if a man have long hair, it is a shame unto him? But if a woman have
long hair, it is a glory to her: for *her* hair is given her for a covering" (1 Cor 11:14–15).

27. See Kerrigan, Rumrich and Fallon, eds., *Paradise Lost*, xxxvi–xxxvii.

28. See Sammons, "'As the Vine Curls Her Tendrils,'" 117.

29. For Sammons a symbol of "eroticism, usually extramarital" (ibid.)

30. Ibid.

31. See Brown, "*Paradise Lost* and John 15," 127. Here Brown regards marriage as
anti-typical of the relationship between Christ and the church. Cf. Eph 5:22–33.

32. 1 Cor 11:3.

the man in the Lord."[33] Eve's ensuing thought paves the way for the unfolding of the worst scenario:

> And Eve first to her husband thus began.
> Adam, well may we labor still to dress
> This garden, still to tend plant, herb and flow'r,
> Our pleasant task enjoined, but till more hands
> Aid us, the work under our labor grows,
> Luxurious by restraint; what we by day
> Lop overgrown, or prune, or prop, or bind,
> One night or two with wanton growth derides
> Tending to wild. (9.205–13)

Milton thus lifts the curtain over the separation scene, whose consummation ineluctably stems from Eve's seeking autonomy:

> . . . Thou therefore now advise
> Or hear what to my mind first thoughts present;
> Let us divide our labors, thou where choice
> Leads thee, or where most needs, whether to wind
> The woodbine round this arbor, or direct
> The clasping ivy where to climb, while I
> In yonder spring of roses intermixed
> With myrtle, find what to redress till noon:
> For while so near each other thus all day
> Our task we choose, what wonder if so near
> Looks intervene and smiles, or object new
> Casual discourse draw on, which intermits
> Our day's work brought to little, though begun
> Early, and th'hour of supper comes unearned. (9.214–25)

Eve's symmetrical picture of their separate work as involving Adam with woodbine, tree and clasping ivy and Eve with roses and myrtle does nothing but enhance the anticipation of a parting far graver than a merely geographical one.

Efficiency is behind Eve's suggestion to part ways with Adam: the work would get done better and faster if they attended to separate tasks without the distraction of each other's "fit society."[34] "Looks," "smiles" and "Casual discourse" would bring their work "to little" and "th'hour of supper" would come "unearned." Eve's outlook is a legalistic one. The

33. 1 Cor 11:11.

34. For a reading of Eve and Adam's solitude in the separation scene and Eve's temptation, see Long, "Contextualizing Eve's and Milton's Solitudes."

idea of the growth of vegetation overnight deriding their daily efforts, as well as the thought of having to earn their wages by discarding all ease and pleasant company does not speak of filial freedom, but of freedom achieved through strict compliance with an external law. A subtle dramatic irony surfaces as Adam hastens to "prop, or prune, or bind" Eve's misapprehension:

> Sole Eve, associate sole, to me beyond
> Compare above all living creatures dear,
> Well hast thou motioned, well thy thoughts employed
> How we might best fulfill the work which here
> God hath assigned us, nor of me shalt pass
> Unpraised: for nothing lovelier can be found
> In woman than to study household good,
> And good works in her husband to promote.
> Yet not so strictly hath our Lord imposed
> Labor, as to debar us when we need
> Refreshment, whether food, or talk between,
> Food of the mind, or this sweet intercourse
> Of looks and smiles, for smiles from reason flow,
> To brute denied, and are of love the food,
> Love not the lowest end of human life.
> For not to irksome toil, but to delight
> He made us, and delight to reason joined.
> These paths and bowers doubt not but our joint hands
> Will keep from wilderness with ease . . . (9.227–45)

For Adam and Eve to attend to the good works of dressing and keeping the garden was God's will for them (Gen 2:15). Hence Adam may praise Eve's solicitude as most becoming. Even more so, Adam may rightfully stress the pervasive biblical theme of woman's virtue. Like the virtuous woman of Proverbs 31, Eve does well "to study household good." However, Adam's words largely function as a *captatio benevolentiae* preluding diverging instruction. To be sure, all Adam's indications and warnings henceforth have a proleptic function aiming to make Eve utterly inexcusable and her fall all the more tragic. In commenting on Genesis 2:15, Calvin had stressed the active position God had envisioned for man in the garden, while defining the nature of prelapsarian labor:

> Moses now adds, that the earth was given to man, with this condition, that he should occupy himself in its cultivation. Whence it follows, that men were created to employ themselves in some

work, and not to lie down in inactivity or idleness. This labour,
truly, was pleasant, and full of delight, entirely exempt from all
trouble or weariness . . .[35]

Accordingly, Adam points out the praiseworthy zeal that informs Eve's
laborious stance, only to direct it under the gracious spirit of creational
purpose. "not so strictly," as Eve depicts it, "hath our Lord imposed /
Labor." On the contrary, "not to irksome toil, but to delight / He made
us." Labor is therefore rightfully accompanied by refreshments, whether
they be food or conversation, or "sweet intercourse / Of looks and smiles."
Conversation, looks and smiles are assimilated to food, as they are respectively "Food of the mind," and "of love the food." Just as the body
needs food for its physical sustenance, so does man's inner being need
the ethereal food of words, looks and smiles. Not only so, but Milton
ties the latter to reason. Particularly, "smiles from reason flow." All such
refreshments are, and ought to be, as it were, the expression of reason, as
opposed to an uncontrolled display of lesser faculties. In denying solace,
Eve is denying reason, Adam seems to be saying. Not only is all such
delight not incompatible with work, but it is its complement. In fact, it
is the milieu within which work has to unfold. It follows delight defines
the spirit of the imposition. The poet appears to counter the generally re-
pressive puritanical spirit here by elevating the human enjoyment of life
to the status of that which glorifies God. To this same effect, the highest
creational expression of delight is undoubtedly prelapsarian sexual intercourse.[36] Even such an ultimately sensual experience does not entail
the momentary eclipse of reason, but is delight to reason joined.

In the final analysis, Eve's very presupposition is wrong. The strict
observance envisioned by Eve is not necessary to keep the garden from
growing wild. As it is true with the free service of God in heaven, love
has devised a way for Adam and Eve's joint labor to keep Eden "from
wilderness with ease." For all their mutability, Adam and Eve, too, can
keep from going wild, yet not apart from the ease of filial freedom allow-

35. Calvin, *Commentaries: Genesis*, 1.2.125.

36. Both Turner (*One Flesh*) and Lindenbaum ("Lovemaking in Milton's Paradise")
do much to stress the reality of prelapsarian sexual solace as a divinely bestowed gift.
Luxon ("Milton's Wedded Love"), on the other hand, denies the latter as he tries to
align Milton with a derogatory medieval view of sexuality. Instead of establishing or
disproving the fact of prelapsarian sexuality, in "'Nor turnd I weene': *Paradise Lost* and
Prelapsarian Sexuality," Lehnhof builds on it, examining how prelapsarian intimacy
sheds light on other aspects of Milton's work.

ing for the solace of unity. To this very unity, other than to joint effort, do "joint hands" point, a sign before the fall of communion of intent and spirit. With joint hands had they paraded before Satan in book 4 (321–22). For all the burden of free and fortifying unity, however, Adam now acknowledges the value of solitude in the face of "much converse," if for just a short time. "short absence" or "short retirement" will urge "sweet return" (9.247–50).

The clearing is yet perturbed by more looming clouds. Adam fears the threat posed by God's adversary. The way in which the threat is bound to unfold is defined by a number of key-terms: "malicious," "sly" and "circumvent" all point to the length to which the foe is resolved to go. Violence or open evil will not do. Deceit is that which alone may render the test effective, yet all the more so were Adam and Eve found asunder. Adam perceives the menace as "nigh at hand," he senses greedy looks, hopeful as Satan is to find them severed, his "best advantage." If deceiving reason is the only way for Satan to affect human choice, Satan's advantage is gained by confronting a single reason unaided. He would be no match for two reasons coming to each other's rescue. Not only so, but by her creational purpose, Eve is better off not leaving "the faithful side" that gave her being. All derogatory adjectives and terms describing Satan's envisioned assault are aptly contrasted to ones defining Adam's role with respect to the one who alone is his true companion and kindred soul, his "associate sole;" "faithful," "shades," "protects," "guards" and "endures" match the safest and seemliest countenance as that of the wife who "by her husband stays" when danger or dishonor approach (9.251–60, 265–69).

In reply to this, Eve testifies to possessing that same knowledge which Adam himself has obtained (9.273–89). She has received it from Adam himself and she has gleaned part of it from an overheard conversation between Michael and Adam. Hence she knows about their foe, but reads Adam's fear of circumvention as doubting her own "firmness." Her misunderstanding is a direct witness to reason's capability to read inputs in ways that are not fixed or codified. By this, also, the poet begins to portray a movement toward self, which, if not yet sinful, closely matches Lucifer's own. Such movement in Eve is reminiscent of her identitarian epiphany, as she contemplates her image reflected in the liquid plain:

> As I bent down to look, just opposite,
> A shape within the wat'ry gleam appeared

> Bending to look on me, I started back,
> It started back, but pleased I soon returned,
> Pleased it returned as soon . . . (4.460–64)

The inversion of the word order "pleased I soon returned, / Pleased it returned as soon" matches the movement of Eve and her reflection. For the first time here Eve becomes acquainted with her self. While no shadow of sin is cast by the scene, Eve's pleased movement toward self retains a proleptic significance in relation to the mounting sense of self in book 9.[37] A self-centered rationalization of Adam's words now appears in her logic: since violence or pain cannot affect them, it must be Satan's "fraud" Adam fears. The implication is one of fear for her faith and love to be "by his fraud . . . shaken or seduced." Adam is thus compelled to draw a distinction between her character and the attempt itself. It is the latter he wants to avert, while not questioning the virtue of the former. Though proving vain and ineffectual, an assault would cast shadows of dishonor on the one "supposed / Not incorruptible" (9.297–98), bring resentment and expose her to "malice" and "false guile" (9.306). The progress of Adam's argument as to the reality of the threat posed by the adversary is verified by the fall of the angels in heaven and leads us straight back to the nature of liberty:

> . . . Eve, who thought
> Less attributed to her faith sincere,
> Thus her reply with accent sweet renewed.
> "If this be our condition, thus to dwell
> In narrow circuit straitened by a foe,
> Subtle or violent, we not endued
> Single with like defense, wherever met,
> How are we happy, still in fear of harm?
> But harm precedes not sin: only our Foe
> Tempting affronts us with his foul esteem
> Of our integrity: his foul esteem
> Sticks no dishonor on our front, but turns
> Foul on himself; then wherefore shunned or feared
> By us? Who rather double honor gain
> From his surmise proved false, find peace within,
> Favor from Heav'n, our witness from th' event.
> And what is faith, love, virtue unassayed
> Alone, without exterior help sustained?

37. Cf. Earl, "Eve's Narcissism."

> Let us not then suspect our happy state
> Left so imperfect by the Maker wise,
> As not secure to single or combined.
> Frail is our happiness, if this be so,
> And Eden were no Eden thus exposed. (9.319–41)

To grant Adam's suggestions is to Eve to question the Maker's own integrity. In regarding his words as projecting fear, she is subtly implying Adam's mystification of reality. Freedom proves under attack. Is that liberty which is confined within boundaries of fear liberty at all? Reacting to this possibility, Eve argues that they need fear no evil for, if tempted, their integrity would prevail and, in prevailing, it would cause for Satan's malice to backfire. The dishonor of being deemed liable to temptation would prove to find no province in them, as they reject the temptation. On the contrary, while returning to its source, the dishonor of temptation would testify to the double honor of them who not only obey God, but do so in the midst of the trial. The test thus proves necessary, for it paves the way for the truthful display of faith, love and virtue. In fact, "what is faith, love, virtue unassayed?"

We know Eve's argument to be Milton's own, for in its very words the distinct echo is heard of *Areopagitica* and God in book 3. Another echo yet reverberates. It is that of *Comus*. Adam and Eve's entire discussion closely redoubles the tit for tat of the two brothers in the Masque, with Adam matching the "Second Brother" and Eve the "Elder." The younger brother fears for his sister facing the ominous night in solitude. The elder brother yet reassures him that

> He that hath light within his own clear breast
> May sit i' the centre, and enjoy bright day;
> But he that hides a dark soul and foul thought . . .
> Himself is his own dungeon (381–84)[38]

We have noted the latter (line 384) to be true of Satan and the poet, yet the former (line 382) is true of the person who has light within. Even so, the younger brother's concern for his sister is scarcely mitigated as he, with Adam, adumbrates the threat as coming from some sinister presence looming large:

> Of night or loneliness it recks me not;
> I fear the dread events that dog them both,

38. Campbell, ed., *Complete English Poems*, 57–91.

> Lest some ill-greeting touch attempt the person
> Of our unownèd sister. (404–7)

The Elder's reply recalls Eve's peroration of the superiority of their integrity and freedom:

> Virtue may be assailed, but never hurt,
> Surprised by unjust force, but not enthralled;
> Yea, even that which mischief meant most harm
> Shall in the happy trial prove most glory. (589–92)

Lady will prove both the elder brother and Eve's argument right as the external threat materializes and Comus makes his attempt on her virtue:

> Fool, do not boast;
> Thou canst not touch the freedom of my mind
> With all thy charms, although this corporeal rind
> Thou hast immanacled . . . (663–5)[39]

The parallel between Eve and Lady yields a proleptic contrast, as Eve falls short of that measure of integrity which she shares with Lady. Lady would in fact prove the prototype of a new Eve by reversing the genitor's first disobedience through her Christ-like integrity before temptation. The contrast works here to the effect of magnifying the tragic nature of Eve's future demise, while also attaching dramatic weight to the words of Adam.

For all its surpassing prerogative to reject outward sources of enthrallment, inward freedom does not exclude Adam's argument. In fact, unity and mutual help, let alone the husband's prerogative to shield his wife, corroborate Eve's conclusions. Milton is far from picturing woman as a helpless and utterly dependent creature and nothing short of according Eve inward rational integrity and liberty apart from Adam. The complementariness of unity and reason should yet be sought as the result of Eve's love-informed free choice. Confirmation now comes in the words of Adam:

> Oh woman, best are all things as the will
> Of God ordained them, his creating hand
> Nothing imperfect or deficient left
> Of all that he created, much less man,
> Or aught that might his happy state secure,

---

39. For Moore ("The Two Faces of Eve"), *Comus'* Lady yields the backdrop for the portrait of Eve's virtue.

> Secure from outward force; within himself
> The danger lies, yet lies within his power:
> Against his will he can receive no harm.
> But God left free the will, for what obeys
> Reason, is free, and reason he made right,
> But bid her well beware, and still erect,
> Least by some fair appearing good surprised
> She dictate false, and misinform the will
> To do what God expressly hath forbid. (9.343–56)

After stressing the perfection of God's plan and creation, Adam breaks down Eve's contention as well as his own. All external threats must remain external, inasmuch as they cannot affect man's inner microcosm of liberty against his will. The ultimate danger is not to be traced to the external assault per se, but to a defection of the will allowing for the efficacy of the assault. To be sure, rejection of all external solicitation lies in man's power, for the will is free insofar as it obeys right reason. And if the decree which ordained man's freedom allows for the will to disregard the dictates of reason, hence absolute freedom in man, creational rectitude is to inform his ultimate choice. No room seems to be left for fear but for the mutability of knowledge. The question indeed rises again, what if evil were to take on the appearance of good and misguide reason? The ensuing misinformation would pass on to the will, thus inducing it to follow the false dictates of reason. While in a perfect environment all this would pertain to the mere realm of speculation, the looming presence of the "angel of light"[40] makes it a genuine possibility:

> Firm we subsist, yet possible to swerve,
> Since reason not impossibly may meet
> Some specious object by the foe suborned,
> And fall into deception unaware,
> Not keeping strictest watch, as she [reason] was warned.
> Seek not temptation then, which to avoid
> Were better, and most likely if from me
> Thou sever not: trial will come unsought.
> Wouldst thou approve thy constancy, approve
> First thy obedience; th' other who can know,
> Not seeing thee attempted, who attest?
> But if thou think, trial unsought may find
> Us both securer than thus warned thou seem'st,
> Go; for thy stay, not free, absents thee more . . . (9.359–72)

40. 2 Cor 11:14.

Adam here foreshadows the deception of reason. One last time he urges Eve to avoid temptation and stay with him, while subordinating the completeness of constancy to obedience. Once again, Adam is not excluding Eve's argument. Virtue must be refined as through fire and temptation alone may afford what virtue is called to discard. While they need not seek temptation, but rather avoid it, trial "will come unsought." Adam must allow Eve to choose freely whether to go or to stay. Freedom and unity go hand in hand, to the extent that there cannot be unity without freedom: freedom allows for true unity; external restraint, though uniting, severs. Eve chooses to part ways with Adam, she chooses to go. The conjunction of "Go" and "stay" in the passage ideally raises the curtain over that poetical process of mutual estrangement which will prove inverted at the end of the poem. That principle whereby for her to stay is to go will in due course be inversely verified by the inward transformation whereby for her to go is to stay.

The Fall

> As soon as we begin asking why God has commanded this or that, the devil has already won, as is plain from the case of Eve in Paradise! She had the command not to eat from a certain forbidden tree. When she lost sight of that command, and lent an ear to the devil's explanation of God's motives, she was already guilty of that terrible disobedience from which we all suffer today.[41]

These words of Martin Luther largely summarize Milton's account of the fall. The command was indeed simple and not liable to interpretation, yet a misinformed rationalization of the motives behind it would be able to undermine its solidity.

Satan's deceptive strategy is devised as a direct attack to reason: while taking advantage of the solitude and unaided independence of Eve's reason, the adversary purposes to misinform and impair reason by carrying out a tri-fold agenda. This agenda entails inducing Eve to turn her eyes on herself, gross deceit, and the elevation of Eve's lower faculties through appeal to the senses.

As Satan contemplates his prey and first addresses her, the words "alone" (480), "sole" (533), "single" (536), and "one" (545–46) define his attempt. The snare is not physical, but mental. The arena is the intel-

41. Luther, "Luther's House Postils," 180.

lect. Not only does Eve's isolation yield a favorable predicament for the assault in that it prevents her reason from availing itself of Adam's virtue, but inasmuch as that vessel is thus exposed which Satan deems the weaker for his purpose:

> ... behold alone
> The woman, opportune to all attempts,
> Her husband, for I view far round, not nigh,
> Whose higher intellectual more I shun (9.480–83)

While Satan echoes Augustine in comparing Eve's lower intellect and greater credulity to Adam's higher faculties and virtue,[42] little can be done but note that Eve's creational status informed by love and subjection matches Lucifer's own. Satan knows this, so having approached solitary Eve, he seeks to dignify her beyond her creational status and thus turn her gaze on her ego:

> Who sees thee? (and what is one?) who shouldst be seen
> A goddess among gods, adored and served
> By angels numberless, thy daily train. (9.5468)

A similar portrait begins to pile up misinformation which Eve's reason knows not how to filter. This new image of Eve which Satan projects makes its way past reason into her heart (550). Most of all, however, she is led to wonder about the serpent's unexpected ability to talk. She sees in the serpent's "looks / Much reason" (558–59). Having forfeited the aid of Adam's reason, she now finds a complement to personal reason in the serpent. In addressing Eve's enquiry into its rational ability, Satan's deceit now fully unfolds:

> Empress of this fair world, resplendent Eve,
> Easy to me it is to tell thee all
> What thou command'st, and right thou shouldst be obeyed:
> I was at first as other beasts that graze
> ... and apprehended nothing high:
> Till on a day roving the field, I chanced
> A goodly tree far distant to behold
> Loaden with fruit of fairest color mixed,
> Ruddy and gold: I nearer drew to gaze;
> When from the boughs a savory odor blown,
> Grateful to appetite, more pleased my sense
> Than smell of sweetest fennel or the teats

42. Augustine, *De Civitate Dei*, 14.11.

Of ewe or goat dropping with milk at ev'n,
Unsucked of lamb or kid, that tend their play.
To satisfy the sharp desire I had
Of tasting those fair apples, I resolved
Not to defer; hunger and thirst at once,
Powerful persuaders, quickened at the scent
Of that alluring fruit, urged me so keen.
About the mossy trunk I wound me soon,
For high from ground the branches would require
Thy utmost reach or Adam's: round the Tree
All other beasts that saw, with like desire
Longing and envying stood, but could not reach.
Amid the Tree now got, where plenty hung
Tempting so nigh, to pluck and eat my fill
I spared not, for such pleasure till that hour
At feed or fountain never had I found.
Sated at length, ere long I might perceive
Strange alteration in me, to degree
Of reason in my inward powers, and speech
Wanted not long, though to this shape retained.
Thenceforth to speculations high or deep
I turned my thoughts, and with capacious mind
Considered all things visible in heav'n,
Or Earth, or middle, all things fair and good;
But all that fair and good in thy divine
Semblance, and in thy beauty's heav'nly ray
United I beheld; no fair to thine
Equivalent or second, which compelled
Me thus, though importune perhaps, to come
And gaze, and worship thee of right declared
Sov'reign of creatures, universal dame. (9.568–71, 574–612)

Satan opens and closes his speech with what is more than a *captatio benevolentiae*. His ultimate purpose is, as I initially suggest, to induce Eve to question God's motives. To do so, he prompts the woman to gaze upon herself and see herself as potentially equal to God. He does so by describing her as worthy of obedience and worship. On the other hand, he aims to persuade her of the positive effects of eating of that same tree from which God has forbidden them to eat. Hence he relates his ability to speak to the virtue infused by the fruit, while also claiming the empowerment of his speculative faculties.

Finally, Satan aptly intertwines overt misinformation with the progressive numbing of reason. Sight, taste, smell, hearing and feel are stimulated by an overwhelming cascade of colors, images, odors, sounds, sensual references and synaesthetic irrationality, "behold / Loaden with fruit," "of fairest colors mixed, Ruddy and gold," "gaze," "savory odor blown" (a synaesthesia), "appetite," "please," "sense," "smell of sweetest fennel or the teats /Of ewe or goat dropping with milk at ev'n, / Unsucked," "Satisfy the sharp desire I had / Of tasting those fair apples," "hunger," "thirst," "scent," "alluring fruit," "mossy trunk . . ."

Having thus appealed to the senses apart from reason, Satan involves Eve's imagination in the act of plucking and eating. He first relates the possibility to reach the branches of the tree to Adam and Eve's superior stature, then he leads Eve through the motions. He thus builds on the extant foundation of the dream, by envisioning the fallacious deed and his subsequent indulgence in it. Only once the oneiric picture is complete and confirmed and the sieve of reason eluded by the stirring of the senses does Satan turn to reason. He does so by pointing Eve to the phony evidence of his own positive evolution. For all the charming arts of the adversary, however, Eve's natural constitution is still sufficient to recall heaven's firm command:

> . . . of this Tree we may not taste nor touch;
> God so commanded, and left that command
> Sole daughter of his voice; the rest, we live
> Law to ourselves, our reason is our law. (9.651–54)

Eve specifically recalls how God's command contrasts the senses with reason. The former define the prohibition ("not taste nor touch"), the latter human authority and freedom ("Law to ourselves"). The command, that is to say, calls man to discard the unfiltered allurement of the senses to embrace right reason and be free. Satan's fraud aims to undermine all truth and right reason to usher in slavery. To this very end, when Eve calls to mind the nature of the punishment to ensue from a breach of the command, Satan urges her to discard reason, her law, to rely on the evidence supplied by the senses:

> . . . do not believe
> Those rigid threats of death; ye shall not die:
> How should ye? By the fruit? It gives you life
> To knowledge. By the threat'ner? *Look* on me,
> Me who have *touched* and *tasted*, yet both live (my italics,
> 9.684–88)

Eve is urged to trust in sight ("Look on me"). The evidence provided by
this sense is there to prove that the serpent's resort to the senses (touched
and tasted), as opposed to reason, yielded, contrary to what God had
said, the benefit of a higher degree of life. Satan's subsequent rationalization aims to relativize the bearing of the command while ironically
promising Eve that his destiny can be hers:

> Why then was this forbid? Why but to awe,
> Why but to keep ye low and ignorant,
> His worshipers; he knows that in the day
> Ye eat thereof, your eyes that seem so clear,
> Yet are but dim, shall perfectly be then
> Opened and cleared, and ye shall be as gods,
> Knowing both good and evil as they know.
> That ye shall be gods . . .
> So you shall die perhaps, by putting off
> Human, to put on gods, death to be wished (9.703–14)

The thought of the divine greatness and completeness of self "Into her
heart too easy entrance won" (734). Eve now sets right reason aside and
allows herself to be fully absorbed by her senses:

> Fixed on the fruit she *gazed*, which to *behold*
> Might tempt alone, and in her ears the *sound*
> Yet *rung* of his persuasive words, impregned
> With reason, to her seeming, and with truth (my italics, 9.735–38)

Utter irony informs this passage as Eve now perceives reason and truth
through the sense of hearing ("sound," "rung"). Reason being thus subordinated to the senses, a fatal symmetry with Satan's sensual depiction
of the tree and its fruit now defines Eve:

> An eager *appetite*, raised by the *smell*
> So *savory* of that fruit, which with *desire*,
> Inclinable now grown to *touch* or *taste*,
> Solicited her *longing eye* . . . (my italics, 9.740–43)

Her sense solicited, everything is ready for Eve's rationalizations to feed
on deceit and definitively forfeit right reason. As Luther has it, "As soon
as we begin asking why God has commanded this or that, the devil has
already won, as is plain from the case of Eve in Paradise!" For the first
time, Eve is portrayed as musing in an inward soliloquy ("thus to herself she mused," 744), for the battle for freedom is not fought on grassy

battlegrounds, nor in the Commons nor in courts of law, but it is lost or won within. The question largely pervading Eve's words is whether we are truly free without completeness, that is, without experiential knowledge of both good and evil. Are we not bound by our limitations? Eve has thus identified the answer:

> Here grows the cure of all, his fruit divine,
> Fair to the eye, inviting to the taste,
> Of virtue to make wise: what hinders then
> To reach, and feed at once both body and mind?
> So saying, her rash hand in evil hour
> Forth reaching to the fruit, she plucked, she ate (9.776–81)

After so many exhaustive and long arguments, the doom of the earth is consummated in but one line. Reason no longer serving Eve, a paratactic syntax matches the instinctive nature of Eve's act as her swift hand reproduces what dream and temptation have suggested. Paradise lost.[43]

The Slavery of Sin

Recalling Romans 8:22,[44] creation felt the blow "That all was lost." The same wound is shared by Eve, marking a now detrimental identification of outward and inward.[45] Eve is now a prey to her senses and, in fact, to her self:

> . . . Eve
> Intent now wholly on her taste, naught else
> Regarded, such delight till then, as seemed,
> In fruit she never tasted, whether true
> Or fancied so, through expectation high
> Of knowledge, nor was Godhead from her thought.
> Greedily she engorged without restraint,
> And knew not eating death: satiate at length,
> And heightened as with wine, jocund and boon,

---

43. In Sir Walter Raleigh's reading, the unfolding of *Paradise Lost* "radiates" either backward or forward from Eve's act of plucking and eating the forbidden fruit (Raleigh, *Milton*, 81–2). This narrative point of view was subsequently adopted by J. H. Hanford (*A Milton Handbook*, 213), E. M. W. Tillyard (*Milton*, 245–49) and A. J. A. Waldock (Paradise Lost *and Its Critics*, 25–64).

44. "For we know that the whole creation groaneth and travaileth in pain together until now."

45. See Hiltner, "Place, Body and Spirit Joined." Cf. also Hiltner, *Milton and Ecology*.

Thus to herself she pleasingly began.
O sov'reign, virtuous precious of all trees
In Paradise, of operation blessed
To sapience, hitherto obscured, infamed,
And thy fair fruit let hang, as to no end
Created; but henceforth my early care,
Not without song, each morning, and due praise
Shall tend thee . . . (9.785–801)

The first consequences of the fall in Eve can be summed up by the word "idolatry." As Lewis has it, Eve "now worships a vegetable."[46] In so doing, she does not only reveal her degeneration, but her subservience to that which feeds her self. Like a drug addict, she has developed an addiction to the virtuous food at once for body and mind. She is compelled to satiate her hunger and thirst by indulging in the fruit of the tree while also greedily expecting higher knowledge and divine nature to pervade her. Her idolatry is idolatry of self and her slavery is, like Satan's, slavery to self. The word "sapience" in turn bespeaks subtle irony, for the higher wisdom to which Eve aspires is but an increase in the scope of her senses (sapience deriving from the Latin *sapere* for "to taste"). The higher she expects to ascend, the lower she falls. Ultimately, "knowledge" (804) and "Experience" (807), which were to present Eve with greater freedom, have deprived her of freedom by binding her to the satisfaction and enhancement of self. The passage from songs of innocence to songs of experience could not be more abrupt. As Eve perceives a gap between her condition of experience and Adam's, she only projects utter loss:

. . . But to Adam in what sort
Shall I appear? Shall I to him make known
As yet my change, and give him to partake
Full happiness with me, or rather not
But keep the odds of knowledge in my power
Without copartner? So to add what wants
In female sex, the more to draw his love,
And render me more equal, and perhaps,
A thing not undesirable, sometime
Superior; for inferior who is free? (9.816–25)

The unity with Adam is lost which resulted from Eve's positive freedom. For the first time, Eve perceives creational differences between herself

46. Lewis, *A Preface to* Paradise Lost, 122.

and Adam in hierarchical terms, in terms, that is, of equality and subalternation, superiority and inferiority. In turn, ambitious pride prompts her to cherish the possibility not to have Adam partake in that which she considers a precious source of power, capable of filling the constitutional gap that separates her from contemplative Adam. The very concept of the rule of men is thus ushered in and freedom defined in terms of absence of outward limitation. Prelapsarian submission implied true freedom, as the former was freely yielded and gently received. If outward limitation is now regarded as a restraint to freedom, it is only because Eve senses independence and superiority as her true freedom.[47] Along the same lines, Satan had previously maintained:

> At first I thought that liberty and Heav'n
> To Heav'nly souls had been all one; but now
> I see that most through sloth had rather serve,
> Minist'ring spirits, trained up in feast and song;
> Such hast thou armed, the minstrelsy of Heav'n,
> Servility with freedom to contend (6.164–9)

The question underlying these lines has to do with the nature of true freedom: is true freedom serving in heaven or ruling in hell? Milton's answer is that true freedom is not about absence of external limitations to self, but about inward filial fellowship with God. If the question is rather whether prelapsarian Eve is complete and free apart from Adam, the answer is yes, as she is wrapped in filial freedom, and the answer is no, for her freedom is to serve love. Eve next envisions death and denies Adam completeness and freedom apart from herself:

> . . . Confirmed then I resolve;
> Adam shall share with me in bliss or woe:
> So dear I love him . . . (9.830–32)

The irony behind these words cannot be overstated, for the love that informs Eve's resolution is nothing but love of self, in fact, the only kind of love that inward enthrallment can produce.

The next effect of the fall on Eve is illustrated by her report of what has of late occurred. Her discernment is completely obscured. Reason

---

47. In "'Render Me More Equal,'" Interdonato argues to the contrary that the fall has not brought about a radical change in Eve. Eve's desire for equality and superiority rather mounts "from a seemingly genuine sense of incompleteness and inferiority" (95). The idea that "Full happiness" (line 819) may rest "in my power" (line 820), however, seems to strongly argue for selfish assertion.

can no longer apprehend truth. Falsity, fraud and deceit suffocate objectivity and project a counterfeit reality. For one, Eve now openly questions God, "This tree is not as we are told" (863). She thus proves to have fully embraced Satan's lies. To be sure, as Satan had promised, her eyes have been opened. Indeed, she has become in a way like God. But the way in which all this has come to pass is to the detriment of freedom and love, in fact, those very elements which allow man to see and partake in God. Adam's reaction to Eve's words is one of utter bewilderment, "horror chill," "the garland wreathed for Eve / Down dropped," "all the faded roses shed," "Speechless," "pale," "lost," "Defaced, deflow'red, and now to death devote," "transgress," "violate," "cursèd fraud," "enemy," "beguiled," "ruined," "die." These words and phrases show to what extent the fall has called for a modification of human lexis.

Adam's ensuing resolution is to die with Eve, for their "state cannot be severed, we are one" (958). Criticism has rightfully identified in Adam's choice of Eve over God the core of Adam's fall.[48] Danielson, Waldock and Lewis have variously argued for what Adam should or should not have done after Eve's fall. Danielson raises the fundamental question, "Given Eve's fall, does Adam face a dilemma: either to disobey God or else to break the bond of human love, whose goodnesss we perceive as fundamental? And if Adam has no choice but to reject the sinner with the sin, or else to accept the sin with the sinner, then will most of us applaud Adam's choosing the latter?"[49] Waldock argues that Adam's acceptance of the sin with the sinner is a display of "one of the highest . . . of all human values: selflessness in love."[50] Lewis, for his part, suggests that Adam should have "scolded or chastised Eve and then interceded with God on her behalf."[51] Danielson follows in Lewis' footsteps and, moving from a theodical premise, argues that though Adam and Eve

---

48. In *A Preface to* Paradise Lost, 126, Lewis argues for Adam's uxuriousness, whereas in *One Flesh*, 8, Turner underscores idolatry. Genuine love for Eve is identified as the motive behind Adam's fall in Waldock, Paradise Lost *and its Critics*, 51–52. In "Adam and His 'Other Self' in *Paradise Lost*," Champagne traces the ultimate reason for Adam's fall to a genuine sense of emptiness in Adam which closely parallels Eve's sense of incompleteness apart from Adam and which can only be filled by the woman.

49. Danielson, "Through the Telescope of Typology," 121.

50. Waldock, Paradise Lost *and Its Critics*, cited in Danielson, "Through the Telescope of Typology," 121.

51. Lewis, *A Preface to* Paradise Lost, 127, cited in Danielson, "Through the Telescope of Typology," 121.

"did *not* avoid falling . . . we are meant to feel that they could have, and should have."[52]

Far from saying that Adam's course of action was inevitable, and granted that the act of disjoining love for God from love for Eve as well as that of disrupting the unity of the couple do pose a problem, I wish to maintain that the true ground of contention is not about what Adam should or should not have done, but rather about what Adam could or could not do. In other words, I am willing to concede Tillyard's argument that through the sleep of reason Adam allows his passion for Eve to prevail over his will.[53] If Adam is not himself exempt from rationalizations that call the very nature of God and truth into question, not Satan's deception or misinformation have clouded all understanding, but "female charm" (997–99). In the final analysis, Adam's reasoning appears to amount to little more than a number of rational justifications for an act that he has already resolved in himself to carry out for the pursuit of Eve.

Again echoing Romans 8:22, the poem remarks the devastating effects of original sin on all creation as well as on Adam's rational ability after his fatal bite:

> Earth trembled from her entrails, as again
> In pangs, and Nature gave a second groan;
> Sky loured, and muttering Thunder, some sad drops
> Wept at completing of the mortal sin
> Original; while Adam took no thought,
> Eating his fill, nor Eve to iterate
> Her former trespass feared . . .
> As with new wine intoxicated both
> They swim in mirth, and fancy that they feel
> Divinity within them breeding wings
> Wherewith to scorn the earth . . . (9.1000–1001)

Once again, Milton is called to illustrate the passage from reason to senses, "Adam took *no thought* / *Eating* his fill." The image of drunkenness returns which Milton had exploited to describe Eve after her fall. Intoxicated, reason deserts them, while fancy, a lower faculty, takes over, suggesting that humanity is being put off and divinity on. In the full replacement of reason, the senses work instrumentally as channels for uncontrolled passions:

52. Danielson, "Through the Telescope of Typology," 121.
53. See Tillyard, *Milton*, 23.

. . . but that false fruit
Far other operation first displayed,
Carnal desire inflaming; he on Eve
Began to cast lascivious eyes, she him
As wantonly repaid; in lust they burn:
Till Adam thus gan Eve to dalliance move.
Eve, now I see thou art exact of taste,
And elegant, of sapience no small part,
Since to each meaning savor we apply,
And palate call judicious; I the praise
Yield thee, so well this day thou hast purveyed.
Much pleasure we have lost, while we abstained
From this delightful fruit, nor known till now
True relish, tasting . . .
. . . never did thy beauty since the day
I saw thee first and wedded thee, adorned
With all perfections, so inflame my sense (9.1011–24, 1029–31)

Images of fire are here juxtaposed to ones of taste. As the word "sapience" again well suggests, the meaning reason attaches to things has been reduced to sensual perception. And so has judgment. Loss of meaning and right understanding has thus paved the way for the rule of sensual pleasure, which is only enhanced by unruly affections. If prelapsarian sexual intercourse was the climactic expression of pure love and freedom, its postlapsarian counterpart is now the apical manifestation of their slavery to passions. Even more so, it is "of their mutual guilt the seal" (1043), for they are one—as both Adam and Eve desire to remain—yet one only in guilt:

Her hand he seized, and to a shady bank,
Thick overhead with verdant roof embow'red
He led her nothing loath; Flowers were the Couch,
Pansies, and Violets, and Asphodel,
And Hyacinth, earth's freshest softest lap . . .
There they their fill of love and love's disport
Took largely . . . (9.1037–43)

Adam's once gentle request now turns into seizing and the couple indulges in selfish intercourse ("their fill . . . / Took largely") much as they had previously engorged the fruit without restraint.[54] If the outward site

54. In "'That Fallacious Fruit,'" Savoie distinguishes between pre- and post-lapsarian sexual intercourse only to assimilate Adam and Eve's act of eating the fallacious fruit to lapsarian oral sex as the disengagement of sexual pleasure from "God's larger plan"

of their sinful solace closely resembles the prelapsarian, not so the inward. The sharp contrast between the bed of flowers upon which they lie and the ensuing description of their inward state points to the disjoining of outward and inward as the ultimate effect of the fall. If for Lewis the contrast between unfallen and fallen sexual intercourse "is not so sharp as it ought to have been,"[55] it is because he is looking in the wrong place. It is not in outward images that the contrast can be seen, but in the disruption of the continuity of inward and outward. To this effect, the fruit of the new rule of the passions is indeed apparent:

> The solace of their sin, till dewy sleep
> Oppressed them, wearied with their amorous play.
> Soon as the force of that fallacious fruit,
> That with exhilarating vapor bland
> About their spirits had played, and inmost powers
> Made err, was now exhaled, and grosser sleep
> Bred of unkindly fumes, with conscious dreams
> Encumbered, now had left them, up they rose
> As from unrest, and each the other viewing,
> Soon found their eyes how opened, and their minds
> How darkened; innocence, that as a veil
> Had shadowed them from knowing ill, was gone,
> Just confidence, and native righteousness
> And honor from about them, naked left
> To guilty Shame . . . (9.1044–58)

For the first time, Adam and Eve feel tired. For the first time, they feel weary and oppressed. Their minds are now the seat of darkness and their conscience cannot find rest, burdened as it is with shame. So quick had Adam been to praise Eve's choice upon experiencing the immediate effects of eating the fruit as now to turn against her and charge her with the loss of all "good," "honor," "innocence," "faith," and "purity." Man and woman bear on their faces the very marks "Of foul concupiscence" and "shame" (1072–9). Loss and foul gain are all the more destabilizing as they inform both Adam's alienation from Eve, as is evident from Adam's charges, and from God, "How shall I behold the face / Henceforth of God or angel, erst with joy / And rapture so oft beheld?" (1080–2). Their

---

through the continuum of "pregnancy, children, family, and a fully realized society" (161).

55. Lewis, *A Preface to* Paradise Lost, 66.

shame in part covered with fig leaves, Adam and Eve's unrest must remain, for

> ... not at rest or ease of mind,
> They sat them down to weep, nor only tears
> Rained at their eyes, but high winds worse within
> Began to rise, high passions, anger, hate,
> Mistrust, suspicion, discord, and shook sore
> Their inward state of mind, calm region once
> And full of peace, now tossed and turbulent:
> For understanding ruled not, and the will
> Heard not her lore, both in subjection now
> Of sensual appetite, who from beneath
> Usurping over sov'reign reason claimed
> Superior sway: from thus distempered breast (9.1120–31)

The theory of the passions is plainly laid out in these words. The list of tormenting affections, however, is not exhausted here, but it expands throughout book 9 only to be integrated in book 10. Here, confronted with the Son, Adam and Eve are found

> ... discount'nanced both, and discomposed;
> Love was not in their looks, either to God
> Or to each other, but apparent guilt,
> And shame, and perturbation, and despair,
> Anger, and obstinacy, and hate, and guile. (10.110–14)

The passions have taken over the control of man from reason and rightly informed will, thus unsettling the mind once free. The mind is the region where liberty resided with peace and rest under the right rule of reason, its king. The king has now been overthrown by sinful affections and man is sold out in slavery to sin. Just as inward peace and freedom mutually irradiated outwardly from the minds of Adam and Eve, thus producing harmony and perfect unity, so does disruption now involve the inward realm as well as Adam and Eve's mutual relationship and fellowship with God. A sequence of mutual charges witnesses the human characters' attempt at saving one's self at the expense of the other, which culminates in the discharging of all responsibility on the external source of temptation: Eve for Adam, and the serpent for Eve.

It is, however, given to book 10 to present us with the highest dramatic expression of that which Benet calls "the agony of alienation," in Adam's soliloquy.[56] As Benet persuasively argues, the latter closely parallels Satan's in book 4. Like Satan, Adam, too, is caught in the circular motion of inward speculative enthrallment. Like Satan, Adam questions God's justice and love (10.743–55). Like Satan, Adam is bound to acknowledge God's fairness in the dialectic of grace and punishment (10.755–68). It is the latter which he now seeks in the form of ultimate extinction. Doubt over the nature of death, however, assails him. He fears that death "be not one stroke" (10.809). He fears that which he knows not and which he cannot control. The idea of dying "a living death" (10.788) is a "thought / Horrid, if true!" His ensuing rationalization that "It was but breath / Of Life that sinned; what dies but what had life / And sin?" (10.789–91) cannot put an end to the spiral of doubt which from himself extends to the doom awaiting his descendants. The one solution envisioned, death, too, only amounts to Adam's attempt at saving himself. Whereas Satan ultimately chooses to challenge the limit, Adam cherishes the passive way. Not free, the human characters, like Satan, find themselves alone. A liberator is needed to overthrow sin, the new despot, and restore the inward boundaries to the guidance of right reason.

A Transmuted Lump of Futurity

Criticism has largely argued for books 11 and 12 of *Paradise Lost* as a poetical anti-climax. Whereas Lewis regards them as "an untransmuted lump of futurity,"[57] Rogers points to the loss of the humanistic and physical element which so strongly informs the rest of the poem as the reason why these books "strike most readers as a disappointment."[58] Explanations for this sudden turn in the poem have ranged anywhere from Milton's loss of poetic energy to his desire to destabilize and redefine Adam's apprehension of reality. I wish to argue that the answer lies in the shift itself. The passage to books 11–12 marks the turn from a largely horizontal dimension of humanity and the physical world to the soteriological dimension of liberty. Once again, the poetic expectation

56. Benet, "Adam's Evil Conscience and Satan's Surrogate Fall," 2.

57. Lewis, *A Preface to* Paradise Lost, 125.

58. Rogers, "Milton and the Mysterious Terms of History," 282. Here Rogers examines the relationship between voluntarism and the humanistic and naturalistic outlook in the unfolding of Milton's philosophy of history.

gives way to the spiritual, so that the limit of derivation in prelapsarian Adam and the sin-bound impairment of postlapsarian Adam are ultimately superseded in the liberty of the Spirit of grace.

As Regina Schwartz persuasively argues in *Remembering and Repeating: Biblical Creation in Paradise Lost*, a theology of re-creation underlies the poem. Accordingly, Michael's account of the progress of history in books 11 and 12 amounts to a lesson in hermeneutics aiming to present Adam with the big picture of history.[59] Adam need not be tossed from despair to elation by the progress of revelation, but the redemptive pattern of history should produce sobriety, that is, sorrow mitigated by hope. To this very effect, in Schwartz's words, "this balance of sorrow and hope, deeply considered by Milton theologically, informs the many yoked contraries in the final lines of the poem . . ."[60]

For all the merit of this view, in this final section I take the redemptive pattern to define both history and characters in terms of inward freedom. Far from merely undergoing an intellective process of self-sobering realization through progressive exposure to the big picture of redemptive history, Adam is to spiritually partake in the final reality. To this effect, re-creation does not only affect the course of history, but Adam and Eve as well. If death calls for Adam and Eve's re-creation, slavery calls for their liberation. The juxtaposition of creation and new creation in books 1, 3 and 7 marks a passage from natural to spiritual, from law to grace and from slavery to the actualization of adoption with respect to the poet and the poetical creation (see ch. 3). The disruption of Adam and Eve's creation calls for the superimposition of Adam and Eve's present dispensation to the dispensation of grace as well as for the ensuing present application of all that the terms of Christian liberty entail.

While generally inclined to read the history of salvation as a unity under the overarching umbrella of Christ's atoning work, Protestant divines variously distinguished between what preceded and what followed the full manifestation of the covenant of grace in terms of a shift from types or shadows to truth, from the bondage of law to the freedom of more apparent grace. Among those who further subdivided theological history were the likes of Girolamo Zanchi and William Ames, who de-

59. See Schwartz, "Milton on the Bible," 52.
60. Ibid., 54.

tected ulterior discontinuity within the first of the two major divisions.[61] Whereas *De Doctrina Christiana* appears to follow in the general strand of Reformed divinity, the theology of history informing *Paradise Lost* appears to argue more conspicuously for dispensational shifts in God's dealings with man. Even these, however, manifestly relate to the ultimate soteriological unfolding of grace.[62]

Two phases characterize Adam and Eve's participation in Christian liberty: book 10 envisions Adam and Eve's experience of grace under the Adamic administration, whereas books 11 and 12 depict Adam's journey through the dispensations and participation in the fullness of God's pro-

61. E.g., for Ames the "manner of administration of the covenant, with respect to the coming of Christ, was one before Moses and another from Moses to Christ," and again, "there was some difference of dispensation from Adam to Abraham from that of the time from Abraham to Moses" (*Marrow*, 203).

62. While the chapter of *De Doctrina* devoted to a discussion of the covenant of grace and its expression before the unveiling of its fullness simply refers to the time between Adam and Moses in terms of the variations in the law (*CPW* 6.515–41), Ames' *Marrow of Theology*, like *Paradise Lost*, deals with it extensively from the very point of view of redemptive history (202–10). In the poem, images of Enoch's rapture as a token of the *parousia* and a Trinitarian "triple-colored bow whereon to look / And call to mind His covenant" anticipate, in Gordon Teskey's words, "the better covenant of the new testament in Christ" (Milton, *Paradise Lost*, ed. Teskey 2005, endnote 874–78, 283). In light of this, Gordon Campbell is right when he identifies stock as in "man as from a second stock proceed" (12.7) as "literally Noah, and typologically Christ, in whom believers were said to be 'engrafted'" (Campbell, ed., *Complete English Poems*, endnote 7, 423). The world's refoundation by Noah and his children will bring about an age of prosperity, equanimity and peace, yet not free from the necessity of "sacrificing bullock, lamb or kid / With large wine off'ring and sacred feast" (20–21). While *De Doctrina* generically speaks of "sacrifices and . . . priests" as mere "*symbols* [my italics] of expiation and redemption both before and during the time of Moses" (*CPW* 6.517), Ames' *Marrow* specifies that "the way of justification was *set forth* [my italics] by expiatory sacrifices offered and accepted for sins" and "sanctification was . . . foreshadowed by *typical* [my italics] oblations and rites of sacrifice" (Ames, *Marrow*, 203), thus pointing to the benefits of Christ's ultimate sacrifice. Not only so, but while *De Doctrina* proves largely uninterested in pre-Mosaic times (after the reference above, *De Doctrina* immediately turns to Mosaic times: "Under the law the type of the Lord's Supper was the manna, and the water which flowed from the rock," *CPW* 6.554), for Ames "in many sacrifices there was something like a sacrament, for those who sacrificed commonly partook of a holy banquet at a holy place with joy before God in their sacrifices" (*Marrow*, 204). Little can be done but observe how Ames' "holy banquet" turns into "sacred feast" in *Paradise Lost* (21). For all the discontinuity, everything in the poem, from the very beginning of Michael's representation of history, looks forward to the Son, Adam's deliverer.

vision for his liberty. The *trait d'union* is provided by the obscure terms of the *protevangelium*, whose full bearing is for Michael to unravel.

Adam and Eve's fall entails the loss of innocence and of both inward and outward freedom with it. While at the earliest stage of progressive revelation they cannot identify the divine figure who visits them nor do they know the full significance of his words and actions, that same liberator around whom the restoration of all history revolves is indeed present with them and so must be the future terms of their restoration. Hence after the pronouncement of judgement and of the veiled promise of salvation to come by the seed of the woman, we read:

> So judged he Man, both Judge and Savior sent,
> And th'instant stroke of death denounced that day
> Removed far off; then pitying how they stood
> Before him naked to the air, that now
> Must suffer change, disdained not to begin
> Thenceforth the form of servant to assume
> As when he washed his servants' feet, so now
> As father of his family he clad
> Their nakedness with skins of beasts, or slain . . .
> And thought not much to clothe his enemies:
> Nor he their outward only with the skins
> Of beasts, but inward nakedness, much more
> Opprobrious, with his robe of righteousness,
> Arraying covered from his Father's sight. (10.209–17, 219–23)

The grace informing these lines has hardly been underscored. By drawing on the images of the servant washing his disciples' feet and the Creator pitying his children's condition of outward and, more importantly, inward nudity, Milton affords a picture of great moment of God's love for mankind. The one who is judge of man is also his Savior. His presence with him, therefore, means that the passive application of salvation need not await the fulfillment of the promise. Not so the display of grace, which the present economy conceals in typical forms. The Son's own ultimate sacrifice and his righteousness are respectively for the sacrifice of animals and their skins to signify. Even so, while skins, as types, can only cover outward nakedness, the Son's robe of righteousness, to which those same types point, is presently given to cover that nudity of shame, fear, oppression, cold, hate, anger, turbulence, perturbation, despair, guilt and weariness which only lies within.

After the lacerating sequence of mutual charges (end of book 9–beginning of book 10) and after Adam's long-entertained Hamlet-like thoughts of suicidal remedy (end of book 10) seeking the salvation of self, Milton points to loss of self as the only way to embracing the Son's righteousness. Eve, accordingly, seeks Adam in her frailty and loneliness and, first to fall, she is first to lay herself bare:[63]

> . . . Eve
> . . . with tears that ceased not flowing,
> And tresses all disordered, at his feet
> Fell humble, and embracing them, besought
> His peace (10.909–13)

Eve's hair has proven to turn to wild ("tresses all disordered") apart from her free subjection to Adam's tending. Having perceived the distance that separates her from Adam and which she has contributed to augment, Eve now gives her self up. In one of Milton's superior symmetries, she confesses the two-fold nature of her sin:

> . . . both have sinned, but thou
> Against God only, I against God and thee (10.930–31)

In these words Eve cherishes the restoration of that unity in diversity which defines God's creational order, "He for God only, she for God in him." Notwithstanding her renewed unresisting countenance, however, Adam is not in the least moved by her confession. His reaction is nothing short of commiseration. For their unity to be restored, first their minds and hearts need to undergo individual renewal. And for their hearts and minds to be renewed, they are to abase themselves and turn to the one who is both judge and savior. Unsurprisingly, thoughts of repentance solely ensue from a renewed focus on the uttering of the *protevangelium* and early experience of God's grace:

> . . . Remember with what mild
> And gracious temper he both heard and judged
> . . . his timely care
> Hath unbesought provided, and his hands
> Clothed us unworthy, pitying while he judged;
> How much more, if we pray him, will his ear
> Be open, and his heart to pity incline,

63. As regards Eve as peace-making agent in book 10, see Doerksen, "'Let There Be Peace.'"

. . .
> Undoubtedly he will relent and turn
> From his displeasure; in whose look serene,
> When angry most he seemed and most severe,
> What else but favor, grace, and mercy shone?
> So spake our father penitent, nor Eve
> Felt less remorse: they forthwith to the place
> Repairing where he judged them prostrate fell
> Before him reverent, and both confessed
> Humbly their faults, and pardon begged, with tears
> Watering the ground, and with their sighs the air
> Frequenting, sent from hearts contrite, in sign
> Of sorrow unfeigned, and humiliation meek.
> (10.1046–47, 1057–61, 1093–1104)

In line 1086, Adam asks, "What better can we do" than to repent with "hearts contrite, in sign / Of sorrow unfeigned, and humiliation meek?" The question requires no answer. In their present dispensation there is nothing better to do than go to God in confession, repentance and humility, having yet experienced his favor and grace (as he clothed them) and retaining hope that comes from the promise contained in the *protevangelium*. Veiled and initiatory though Adam and Eve's knowledge of God's nature and providence is, repentance, faith, grace and hope provide the coordinates for a new relationship with God. No sooner are these virtues displayed in the human characters, however, than the poem hastens to trace their origin to the outpouring of grace prevenient,[64] or

---

64. Not once does the expression appear in *De Doctrina*, albeit the underlying concept is thought to be akin to that which *De Doctrina* labels "sufficient grace" (*satis gratia*, CPW 6.192–94). Benjamin Myers assimilates the two by pointing out how in the treatise regenerating grace "restores a person's natural faculties of right judgement and free will" (CPW 6.461) and adding, "This is precisely the meaning of prevenient grace in *Paradise Lost*" (Myers, *Milton's Theology of Freedom*, 151–52). For Myers, prevenient grace provides the key to true liberty, seen as freedom to choose among alternatives (for Myers' full treatment of prevenient grace, see *Milton's Theology of Freedom*, 145–55; "Prevenient Grace and Conversion in *Paradise Lost*," 20–36. For a parallel argument, also see Fallon, "Milton's Arminianism and the Authorship of *De Doctrina Christiana*," 103–27; and "*Paradise Lost* in Intellectual History," 330–34). Both Myers and Fallon, nevertheless, fail to ascribe to Milton's use of so highly distinctive a terminology (*gratia praeveniens*) its proper significance. While *De Doctrina* seems to steer clear of the specific phrase in order to stress the unity and universal extent of grace (although bestowed to all in different measure according to God's will, grace is, in the Latin treatise, sufficient for all to attain to salvation), *Paradise Lost* appears to distinguish between prevenient grace and grace efficacious (saving grace), the former being merely functional to

that quality of grace whereby the effects of the fall on the heart's ability
to turn to God are reversed:

> Thus they in lowliest plight repentant stood
> Praying, for from the mercy-seat above
> Prevenient grace descending had removed
> The stony from their hearts, and made new flesh
> Regenerate grow instead . . . (11.1–5)

From Augustine to Calvin, Arminius and Amyraut, the understanding that grace was to precede the salvific choice of fallen mankind was
largely shared. For Adam and Eve to be able to turn to God, first their
hearts of stone were to undergo transformation. The oracle of Ezekiel
was to find fulfillment by the regenerating work of grace[65] ushering in
the saving imputation of the Son's both passive and active righteousness:

> See Father, what fruits on Earth are sprung
> From thy implanted grace in man, these sighs
> And prayers, which in this golden censer, mixed
> With incense, I thy priest before thee bring,
>
> . . .
>
> . . . Now therefore bend thine ear
> To supplication, hear his sighs though mute;
> Unskillful with what words to pray, let me
> Interpret for him, me his advocate
> And propitiation, all his works on me
> Good or not good ingraft; my merit those
> Shall perfect, and for these my death shall pay.
> Accept me, and in me from these receive
> The smell of peace toward mankind, let him live
> Before thee reconciled, at least his days
> Numbered, though sad, till death, his doom . . .
>
> . . .
>
> To better life shall yield him, where with me
> All my redeemed may dwell in joy and bliss,
> Made one with me as I with thee am one.

---

the reception of saving grace as the sole source of true liberty. To this effect, the poem
is particular in distinguishing between God pre-emptively molding the heart of Adam
and Eve so they can seek his face and the Son pointing to his merit and to the price
his death shall pay to obtain reconciliation. The idea thus appears unwarranted that
"Milton made little distinction between them [grace actual and habitual]" (Boswell,
"Milton and Prevenient Grace," 83–94).

65. The turning of the human characters' hearts into hearts of flesh sharply contrasts
with the obduracy of Satan's heart. See Swiss, "Satan's Obduracy in *Paradise Lost.*"

To whom the Father, without cloud, serene.
All thy request for man, accepted Son,
Obtain, all thy request was my decree (11.22–25, 30–40, 42–47)

High-priest of a better covenant, the Son is here seen as interceding with the Father on Adam and Eve's behalf. As their advocate, he pleads their case by producing himself as propitiatory argument. The doctrine of substitution[66] underlies the words of the Son. To be ingrafted in the Son is to have one's works wrought in his righteousness, yielding peace with God and reconciliation. In a reversed perspective, the words that testify to John Bunyan's passage from fear and doubt to confidence shed light on the role of the Son as well as on the response of the Father:

> Sinner, thou thinkest that because of thy sins and infirmities I
> cannot save thy soul, but behold my Son is by me, and upon him
> I look, and not on thee, and will deal with thee according as I am
> pleased with him.[67]

The Father's response cannot be anything other than to treat the sinner in conformity with the way in which he is pleased with his Son. In fact, the Son requests nothing but that which the Father has fore-ordained.[68] This proves to be the seal on Adam and Eve's turn from the slavery of sin to God, for the very terms that would be revealed upon the full manifestation of the covenant of grace are those which have concealed them in God since before the foundation of the world and which inform their present conversion. This reality, none the less, seems to merely pertain to the realm of God's sovereign decrees as lack of knowledge prevents Adam and Eve from fully actualizing the freedom that is theirs in the Son. A dispensational gap separates them from clear vision and maturity.

This gap is now filled by Michael. Through visions in book 11 and narration in book 12, Michael unfolds the progress of history towards the manifestation of the *evangelium* and the culmination of the ages. The passage from visions to narration is marked by the end of the pre-Noahic creation and the ensuing re-creation. The limits of revelation are the limits of man, whether as conveyor or as recipient of that same

66. Cf. e.g., 2 Cor 5:21: "For he hath made him sin for us, who knew no sin; that we might be made the righteousness of God in him."

67. Bunyan, *Grace Abounding*, §§ 257–58, 65.

68. For Ames "the agreement between God and Christ was a kind of advance application of our redemption and deliverance" (Ames, *Marrow*, 149).

revelation. The impotence of the three times blind poet to see and tell of that which is invisible to mortal sight is the impotence of Adam to see it and receive it. As the poet is to come to terms with the failure of his sense-bound faculties for generative light to fill him, so are the preroga- tives of Adam's sight to be discarded if he is to receive the full unfolding of God's nature and will through the light of the Word.

The passage from what is perceived through the senses in visions to the knowledge of God involving conscience and intellect through narra- tive revelation significantly parallels "the bipartite structure of Milton's ideal [program of] education."[69] As the celestial light both *is* and *conveys* God, so is the identification of the Logos with the words of Scripture a spiritual necessity if Adam is to know God without the cloud of deriva- tion, law and sinful impairment. God's Word, presently uttered through his messenger and subsequently crystallized in Scripture—it is, to this effect, no wonder that Michael's and Adam's pronouncements largely prove to paraphrase Scripture—establishes "a relationship between man and God in a way which authorizes the words of the Word not merely to signify but to effect."[70] The words of the Word in Michael's narration are indeed called to effect, as well as signify, the ultimate encounter with God for Adam and for the reader with him. In relating revelation to Adam, therefore, Michael devises a whole narrative strategy aiming to pave the way for the *kerygmatic* encounter. In Patrides' words:

> Michael's failure to be precise is calculated; being an excellent story-teller, he increases suspense by withholding the informa- tion Adam is seeking until the appropriate moment. So the gradual identification of the "seed" continues.[71]

For all the merit of Patrides' observation, it should be noted that Michael's strategy not only seems to work to the effect of withholding information from Adam until the appropriate time, but it also appears to make Adam the center around which the whole process revolves. Michael's narration indeed inspires and feeds off Adam's reactions, inquiries and misappre- hensions. Yet to what end? Once again, far from being a mere lesson

---

69. See Coiro, "'To repair the ruins of our first parents,'" 133. Coiro indeed argues that "in Books XI and XII of *Paradise Lost* Michael leads Adam through an education that exactly parallels, down to the smallest detail, the 'methodical course' that Milton had delineated with such precision in his educational tractate."

70. So Luther for Reisner, *Milton and the Ineffable*, 88.

71. Patrides, "The 'Protevangelium,'" 19–30.

in hermeneutics intending to mitigate Adam's excesses and elicit sober understanding, the whole process plunges Adam deeper and deeper into the subsequent stages of the *Heilgeschichte* that he may fully appropriate the reality of redemption in which he and Eve already share. While the *protevangelium* unfolds in the typical pre-figurations of the Abrahamic and Davidic covenants, the slavery of sin, with human childhood under the bondage and impotence of the law and the rule of men, informs both the course of salvation history and Adam's own apprehension of the terms of his own liberty.

Walker persuasively argues that the burden of typology is central to the two final books of *Paradise Lost*, while turning "on the claim that this centrality effects a coherent vision of history as an image of eternity."[72] More than that, however, the final section of the poem appears to collapse the image of eternity with the human characters' present liberty in an inaugurated eschatology. Only a journey through the dispensations may alert Adam to the pervasive ramifications of the fall and thus to the image of eternity which is being formed in him. Just as it was for the historical Milton and for Milton's reader, a similar journey was only to occur through personal, Spirit-led interaction and confrontation with verbal revelation. In fact, it was to occur through personal involvement in a process of induction and deduction that would lead his spirit and intellect to know Jesus, as opposed to self, law or human government, as the only source of true freedom and his present liberator.

Along these lines, Adam's progress matches the progress of theological revelation as it unfolds in book 12. When Michael first stresses the anticipatory terms of the *evangelium* in Abraham's faith[73] and in the Abrahamic covenant (12.125–28, 146–51), Adam exults as both the darkness of his vision and that of his ignorance begin to dissipate:

---

72. Walker, "Typology and *Paradise Lost*, Books XI and XII," 246. Regina Schwartz, for her part, regards the forth-looking types of book 12 as manipulated by Michael to the effect of leading Adam to more unendings. Like Moses on Mt. Pisgah, Adam is granted, in Schwartz's understanding, the vision of the promised land from afar. Unlike Moses, though, he does not see Canaan, but only more shadows. He thus fails to apprehend the true substance of things. I intend to argue that Adam's misapprehensions and short-sighted conclusions testify not so much to a negative circular movement as to a progressive approach alongside a persistent attempt to relate revelation to one's personal condition and to that of mankind.

73. In Ames' words, "Father and pattern of all who should believe" (*Marrow*, 204).

> O sent from Heav'n,
> Enlight'ner of my darkness, gracious things
> Thou hast revealed, those chiefly which concern
> Just Abraham and his seed: now first I find
> Mine eyes true op'ning, and my heart much eased
> Erewhile perplexed with thoughts what would become
> Of me and all mankind; but now I see
> His day, in whom all nations shall be blest,
> Favor unmerited by me, who sought
> Forbidden knowledge by forbidden means. (12.270–9)

The *protevangelium* begins to acquire substance in Adam's eyes as the identification occurs of the seed of the woman as the seed of Abraham. Adam now sees the highway of grace ("gracious things") as running through "Just Abraham" and his descent.[74] This knowledge affects him personally in that it redefines both his sense of responsibility for the destiny of mankind and his perception of his own. Not only are his eyes now partially opened, but his heart is eased. In other words, that same mind and that same conscience which have been perplexed with doubt and fearful uncertainty have now gained a measure of light from revelation. Not only does Adam now see the day of him in whom all nations will be blessed, but he is able to relate the future benefit to his own condition. In other words, such is Adam's identification with the progressive terms of Christian liberty that the unmerited favor produced by the future seed begins to be retained as his present grace.

After stressing Abraham's significance with respect to the history of salvation, Michael next accounts for the dispensation of the law as itself pointing to the ultimate unfolding of the *protevangelium* (12.227–42).[75] The very mention of laws, however, perplexes Adam and paves the way for a fresh insight into the rule of law:

---

74. "From Adam to Abraham . . . redemption by Christ and the application of Christ . . . was to be carried out by the seed of the woman . . . From the time of Abraham . . . redemption along with its application was majestically shown . . . in the promise and covenant of blessing to come to all nations from the seed of Abraham" (Ames, *Marrow*, 204).

75. "From the time of Moses to Christ, these same things [things pertaining to the covenant] were further adumbrated by extraordinary and ordinary means" (Ames, *Marrow*, 204).

> This yet I apprehend not, why to those
> Among whom God will deign to dwell on Earth
> So many and so various laws are giv'n;
> So many laws argue so many sins (12.280–3)

So many laws argue so many sins as they both expose sin and make sin exceedingly sinful. External laws, that is, set a standard which man is incapable of meeting and thus deprive him of all moral strength in the very pursuit of obedience. In the words of Paul of Tarsus, "For when we were in the flesh, the sinful passions which were aroused by the law were at work in our members to bear fruit to death."[76] Not that the law was bad in itself, but "sin, that it might appear sin, was producing death in me through what is good, so that sin through the commandment might become exceedingly sinful."[77] Michael grants Adam's argument and hinges the progress of revelation on it. In so doing, he meets Adam where he is and leads him where he wants him to go. The final destination has not changed. The law itself had but a functional end, aiming to point sinful man to a justice apart from himself or the law. Accordingly,

> . . . shall not Moses, though of God
> Highly beloved, being but the minister
> Of law, his people into Canaan lead;
> But Joshua whom the Gentiles Jesus call (12.307–10)

Not to Moses, as the minister of the law, is it given to be the rightful type of the savior, but to Joshua, whose name identifies him with the woman's seed. Only one stage is now left before the full unveiling of the obscure terms of the promise. The Davidic covenant yields the final typological piece of the puzzle. David's regal throne shall endure forever, for a king in David's lineage shall rise whose kingdom will never end. Michael's reference is once again to

> . . . the woman's seed to thee foretold,
> Foretold to Abraham, as in whom shall trust
> All nations, and to kings foretold, of kings
> The last, for of his reign shall be no end. (12.327–30)

Michael thus isolates the *fil rouge* of his revelation to Adam. All is left for him to do is to identify the ultimate seed and everlasting king and unfold the terms of his victory over the serpent. He therefore accounts

76. Rom 7:5.
77. Rom 7:13.

for the virgin birth as the marriage of heaven and earth. If Adam's reactions reveal his full participation in whatever measure of revelation he is accorded, the very identification of the son of promise as born of a virgin fills him with "joy" so sudden (12.372) as the outburst of triumph and discernment it produces:

> O prophet of glad tidings, finisher
> Of utmost hope! Now clear I understand
> What oft my steadiest thoughts have searched in vain,
> Why our great expectation should be called
> The seed of woman . . . (12.375–79)

Adam acknowledges Michael as a "prophet of glad tidings" and "finisher / Of utmost hope." In revealing the advent of the woman's seed, Michael has brought gladness and the consummation of all hope to Adam. The word "finisher" yields the conclusion of his pursuit. His clear-sightedness, to be sure, only refers to "Why our great expectation should be called / The seed of woman." His vision is thus partial, yet not "clouded."[78] In fact, the clarity of Adam's understanding and insight can hardly be questioned as he expands on the words of God's messenger and appropriates the doctrine of the hypostatic union of God and man in the woman's progeny:

> . . . from my loins
> Thou shalt proceed, and from thy womb the Son
> Of God Most High; so God with man unites. (12.380–82)

The first portion of the *protevangelium* being thus revealed, the second now awaits clarification. So Adam:

> . . . say where and when
> Their fight, what stroke shall bruise the victor's heel. (12.384–85)

Whereas for Schwartz "There will be no single duel" as "the battle for obedience must be fought in the hearts of Adam's progeny,"[79] no material fight but a fight for that liberty upon which alone obedience is based will indeed occur at the cross. There the Son, both God and man, will destroy Adam's sin

78. For Schwartz, Adam "is once again overconfident, for his next question—where and when the combat between Christ and Satan will take place—only reveals how clouded his vision still is (12.375–85)" (Schwartz, "From Shadowy Types to Shadowy Types," 125).

79. Schwartz, "From Shadowy Types to Shadowy Types," 125.

> ... by fulfilling that which thou didst want,
> Obedience to the law of God, imposed
> On penalty of death, and suffering death,
> The penalty to thy transgression due (12.396–99)

While for Saurat the crucifixion plays "no noticeable part" in the poem's theology and "vicarious atonement is no Miltonic conception,"[80] it is at the cross that Milton collapses past and future with Adam's present. Just as types find their substance here, so do the future Davidic kingdom and complete glorification. The Son is indeed the ἔσχατος, the end of history, and the consummation of Adam's present search.[81] The disclosure of his identity and work therefore may rightfully project Adam to the end of the ages, when

> On the day of complete glorification, 'the Earth
> Shall all be Paradise, far happier place
> Than this of Eden, and far happier days'. (463–65)

These words disclose the epilogue of book 12 and of the poem as a whole by beginning to pull its loose ends together. By means of a comparison, Michael lets Adam know that God has something even better than Eden in store. As John C. Ulreich points out, the second term of comparison must be unfallen Eden.[82] The indication in lines 464–65 is both eschatological and geographical. The comparison is between two places, unfallen Eden and the new earth, two times, the beginning and the end, and the external happiness they respectively produced and will produce.[83]

Even so, happiness is attributed to a place or a time with respect to the happiness man experiences within that place and time. The question inevitably arises as to why the new paradise would be happier than the old, granted a perfect predicament informs both. To see the answer in the poetical shadows the fall casts on unfallen Eden is to do away with Adam's gloss upon Michael's words. Adam is in fact ready to declare the ultimate good resulting from evil as "more wonderful" (471) than that produced at "Creation" (472). Is Milton rather endorsing the Medieval concept of the *felix culpa*? That would be tantamount to casting doubts

---

80. Saurat, *Milton*, 177–78.

81. The great protagonist of the poem for Woodhouse, *The Heavenly Muse*, 188–90.

82. Ulreich, "'A paradise within,'" 351.

83. For an analysis of millennial eschatology in Milton, see especially Sarah Hutton's "Mede, Milton, and More," 29–41.

over God's nature and providence. Far from it, Adam's reaction to Michael's words reflects man's responsibility for the fall resulting from free choice. While God in his love has to grant the latter, thus also allowing for the fall, his perfections call for love and justice to ultimately saturate his universe. God's saving decree is his preordained response to man's free fall. Hence the key to the fulfillment of theodicy is found in God the Son, for "mercy and justice in [God's] face discerned" (3.407) finally meet at the cross. The latter in turn constitutes the foundation of both incomplete and complete restoration.

Adam's outburst of praise hits the bull's eye as he exalts "goodness infinite, goodness immense" (469). That goodness is thus stressed here which can turn man's evil into something even better than the first unblemished good. In Ulreich's words, "greater goodness comes about not because of but in spite of [and alongside] our transgression."[84] Hence, the ground for the new earth to be even "happier" than Eden need not be traced to concepts of a fortunate fall or to the restored perfectibility of mankind, as Ulreich ultimately suggests, but to the quality of divine grace. As *De Doctrina* has it, "MAN'S RESTORATION is the act by which man, freed from sin and death by God the Father through Jesus Christ, is raised to a far more excellent state of grace and glory than that from which he fell."[85]

One question yet remains: was man really free before acquiring experiential knowledge of evil? He *was* insofar as he was accorded the right to choose evil, that is to choose against God (negative liberty)—a perfect God could grant nothing less, lest he create automata that could only serve necessity, yet nothing more, lest he turn into the author of sin—he *was* in that he was free to pursue all good (positive liberty). He *wasn't* as for the extent of his consciousness of evil or his negative perfectibility. Theoretical knowledge of evil was all that God could grant both before and after the fall and all that Milton could advocate in *Areopagitica*. However, such knowledge was limited to the mind and did not encompass conscience. Alternatives were not therefore equally apprehended and choice in turn not absolutely free.

On the other hand, knowledge as experience of evil would make man whole and the recipient of paramount freedom, were it not for sin and its passions affecting and hindering both wholeness and freedom

84. Ulreich, "'A paradise within,'" 365.
85. *CPW* 6.415.

altogether. "Happier had it sufficed him to have known / Good by itself and evil not at all!," exclaims Milton, thus averting the implicit suggestion that evil is in fact good. The poet has made every possible effort in books 9–11 to depict Eve's desire to know more than she could and should take as morally detestable and the fall with its consequences as absolutely tragic. The quality of grace, however, is such that it can improve that which God by his nature could not make any better when he called "Light out of darkness" (473). The quality of grace can make Adam, and the new earth with him, happier in the end as it frees a now complete but enslaved man from the destitution his first disobedience has brought upon him and puts him in an immensely deeper relationship with God (as infinitely deeper is the expression of divine grace). The new Adam can thus avail himself of completeness and maturity of intellect and conscience while enjoying full freedom from sin and its ramifications in a new union with both Son and Father. Man's ultimate condition under the discipline of the gospel of grace proves therefore by far superior to his first in terms of freedom and authority.[86] In light of such new freedom and authority, the words of Adam come as little surprise as, with Paul,[87] he takes grace to its extreme consequences:

> . . . Full of doubt I stand,
> Whether I should repent me now of sin
> By me done and occasioned, or rejoice
> Much more, that much more good thereof shall spring,
> To God more glory, more good will to men
> From God, and over wrath grace shall abound! (12.473–78)

Michael's response relating the ministry of the Spirit of grace working through love diverts Adam's reason to the rightful ramifications of grace as seen against the backdrop of those false religious guides who would "force the Spirit of Grace" (525). Confronted with such detrimental perspective, Adam proves ultimately ready to discard the rationale pre-

---

86. Marginal though it is, Knott's understanding that the new paradise is happier than Eden for "it includes an awareness of what unhappiness is" (*Milton's Pastoral Vision*, 16) is undoubtedly included in man's new maturity and freedom.

87. Rom 5:20–1; 6:1–2: "Where sin abounded, grace did much more abound: That as sin hath reigned unto death, even so might grace reign through righteousness unto eternal life by Jesus Christ our Lord. What shall we say then? Shall we continue in sin, that grace may abound? God forbid. How shall we, that are dead to sin, live any longer therein."

viously entertained to embrace the spiritual principles that stem from Christian liberty:

> Greatly instructed I shall hence depart,
> Greatly in peace of thought, and have my fill
> Of knowledge, what this vessel can contain;
> Beyond which was my folly to aspire.
> Henceforth I learn, that to obey is best,
> And love with fear the only God, to walk
> As in his presence, ever to observe
> His providence, and on him sole depend,
> Merciful over all his works, with good
> Still overcoming evil, and by small
> Accomplishing great things, things deemed weak
> Subverting worldly strong, and worldly wise
> By simply meek; that suffering for truth's sake
> Is fortitude to highest victory,
> And, to the faithful, death the gate of life;
> Taught by his example whom I now
> Acknowledge my Redeemer ever blest. (12.557–73)

If the terms of Christian liberty had brought "peace / Of Conscience" (12.296–7), they are now said to bring "peace of thought." All spiritual wisdom has ensued from the apprehension of the one whom he now no longer knows as the seed of the woman, but as *his Redeemer*. Whereas Myers identifies conversion as an ongoing dynamic process,[88] Adam's present realization testifies to the actualization of a positional reality. Manifestly discarding the speculative wisdom that Adam had previously sought (in inquiring into the heavenly spheres), Michael in turn identifies that which Adam has acquired as the highest knowledge and the highest wisdom, or else the rightful benefit of education and of positive perfectibility. Only, he bids Adam add

> Deeds to thy knowledge answerable, add faith,
> Add virtue, patience, temperance, add love,
> By name to come called charity, the soul
> Of all the rest: then wilt thou not be loath
> To leave this Paradise, but shalt possess
> A Paradise within thee, happier far. (12.582–87)

Echoing 2 Peter 1:5–7, that given by the archangel is a list of love-defined and love-empowered virtues which saving faith is to pursue by the agen-

---

88. Myers, *Milton's Theology of Freedom*, 156–62.

cy of the Spirit of truth. Freedom and love in turn will yield a paradise within which far surpasses the outer paradise. In Irene Samuel's words:

> Michael compares not the paradise within, which Adam has already lost, with that which he may yet find, but the external Eden with the inner; for the final consequence of the fall is this disjoining of inner and outer state.[89]

It should be noted this passage is indeed related to the previous eschatological happier place and days, but it shows its distinctiveness insofar as it maintains the gap between outer and inner which the other collapses. Adam need not worry about leaving Eden, because far happier is that paradise which is carried within. A spiritually inaugurated eschatology is set forth here, which is only to find its outward counterpart in the final reality. To be sure, overtones of both sorrow and happiness clearly appear throughout book 12 and plainly characterize its conclusion. Even so, if Adam can at present experience a paradise within happier far, it is only because the balance of sorrow and present happiness in the poem is the balance of outward and inward. Inwardly free, Adam can freely confront an outward world that has lost paradise just as the true Christian is to make his way through all external woe.[90]

Adam's first step as a man who has actualized the full reality of his restoration now awaits him. Reconciliation with Eve must ensue as the first fruit of liberty and love. He is to recover that unity with Eve which has been questioned since the very moment she chose independent isolation. To this end, Eve must first be made aware of the full terms of her own redemption. Michael therefore urges Adam to share with her the "great deliv'rance by her Seed to come" (600). As Satan had taken advantage of the sleep of reason in the foul dream, so is Eve now given to experience that "God is also in sleep, and dreams advise" (611). For all the tragic extent of her fall, the Deliverer himself will come from her!

---

89. Samuel, *Plato and Milton*, 121. In *The Paradise Within*, 166, Martz contends that "the promised redemption consists primarily in the renewal of man's inner powers: those powers of the soul by which the bard has . . . pursued his triumphant journey of the mind toward Paradise." Blackburn ("Paradises Lost and Found") and Kaufman (*Paradise in the Age of Milton*) identify the paradise within with the doctrine of incomplete glorification. For an argument contradicting the idea of superiority of the new inward paradise over the old, see Sherry, "'A Paradise Within' Can Never Be 'Happier Farr.'"

90. See Duncan, *Milton's Earthly Paradise*, 266.

Everything is indeed new. Eve need no longer beg nor retain the lexis of separation, discord and self-seeking despair. Rather, for her now

> ... with thee to go,
> Is to stay here; without thee here to stay,
> Is to go hence unwilling; thou to me
> Art all things under Heav'n, all places thou (12.615–18)

The restoration of creational unity can be read in the chiasmic structure of these lines as the reversal of Eve's desire for individual venture. The question returns as to whether Eve is truly complete and free apart from Adam. The dialectic of freedom and love, inward and outward, once again affords the answer. Once again, freedom is not about absence of external restraint, just as Satan was not free though reigning in hell, nor is it about compliance with an external law. Eve's true freedom is not found in her independence from Adam nor is it found in her subordination to Adam. It is rather found in her appropriation of the liberating terms of grace. Endowed with true freedom, Eve is now defined by love for Adam. And if for Satan "Which way I fly is hell," Eve's inward paradise of freedom causes for that same love to be the measure of paradise irrespective of geographical boundaries.[91] The freedom *from* marriage which Milton had envisioned in the divorce tracts as an actualization of inward liberty in the domestic realm now becomes freedom *within* marriage, as Adam and Eve's hands, long clenched, intertwine again and the pair takes to its solitary way.

Their ultimate destination is unknown. It is now up to them "to choose / Their place of rest" (646–47), the whole world lying before them (646). Whereas the boundaries of prelapsarian Eden are those of incomplete and law-bound freedom, the grace-bound maturity and unconditionality of postlapsarian inward liberty opens them up to the world as it allows them to choose the good amidst potentially infinite and equally apprehended options. The poet has little doubt about Adam and Eve's ability to find their place of rest, for rest is what they carry within. If the outward place will itself be defined by rest, therefore, it is only because inward liberty yields the power to effect the awaited restoration of the prelapsarian match of outward and inward paradise which the fall had disrupted.

91. See Knott, "Milton's Pastoral Vision," 61. Here Knott identifies the superiority of the new inward paradise over the old in the former's self-attainment and independence from the external world.

Conclusion

In a final appeal to the nation in 1659, Milton had urged the people of England "to become children of reviving libertie; and may reclaim, though they seem now chusing them a captain back for Egypt."[92] In envisioning the apparent choice of "a captain back for Egypt," *The Ready and Easy Way* was pointing to the restoration of monarchy as a return to tyranny. In so doing, it appeared to tie outward liberty to political emancipation rather than to inward restoration. The context, however, redefines this reading. Egypt signified both Israel's condition of material slavery and, figuratively, slavery to sin. Just as Israel had been liberated from the slavery of historical Egypt, so was the Christian free from spiritual Egypt. Milton appears to make no distinction between the political and the spiritual level. On the contrary, a juxtaposition occurs to underscore the inextricable connection between the two. Such connection, however, does not entail interdependence, but the subservience of the former to the latter. If "chusing . . . a captain back for Egypt" is directly contrasted to becoming "children of reviving libertie," it is because the effect (political liberty) is the necessary result of a cause (spiritual liberty). The nation's lament that her past condition of slavery was preferable to the present one and her longing for a return to Egypt therefore testifies to lack of spiritual liberty.[93] The failure of England to fully appropriate external liberties in the years of the Interregnum likewise only resulted from its forfeiting the discipline of grace for inward servitude to self-enhancing affections:

92. *CPW* 7.463.

93. Algernon Sidney would argue much to the same effect, "God hath deliver'd us from slavery, and shewd us that he would be our King; and we recall from exile one of that detested race" (*Court Maxims* (1665–66); cited in Scott, *Algernon Sidney*, 186). Here the liberating rule of heaven's king is contrasted to the slavery of "that detested race." If God's rule entailed liberty from the rule of men, it signified his sovereignty over the soul. Such rule, however, as Milton had long acknowledged, was but a mild yoke.

> But what more oft in Nations grown corrupt,
> And by thir vices brought to servitude,
> Than to love Bondage more than Liberty,
> Bondage with ease than strenuous liberty. (SA 268–71)

Liberty, to be sure, was not easy to abide by. Once received, Christian liberty was to be chosen again and again over the bondage of sin, law and men. It was to be chosen again and again to allow for the paradise within to flourish and, accordingly, see God's kingdom come.

In adumbrating "peace, justice, plentifull trade and all prosperitie" to ensue from political reform and progress "even to the coming of our true and rightfull and only to be expected King . . . the Messiah, the Christ,"[94] *The Ready and Easy Way* bore the long echo of Milton's initial prophetic cry:

> presse on hard to that *high* and *happy* emulation to be found the *soberest, wisest,* and *most Christian People* at that day when thou the Eternall and shortly-expected King shalt open the Clouds to judge the severall Kingdomes of the World, and distributing *Nationall Honours* and *Rewards* to Religious and just *Commonwealths,* shalt put an end to all Earthly *Tyrannies,* proclaiming thy universal and milde *Monarchy* through Heaven and Earth.[95]

In 1659 as in 1641 that political reform which would be matched by Christ's mild rule could still be cherished as the outward counterpart of the Canaan within. *Paradise Lost* was no step backwards. It was not the initial expression of the experience of defeat, to use Hill's words. It was rather the climax of Milton's libertarian aspirations. Outward demise was strictly related to the failure of individuals to embrace inward liberty. If the battle for liberty could no longer be fought in the public arena, it was because liberty had been defeated in the inward. The latter therefore needed to be reclaimed for liberty. Accordingly, Milton's message should no longer address the parliament, but the heart of man. It should no longer envision the passing of liberal laws, but the restoration of Christian liberty. Likewise, the pursuit of liberty would cease to be the contingent prerogative of the left hand. It would now be entrusted with the right. The message, however, remained the same. Not law nor human government could truly free man, but the free man could free law and human government along with those who were subject to their tyranny.

94. *CPW* 7.445.
95. *CPW* 1.616.

Bibliography

Achinstein, Sharon. *Literature and Dissent in Milton's England*. Cambridge: Cambridge University Press, 2003.

———. *Milton and the Revolutionary Reader*. Princeton: Princeton University Press, 1994.

Achinstein, Sharon, and Elizabeth Sauer, eds. *Milton and Toleration*. Oxford: Oxford University Press, 2007.

Adamo, Pietro, and Giulio Giorello. "La 'tolleranza armata': Politica e Religione nella Rivoluzione Inglese (1640–1660)." In *Modernità, Politica e Protestantesimo*, edited by E. Bein Ricco, 81–136. Turin: Claudiana, 1994.

Ainsworth, David. *Milton and the Spiritual Reader: Reading and Religion in Seventeenth-Century England*. New York: Routledge, 2008.

———. "Spiritual Reading in Milton's Eikonoklastes." *Studies in English Literature* 45/1 (2005) 157–89.

Allen, Michael. "Divine Instruction: *Of Education* and the Pedagogy of Raphael, Michael and the Father." *Milton Quarterly* 26/4 (1992) 113–21.

Allestree, Richard. *The Gentleman's Calling*. London: T. Garthwait, 1660.

———. *The Practice of Christian Graces, or the Whole Duty of Man*. London: J. Beecroft, 1659.

Ames, William. *Medulla Theologica* [*The Marrow of Theology*] (1629). Translated and edited by John D. Eusden. Grand Rapids: Baker, 1968.

———. *The Substance of Christian Religion; or, A Plain and Easie Draught of the Christian Catechism*. London: T. Mabb for T. Davies, 1659.

Amyraut, Moyse. *Apologie pour ceux de la religion sur les sujets d'aversion que plusieurs pensent avoir contre leurs personnes & leur créance*. Saumur: I. Desbordes, 1647.

———. *Brief traitté de la predestination et de ses principales dependances par Moyse Amyraut*. Saumur: J. Lesnier and I. Desbordes, 1634.

———. *De la Justification, contre les opinions de Monsieur de La Milletière, où sont examinées les raisons de l'Eglise romaine sur cette matière et la doctrine des Evangiles défendüe contre elles*. Saumur: J. Lesnier and I. Desbordes, 1638.

———. *De L'Élevation de la Foy et de L'Abaissement de la Raison en la Créance des Mysteres de la Religion*. Saumur: J. Lesnier, 1641.

———. *De mysterio trinitatis, deque vocibus ac Phrasibus quibus tam Scriptura quam apud Patres explicatur, Dissertatio, septem partibus absoluta*. Saumur: Isaac Desbordes, 1661.

———. *A Discourse Concerning Religions, in Refutation of the Opinion which Accounts All Indifferent*. London: M. Simmons for Will, 1660.

———. *Dissertationes theologicae quatuor*. Saumur: I. Desbordes, 1645.

————. *Dissertationes theologicae sex, quarum quatuor De oeconomica trium personarum, De jure Dei in creaturas, De gratia universali, De gratia particulari, antehac editae, nunc revisae prodeunt. Duae, De serpente tentatore et De peccato originis, ad superiores additae sunt authore Mose Amyraldo.* Saumur: I. Desbordes, 1660.

————. *Du Règne de mille ans, ou De la prospérité de l'Eglise.* Saumur: Desbordes, 1654.

Anderson, Judith H. "Satanic Ethos and Envy: The Origin of Evil and Death in *Paradise Lost*." *Milton Studies* 51 (2010) 137–64.

[Anon.]. *The Fountaine of Free Grace Opened, by the Congregation . . . Falsely Called Anabaptists.* London, 1645.

Aquinas, Thomas. *The Basic Writings of St Thomas Aquinas.* Edited by A. C. Pegis. 2 vols. New York: Random House, 1945.

————. *Summa Theologiae.* Edited by Thomas Gilby et al. 60 vols. London: Eyre and Spottiswoode, 1964–76.

Arminius, Jacobus. *The Works of James Arminius.* Translated and edited by James Nichols and William Nichols. 3 vols. Grand Rapids: Baker, 1986.

Armitage, David, Armand Himy, and Quentin Skinner, eds. *Milton and Republicanism.* Cambridge: Cambridge University Press, 1995.

Armstrong, Brian G. *Calvinism and the Amyraut Heresy: Protestant Scholasticism and Humanism in Seventeenth-Century France.* Madison: University of Wisconsin Press, 1969.

Arnold, Marilyn. "Milton's Accessible God: The Role of the Son in *Paradise Lost*." *Milton Quarterly* 7 (1973) 65–72.

Arnold, Richard. *Logic of the Fall: Right Reason and (Im)pure Reason in Milton's Paradise Lost.* New York: Lang, 2006.

Ashworth, Ann. "Psyche and Eve: Milton's Goddess without a Temple." *Milton Quarterly* 18 (1984) 52–58.

Aubrey, John. *Brief Lives.* Edited by A. Clark. 2 vols. Oxford: Clarendon, 1898.

Augustine. *The City of God against the Pagans.* Edited and translated by G. E. McCracken et al. Vol. 1, *Books 1–3.* Cambridge, MA: Harvard University Press, 1957.

————. *Contra secundam Juliani responsionem.* In *Patrologia Latina*, edited by Jacques-Paul Migne, vol. 45. Col. 1432. http://www.documentacatholicaomnia. eu/02m/0354-0430,_Augustinus,_Contra_Secundam_Juliani_Responsionem._ Admonitio,_MLT.pdf.

————. *De civitate Dei contra paganos.* In *St. Augustine: Anti-Pelagian Writings*, edited by Philip Schaff. Vol. 2. Grand Rapids: Eerdmans, 1979.

————. *De gratia et libero arbitrio.* In *St. Augustine: Anti-Pelagian Writings*, edited by Philip Schaff. Vol. 5. Grand Rapids: Eerdmans, 1979.

————. *De praedestinatione sanctorum ad Prosperum et Hilarium.* In *St. Augustine: Anti-Pelagian Writings*, edited by Philip Schaff. Vol. 5. Grand Rapids: Eerdmans, 1979.

————. *De spiritu et littera.* In *St. Augustine: Anti-Pelagian Writings*, edited by Philip Schaff. Vol. 5. Grand Rapids: Eerdmans, 1979.

————. *In evangelium Ioannis tractatus.* In *St. Augustine: Anti-Pelagian Writings*, edited by Philip Schaff. Vol. 7. Grand Rapids: Eerdmans, 1979.

Bacon, Francis. *The Advancement of Learning* (1605). Edited by James Spedding, Robert L. Ellis, and Douglas D. Heath. Vol. 6. Boston: Houghton, 1900.

————. *The Advancement of Learning* (1605). Edited by J. Devey. New York: Collier, 1905.

Bainton, Roland H. *The Travail of Religious Liberty.* Philadelphia: Westminster, 1951.

Barbour, Hugh. *The Quakers in Puritan England*. New Haven: Yale University Press, 1964.

Barclay, Robert. "The Possibility and Necessity of the Inward and Immediate Revelation of the Spirit of God." In *Truth Triumphant through the Spiritual Warfare*. London, 1672.

———. *Roberti Barclaii Theologiae Verè Christianae Apologia*. London, 1676. Republished as *Apology for the True Christian Divinity*. London: J. Forbes, 1678.

Barker, Arthur E. "Christian Liberty in Milton's Divorce Pamphlets." *Modern Language Review* 35 (1940) 153–61.

———. *Milton and the Puritan Dilemma, 1641–1660*. Toronto: University of Toronto Press, 1942.

Barton, Carol. "'They Also Perform the Duties of a Servant Who Only Remain Erect on their Feet in a Specified Place in Readiness to Receive Orders': The Dynamics of Stasis in Sonnet XIX ('When I consider How My Light is Spent')." *Milton Quarterly* 32 (1998) 109–22.

Bates, Catherine. "No Sin but Irony: Kierkegaard and Milton's Satan." *Literature and Theology* 11 (1997) 1–26.

Bauman, Michael. "Creation and the Son's Alleged Omnipresence." *Milton Quarterly* 19 (1985) 110–12.

———. *Milton's Arianism*. New York: Lang, 1987.

Bellarmine, Robert. *Disputationes de controversiis christianae fidei, ad versus hujus temporis haereticos*. 4 vols. Rome, 1586–93.

Benet, Diana T. "Adam's Evil Conscience and Satan's Surrogate Fall." *Milton Quarterly* 39 (2005) 2–15.

———. "Satan, God's Glory and the Fortunate Fall." *Milton Quarterly* 19 (1985) 34–37.

Bennett, Joan. *Reviving Liberty: Radical Christian Humanism in Milton's Great Poems*. Cambridge, MA: Harvard University Press, 1989.

Berkouwer, G. C. *Man: The Image of God*. Grand Rapids: Eerdmans, 1952.

Berkowitz, M. S. "Thomas Young's 'Hopes Encouragement' and Milton's Sonnet XIX." *Milton Quarterly* 16 (1982) 94–97.

Berlin, Isaiah. *Four Essays on Liberty*. Oxford: Oxford University Press, 1969.

Berry, Boyd M. *Process of Speech: Puritan Religious Writing and Paradise Lost*. Baltimore: Johns Hopkins University Press, 1976.

Bethell, S. L. *The Cultural Revolution of the Seventeenth Century*. London: Dobson, 1963.

Beza, Theodore. *A Booke of Christian Questions and Answers, Wherein Are Set Foorth the Cheef Points of the Christian Religion*. London, 1572.

———. *Tabula Praedestinationis*. Geneva, 1555.

Biberman, Matthew. "Milton, Marriage and a Woman's Right to Divorce." *Studies in English Literature* 39 (1999) 131–53.

Biddle, John. *A Confession of Faith Touching the Holy Trinity*. London, 1648.

Bignami, Marialuisa. "Milton Dà Spazio alla Mano Sinistra: Si Progetta l'Uomo Nuovo." In *Il Progetto e il Paradosso—Saggi sull'Utopia in Inghilterra*, 31–61. Milan: Guerini, 1990.

———. "Satan Speaks: Public Speeches and Private Utterances in John Milton's *Paradise Lost*." In *Le scritture e le riscritture: discorso religioso e discorso letterario in Europa nella prima età moderna*, edited by Daniele Borgogni and R. Camerlingo, 231–46. Naples: Edizioni Scientifiche Italiane, 2005.

Blackburn, Thomas H. "Paradises Lost and Found: The Meaning and Function of the 'Paradise Within' in *Paradise Lost.*" *Milton Studies* 5 (1973) 191–211.

Blunt, David. "Debate of Redemption at the Westminster Assembly." *British Reformed Journal* (January–March 1996) 5–10.

Boehrer, Bruce Thomas. "Elementary Structures of Kingship: Milton, Regicide, and the Family." *Milton Studies* 23 (1987) 97–117.

Boesky, Amy. "Milton's Heaven and the Model of the English Utopia." *Studies in English Literature* 36 (1995) 91–110.

Bonhoeffer, Dietrich. *Ethics.* Edited by Clifford J. Green. Translated by Reinhard Krauss, Douglas W. Stott, and Charles C. West. Philadelphia: Fortress, 2004.

Borris, Kenneth. "Allegory in *Paradise Lost*: Satan's Cosmic Journey." *Milton Studies* 26 (1991) 101–33.

Boswell, J. C. "Milton and Prevenient Grace." *Studies in English Literature* 7 (1967) 83–94.

Bramhall, John. *Discourse on Liberty and Necessity* (1645). In *Hobbes and Bramhall on Liberty and Necessity,* edited by Vere Chappell, 1–14. Cambridge: Cambridge University Press, 1999.

Brodwin, Leonora Leet. "The Dissolution of Satan in *Paradise Lost*: A Study of Milton's Heretical Eschatology." *Milton Studies* 8 (1975) 165–207.

Brown, Cedric C. *John Milton: A Literary Life.* Basingstoke: Macmillan, 1995.

Brown, Mary Ruth. "*Paradise Lost* and John 15: Eve, the Branch and the Church." *Milton Quarterly* 20 (1986) 127–31.

Bruce, F. F. *The Book of the Acts.* Grand Rapids: Eerdmans, 1988.

———. *The Epistles to the Colossians, to Philemon, and to the Ephesians.* Grand Rapids: Eerdmans, 1984.

———. *The Epistle to the Galatians.* Grand Rapids: Eerdmans, 1982.

———. *The Epistle to the Hebrews.* Grand Rapids: Eerdmans, 1990.

———. *1 & 2 Corinthians.* London: Oliphants, 1971.

———. *1 & 2 Thessalonians.* Waco, TX: Word, 1982.

———. *The Gospel and Epistles of John.* Grand Rapids: Eerdmans, 1983.

———. *Paul: Apostle of the Heart Set Free.* Grand Rapids: Eerdmans, 1977.

———. *Philippians.* Peabody, MA: Heinemann, 1989.

———, ed. *New International Bible Commentary.* Grand Rapids: Eerdmans, 1979.

Bryson, Michael. "'His Tyranny Who Reigns': The Biblical Roots of Divine Kingship and Milton's Rejection of 'Heav'n's King.'" *Milton Studies* 43 (2004) 111–44.

———. "'That Far Be from Thee': Divine Evil and Justification in *Paradise Lost.*" *Milton Quarterly* 36 (2002) 87–105.

———. *The Tyranny of Heaven: Milton's Rejection of God as King.* Newark, NJ: Rosemont, 2004.

Buck, Philo M. *Milton on Liberty.* University Studies of the University of Nebraska 25. Lincoln, 1925.

Buhler, Stephen M. "Kingly States: The Politics of *Paradise Lost.*" *Milton Studies* 28 (1992) 49–68.

Bunyan, John. *Grace Abounding to the Chief of Sinners* (1666). Edited by W. R. Owens. London, 1987.

———. *A holy life, the beauty of Christianity: or, An exhortation to Christians to be holy.* London: B. W., 1684.

Burden, Dennis. *The Logical Epic: A Study of the Argument of* Paradise Lost. Cambridge, MA: Harvard University Press, 1967.

Burgess, Anthony. *The Doctrine of Original Sin, Asserted and Vindicated against the Old and New Adversaries Thereof.* London: A. Miller, 1659.

Burns, Norman T. *Christian Mortalism from Tyndale to Milton.* Cambridge, MA: Harvard University Press, 1972.

Burt, Stephen. "'To the Unknown God': St. Paul and Athens in Milton's *Areopagitica*." *Milton Quarterly* 32 (1998) 23–31.

Bush, Douglas, ed. *The Complete Poetical Works of John Milton.* Boston: Houghton, 1965.

Butler, George F. "The Wrath of Aeneas and the Triumph of the Son: Virgil's Aegaeon and *Paradise Lost*." *Comparative Literature Studies* 34 (1997) 103–18.

Byard, Margaret M. "Divine Wisdom-Urania." *Milton Quarterly* 12 (1978) 134–37.

Cable, Lana. "Shuffling Up Such a God: The Rhetorical Agon of Milton's Antiprelatical Tracts." *Milton Studies* 21 (1986) 3–33.

Calvin, John. *Commentaries.* 22 vols. Translated by John Owen et al. Grand Rapids: Baker, 2003.

———. *Commentaries.* Translated and edited by Joseph Harountunian and Louise Pettibone Smith. Philadelphia: Westminster, 1948.

———. *Institutes of the Christian Religion.* Translated by Henry Beveridge. Edinburgh: Calvin Translation Society, 1863.

———. *Institutio christianae religionis.* Geneva: J. Stoer, 1536.

Cameron, John. *An examination of those plausible appearances which seeme most to commend the Romish Church, and to prejudice the Reformed.* Oxford: J. Lichfield and W. Turner, 1626.

Campbell, Gordon. "Alleged Imperfections in Milton's *De Doctrina Christiana*." *Milton Quarterly* 12 (1978) 64–65.

———. "The Authorship of *De Doctrina Christiana*." *Milton Quarterly* 26 (1992) 129–30.

———. "Milton's Theological and Literary Treatments of the Creation." *Journal of Theological Studies* 30 (1979) 128–37.

———. "The Mortalist Heresy in *Paradise Lost*." *Milton Quarterly* 13 (1979) 33–36.

———, ed. *Complete English Poems, Of Education, Areopagitica.* London: Dent, 1993.

Campbell, Gordon, and Thomas N. Corns. *John Milton: Life, Work and Thought.* Oxford: Oxford University Press, 2008.

Campbell, Gordon, et al. *Milton and the Manuscript of De Doctrina Christiana.* Oxford: Oxford University Press, 2007.

Canfield, J. Douglas. "Blessed Are the Merciful: The Understanding of the Promise in *Paradise Lost*." *Milton Quarterly* 7 (1973) 43–46.

Cantimori, Delio. *Umanesimo e Religione nel Rinascimento.* Turin: Einaudi, 1980.

Caponetto, Salvatore. *La Riforma Protestante nell'Italia del Cinquecento.* Turin: Claudiana, 1997.

Carey, John, ed. *Milton: The Complete Shorter Poems.* Harlow, UK: Longman, 2007.

———. "Milton's Satan." In *The Cambridge Companion to Milton*, edited by Dennis Danielson, 160–74. Cambridge: Cambridge University Press, 1989.

Carey, John, and Alastair Fowler, eds. *The Poems of John Milton.* Harlow, UK: Longman, 1968.

Carlton, Susan R. "The Inward Image." *Milton Quarterly* 15 (1981) 88–92.

Champagne, Claudia M. "Adam and His 'Other Self' in *Paradise Lost*: A Lacanian Study in Psychic Development." *Milton Quarterly* 25 (1991) 48–59.

Chaplin, Gregory. "'One Flesh, One Heart, One Soul': Renaissance Friendship and Miltonic Marriage." *Modern Philology* 99 (2001) 266–92.

Chernaik, Warren. "Civil Liberty in Milton, the Levellers, and Winstanley." In *Winstanley and the Diggers, 1649–1999*, edited by Andrew Bradstock, 101–20. London: Frank Cass, 2000.

Christopher, Georgia B. "Milton and the Reforming Spirit." In *The Cambridge Companion to Milton*, edited by Dennis Danielson, 193–201. Cambridge: Cambridge University Press, 1989.

———. *Milton and the Science of the Saints.* Princeton: Princeton University Press, 1982.

Cicero, Fabio, ed. *Paradiso Perduto.* Translated by Roberto Piumini. Milan: Bompiani, 2009.

Coffey, John. *John Goodwin and the Puritan Revolution: Religion and Intellectual Change in Seventeenth-Century England.* Woodbridge, UK: Boydell, 2006.

———. *Persecution and Toleration in Milton's England, 1558–1689.* Harlow, UK: Longman, 2000.

———. "Puritanism and Liberty Revisited: The Case for Toleration in the English Revolution." *The Historical Journal* 41 (1998) 961–85.

Coiro, Ann Baynes. "'To repair the ruins of our first parents': *Of Education* and Adam." *Studies in English Literature* 28 (1988) 133–47.

Colie, R. L. *Light and Enlightenment: A Study of the Cambridge Platonists and Dutch Arminians.* Cambridge: Cambridge University Press, 1957.

Conti, Brooke. "'That Really Too Anxious Protestation': Crisis and Autobiography in Milton's Prose." *Milton Studies* 45 (2006) 187–209.

Corns, Thomas N. "Bunyan, Milton and the Diversity of Radical Protestant Writing." In *Bunyan: Reading Dissenting Writing*, edited by N. H. Keeble, 21–38. Oxford: Lang, 2002.

———. "Bunyan's *Grace Abounding* and the Dynamics of Restoration Nonconformity." In *History, Language, and the Politics of English Renaissance Prose*, edited by Neil Rhodes, 259–70. Tempe: Arizona State University Press, 1997.

———, ed. *A Companion to Milton.* Oxford: Blackwell, 2001.

———, ed. *The Development of Milton's Prose Style.* Oxford: Clarendon, 1982.

———. "John Milton, Roger Williams and the Limits of Toleration." In *Milton and Toleration*, edited by Sharon Achinstein and Elizabeth Sauer, 72–85. Oxford: Oxford University Press, 2007.

———. *John Milton: The Prose Works.* New York: Twayne, 1998.

———. *Milton's Language.* Oxford: Oxford University Press, 1990.

———. *Regaining Paradise Lost.* London: Longman, 1994.

———. *Uncloistered Virtue: English Political Literature, 1640–1660.* Oxford: Clarendon, 1992.

———. "'With Unaltered Brow': Milton and the Son of God." *Milton Studies* 42 (2002) 106–21.

Costello, W. T. *The Scholastic Curriculum of Seventeenth-Century Cambridge.* Cambridge, MA: Harvard University Press, 1958.

Creaser, John. "Prosodic Style and Conceptions of Liberty in Milton and Marvell." *Milton Quarterly* 34 (2000) 1–13.

Cummins, Juliet. "Milton's Gods and the Matter of Creation." *Milton Studies* 40 (2001) 81–105.

———, ed. *Milton and the Ends of Time.* Cambridge: Cambridge University Press, 2003.

Daiches, David. *Milton.* London: Hutchinson, 1971.

Danielson, Dennis, ed. *The Cambridge Companion to Milton.* Cambridge: Cambridge University Press, 1999.

―――. "The Fall and Milton's Theodicy." In *The Cambridge Companion to Milton*, edited by Dennis Danielson, 144–59. Cambridge: Cambridge University Press, 1999.

―――. *Milton's Good God: A Study in Literary Theodicy.* Cambridge: Cambridge University Press, 1982.

―――. "On Toads and the Justice of God." *Milton Quarterly* 13 (1979) 12–14.

―――. "Through the Telescope of Typology: What Adam Should Have Done." *Milton Quarterly* 23 (1989) 121–27.

―――. "Timelessness, Foreknowledge, and Free Will." *Mind* 86 (1977) 430–32.

Darbishire, Helen, ed. *The Poetical Works of John Milton.* 2 vols. Oxford: Clarendon, 1952–55.

Dell, William. *Christ's Spirit, a Christian's Strength.* London, 1651.

Di Benedetto, Vincent P. "Scripture's Constraint and Adam's Self-Authoring Freedom: A Reading of the Self in *Paradise Lost.*" *Milton Quarterly* 25 (1991) 1–14.

Diekhoff, John S. "Eve's Dream and the Paradox of Fallible Perfection." *Milton Quarterly* 4 (1970) 5–7.

―――, ed. *Milton on Himself: Milton's Utterances Upon Himself and His Works.* New York: Humanities, 1939.

Dillon, Steven C. "Milton and the Poetics of Extremism." *Milton Studies* 25 (1989) 265–83.

Diprose, Ronald E. *Israel and the Church: The Origin and Effect of Replacement Theology.* Waynesboro, GA: Authentic, 2000.

Dobbins, Austin C. *Milton and the Book of Revelation: The Heavenly Cycle.* Birmingham: University of Alabama Press, 1975.

Dobranksy, Stephen. "Burghley's Emblem and the Heart of Milton's *Pro Populo Anglicano Defensio.*" *Milton Quarterly* 34 (2007) 33–48.

―――, ed. *Milton in Context.* Cambridge: Cambridge University Press, 2010.

Dobransky, Stephen, and John P. Rumrich, eds. *Milton and Heresy.* Cambridge: Cambridge University Press, 1998.

Doerksen, Daniel W. "'Let There Be Peace': Eve as Redemptive Peacemaker in *Paradise Lost*, Book X." *Milton Quarterly* 31 (1997) 124–30.

―――. "Milton and the Jacobean Church of England." *Early Modern Literary Studies* 1 (1995) 15–23.

Donne, John. *Poesie.* Edited by Alessandro Serpieri and Silvia Bigliazzi. Milan: Rizzoli, 2007.

Donnelly, Phillip J. "'Matter' versus Body: The Character of Milton's Monism." *Milton Quarterly* 33 (1999) 79–85.

―――. *Milton's Scriptural Reasoning: Narrative and Protestant Toleration.* Cambridge: Cambridge University Press, 2009.

―――. "*Paradise Regained* as Rule of Charity: Religious Toleration and the End of Typology." *Milton Studies* 43 (2004) 171–97.

Dowling, Paul. *Polite Wisdom: Heathen Rhetoric in Milton's Aeropagitica.* Lanham, MD: Rowman and Littlefield, 1995.

Du Moulin, Pierre. *The Anatomy of Arminianisme.* London: T. Snodham, 1620.

Duncan, Joseph E. *Milton's Earthly Paradise: A Historical Study of Eden.* Minneapolis: University of Minnesota Press, 1972.

Durham, Charles W. "'To Stand Approv'd in Sight of God': Abdiel, Obedience, and Hierarchy in *Paradise Lost.*" *Milton Quarterly* 26 (1992) 15–20.

Dzelzainis, Martin. "History and Ideology: Milton, the Levellers, and the Council of State in 1649." *Huntington Library Quarterly* 68 (2005) 269–87.

————. "Republicanism." In *A Companion to Milton*, edited by Thomas N. Corns, 294–308. Oxford: Blackwell, 2001.

Earl, James W. "Eve's Narcissism." *Milton Quarterly* 19 (1985) 13–19.

Earle, John. *Micro-cosmography; or, a Peece of the World Discovered*. London, 1628.

Edwards, Thomas. *Gangraena or, A Catalogue and Discovery of Many of the Errours, Heresies, Blasphemies and Pernicious Practices of the Sectaries of this Time*. 3 parts. London, 1646.

Egan, James. "'As His Own Rhetoric Shall Persuade Him': Refutation and Aesthetic Self-Construction in Milton's Antiprelatical Tracts." *Prose Studies* 24 (2001) 41–64.

————. *The Inward Teacher: Milton's Rhetoric of Christian Liberty*. University Park: Pennsylvania State University Press, 1980.

Ellwood, Thomas. *The History of the Life of Thomas Ellwood*. 2nd ed. London: J. Sowle, 1714.

Emerson, Ralph Waldo. *Nature*. In *The Norton Anthology of American Literature*, edited by Hershel Parker, 1:1072–1100. 5th ed. New York: Norton, 1998.

Empson, William. *Milton's God*. London: Chatto and Windus, 1961.

Endy, Melvin B. *William Penn and Early Quakerism*. Princeton: Princeton University Press, 1973.

Episcopius, Simon. *Apologia per Confessione*. Paris, 1629.

————. *Confessio declaratio sententiae pastorum gui in foederato Beiglo Remonstrantes vocantur super praecipuis artscuf is religionis Christianae*. Paris, 1621.

————. *The Confession or Declaration of the Ministers or Pastors Which in the United Provinces Are Called Remonstrants, Concerning the Chief Points of Christian Religion*. London, 1676.

————. *Opera Theologica*. 2 vols. London, 1678.

Erastus, Thomas. *The Nullity of Church-Censures*. London: G. L., 1659.

Ericson, Edward E., Jr. "The Sons of God in *Paradise Lost* and *Paradise Regained*." *Milton Quarterly* 25 (1991) 79–89.

Erickson, Lee. "Satan's Apostles and the Nature of Faith in *Paradise Lost* Book I." *Studies in Philology* 94 (1997) 382–94.

Erskine, Thomas. *Letters*. Edinburgh: Douglas, 1977.

Escobedo, Andrew. "Milton and the Ends of Time." *Milton Quarterly* 39 (2005) 159–62.

Evans, Helen Ward. "Milton on Liberty of Conscience." PhD diss., Stanford University, 1965.

Evans, J. Martin. "The Birth of the Author: Milton's Poetic Self-Construction." *Milton Studies* 38 (2000) 47–65.

Falcone, Filippo. "More Challenges to Milton's Authorship of *De Doctrina Christiana*." *ACME* 63 (2010) 231–50.

Fallon, Stephen M. "Elect Above the Rest: Theology as Self-Representation in Milton." In *Milton and Heresy*, edited by Stephen Dobransky and John P. Rumrich, 93–116. Cambridge: Cambridge University Press, 1998.

————. *Milton Among the Philosophers*. Ithaca: Cornell University Press, 2006.

————. "Milton's Arminianism and the Authorship of *De Doctrina Christiana*." *Texas Studies in Literature and Language* 41 (1999) 103–27.

————. *Milton's Peculiar Grace: Self-Representation and Authority*. Ithaca: Cornell University Press, 2007.

————. "*Paradise Lost* in Intellectual History." In *A Companion to Milton*, edited by Thomas N. Corns, 329–47. Oxford: Blackwell, 2001.

———. "The Spur of Self-Concernment: Milton in His Divorce Tracts." *Milton Studies* 38 (2000) 220–42.

———. "The Uses of 'Seems' and the Spectre of Predestination." *Milton Quarterly* 21 (1987) 99–101.

———. "'To Act or Not': Milton's Conception of Divine Freedom." *Journal of the History of Ideas* 49 (1988) 425–49.

Ferry, Anne. "Milton's Creation of Eve." *Studies in English Literature* 28 (1988) 113–32.

Festa, Thomas. "Repairing the Ruins: Milton as Reader and Educator." *Milton Studies* 43 (2004) 35–63.

Fiore, Peter A. "Freedom, Liability and the State of Perfection in *Paradise Lost*." *Milton Quarterly* 5 (1971) 47–51.

———. *Milton and Augustine: Patterns of Augustinian Thought in Milton and Augustine.* University Park: Pennsylvania State University Press, 1990.

Fish, Stanley. "Reason in *The Reason of Church Government*." In *Self-Consuming Artifacts: The Experience of Seventeenth Century Literature*, edited by Stanley Fish, 265–302. Berkeley: University of California Press, 1972.

———, ed. *Seventeenth-Century Prose: Modern Essays in Criticism.* Oxford: Oxford University Press, 1971.

———. *Surprised by Sin: The Reader in* Paradise Lost. Cambridge, MA: Harvard University Press, 1998.

Flannagan, Roy, ed. *The Riverside Milton.* Boston: Wadsworth, 1998.

Fletcher, Harris F. *The Use of the Bible in Milton's Prose.* Urbana: University of Illinois Press, 1929.

Forey, Margaret. "Milton's Satan: Wisdom Reversed." *Essays in Criticism* 46 (1996) 302–18.

Forsyth, Neil. "At the Sign of the Dove and Serpent." *Milton Quarterly* 34 (2000) 57–65.

———. "The Fall and Poole's *Idea of the Fall*: A Review Article." *Milton Quarterly* 40 (2006) 48–59.

———. *The Old Enemy: Satan and the Combat Myth.* Princeton: Princeton University Press, 1987.

———. "Rebellion in *Paradise Lost*: Impossible Original." *Milton Quarterly* 30 (1996) 151–62.

———. *The Satanic Epic.* Princeton: Princeton University Press, 2003.

Fox, George. *A Journal of the Life, Travels, Sufferings, Christian Experiences, and Labour of Love, of George Fox.* Edited by Thomas Ellwood. 7th ed. London, 1803.

———. *The Journal.* Edited by Nigel Smith. Harmondsworth, UK: Penguin, 1998.

French, J. Milton. *The Life Records of John Milton.* New Brunswick: Rutgers University Press, 1949–58.

Fresch, Cheryl H. "Milton's Eve and the Problem of the Additions to the Command." *Milton Quarterly* 12 (1978) 83–90.

Fried, Daniel. "Milton and Empiricist Semiotics." *Milton Quarterly* 37 (2003) 117–38.

Frye, Northrop. *The Return of Eden: Five Essays on Milton's Epics.* Toronto: University of Toronto Press, 1965.

Frye, Roland Mushat. "The Dissidence of Dissent and the Origins of Religious Freedom in America: John Milton and the Puritans." Reprint from *Proceedings of the American Philosophical Society* 133/4 (1989).

Gabrieli, Vittorio, ed. *John Milton: Selected Prose.* Bari: Adriatica, 1970.

Gallagher, Philip J. *Milton, the Bible, and Misogyny.* Columbia: University of Missouri Press, 1990.

Garrett, James L. *Baptist Theology: A Four-Century Study.* Macon, GA: Mercer University Press, 2009.

Gay, David. *The Endless Kingdom: Milton's Scriptural Society.* Newark: University of Delaware Press, 2002.

Geisst, Charles R. *The Political Thought of John Milton.* London: Macmillan, 1984.

Gertz-Robinson, Genelle. "Still Martyred after All These Years: Generational Suffering in Milton's *Areopagitica*." *English Literary History* 70 (2003) 963–87.

Giacomantonio, Flavio, ed. and trans. *Il Paradiso Perduto.* Pisa: Serra, 2009.

Gilman, Wilbur E. *Milton's Rhetoric: Studies in His Defense of Liberty.* Columbia: University of Missouri Press, 1939.

Gilson, Étienne. *The Philosophy of St. Thomas Aquinas.* Translated by G. A. Elrington. New York: Arno, 1979.

Giltin, Kevin. "History and Reform in Milton's *Readie and Easie Way*." *Milton Studies* 24 (1988) 17–41.

Goodfellow, William S. "Adam's Encounter with God in *Paradise Lost*." *Milton Quarterly* 7 (1973) 103–7.

Goodman, Ellen. "Human Mastership of Nature: Aquinas and Milton's *Paradise Lost*." *Milton Quarterly* 26 (1992) 9–15.

Goodwin, John. *The Agreement and Distance of Brethren.* London: J. Macock, 1652.

———. *The Banner of Justification Displayed.* London: J. Macock, 1659.

———. *Confidence Dismounted.* London: J. Macock, 1651.

———. *An Exposition of the Nineth Chapter of the Epistle to the Romans.* London: J. Macock, 1653.

———. *Redemption Redeemed.* London: J. Macock, 1651.

———. *The Remedie of Unreasonableness.* London: J. Macock, 1650.

Gray, J. C. "Paradox in *Paradise Lost*." *Milton Quarterly* 7 (1973) 76–82.

Gregerson, Linda. *The Reformation of the Subject: Spenser, Milton and the English Protestant Epic.* Cambridge: Cambridge University Press, 1995.

Grose, Christopher. *Milton and the Sense of Tradition.* New Haven: Yale University Press, 1988.

Grossman, Marshall. "The Genders of God and the Redemption of the Flesh in *Paradise Lost*." In *Milton and Gender*, edited by Catherine Gimelli Martin, 95–114. Cambridge: Cambridge University Press, 2004.

———. "Milton's Dialectical Visions." *Modern Philology* 82 (1984) 23–39.

———. "Subsequent Precedence: Milton's Materialistic Reading of Ficino and Tasso." *Surfaces* 6 (1996) 1–25.

Grotius, Hugo. *De satisfactione Christi adversus Faustum Socinum.* Leiden: I. Patius, 1617.

———. *De veritate religionis Christianae.* Paris, 1627.

———. *Opera Omnia Theologica.* 3 vols. N.p., 1679.

Gulden, Ann Torday. "Milton's Eve and Wisdom: The 'Dinner-Party' Scene in *Paradise Lost*." *Milton Quarterly* 32 (1998) 137–43.

Guss, Donald L. "Enlightenment as Process: Milton and Habermas." *Modern Language Association of America* 106 (1991) 156–69.

Hale, John K. "Neo-Latin Polemic in the 1650s: Milton versus Salmasius and Others." *Classical and Modern Literature* 21 (2001) 1–23.

———. "The Problems and Opportunities of Editing *De Doctrina Christiana*." *Milton Quarterly* 44 (2010) 38–46.

———. "The 1668 Argument to *Paradise Lost*." *Milton Quarterly* 35 (2001) 87–97.

Hale, John K., et al. "The Provenance of *De Doctrina Christiana*." *Milton Quarterly* 31 (1997) 67–117.

Halewood, William H. *The Poetry of Grace: Reformation Themes and Structures in English Seventeenth-Century Poetry*. New Haven: Yale University Press, 1970.

Halkett, John. *Milton and the Idea of Matrimony: A Study of the Divorce Tracts and Paradise Lost*. New Haven: Yale University Press, 1970.

Haller, W. *Liberty and Reformation in the Puritan Revolution*. New York: Columbia University Press, 1963.

———. *The Rise of Puritanism, or the Way to the New Jerusalem as Set Forth in Pulpit and Press from Thomas Cartwright to John Lillburne and John Milton, 1570–1643*. Philadelphia: University of Pennsylvania Press, 1972.

Hamlet, Desmond. *One Greater Man: Justice and Damnation in* Paradise Lost. Lewisburg: Bucknell University Press, 1976.

Hardin, Richard F. "Milton's Nimrod." *Milton Quarterly* 22 (1988) 38–44.

Hart, D. Bentley. "Matter, Monism, and Narrative: An Essay on the Metaphysics of *Paradise Lost*." *Milton Quarterly* 30 (1996) 16–27.

Hawkes, David. "The Politics of Character in Milton's Divorce Tracts." *Journal of the History of Ideas* 62 (2001) 141–60.

Healy, T., and J. Sawday, eds. *Literature and the English Civil War*. Cambridge: Cambridge University Press, 1990.

Helms, Randel. "'His Dearest Mediation': The Dialogue in Heaven in Book III of *Paradise Lost*." *Milton Quarterly* 5 (1971) 52–57.

Henderson, Katherine U. *Half Humankind: Contexts and Texts of the Controversy about Women in England, 1540–1640*. Urbana: University of Illinois Press, 1985.

Henry, Nathaniel H. "Milton and Hobbes: Mortalism and the Intermediate State." *Studies in Philology* 48 (1951) 234–49.

———. *The True Wayfaring Christian: Studies in Milton's Puritanism*. New York: Lang, 1987.

Herman, Peter C. "'Warring Chains of Signifiers': Metaphoric Ambivalence and the Politics of *Paradise Lost*." *Texas Studies in Literature and Language* 40 (1998) 268–92.

Hill, Christopher. *Antichrist in Seventeenth-Century England*. Oxford: Oxford University Press, 1971.

———. *The Experience of Defeat: Milton and Some Contemporaries*. New York: Penguin, 1984.

———. *Intellectual Origins of the English Revolution*. Oxford: Clarendon, 1965.

———. *Milton and the English Revolution*. London: Faber, 1977.

———. "Milton, Bunyan and the Literature of Defeat." *Mosaic* 24 (1991) 1–12.

———. *A Nation of Change and Novelty: Radical Politics, Religion and Literature in Seventeenth-Century England*. New York: Routledge, 1990.

———. "Professor William B. Hunter, Bishop Burgess, and John Milton." *Studies in English Literature* 34 (1994) 165–88.

———. *Puritanism and Revolution*. London: Secker and Warburg, 1958.

———. *The World Turned Upside Down*. Harmondsworth, UK: Penguin, 1975.

Hill, John Spencer. *John Milton, Poet, Priest and Prophet: A Study of Divine Vocation in Milton's Poetry and Prose*. London: Macmillan, 1979.

Hillier, Russell M. "'By Force or Fraud / Weening to Prosper': Milton's Satanic and Messianic Modes of Heroism." *Milton Quarterly* 43 (2009) 17–38.

Hiltner, Ken. "Place, Body and Spirit Joined: The Earth-Human Wound in *Paradise Lost.*" *Milton Quarterly* 35 (2001) 113–17.

Hobbes, Thomas. *The English Works.* 11 vols. Edited by William Molesworth. London: Bohn, 1839–45.

———. *Leviathan* (1651). Edited by C. B. MacPherson. Harmondsworth, UK: Penguin, 1968.

———. *Of Liberty and Necessity* (1645). Translated and edited by Arrigo Pacchi. *Logica, Libertà e Necessità.* Milan: Principato, 1972.

Hobson, Theo. *Milton's Vision: The Birth of Christian Liberty.* London: Continuum, 2008.

Hoffman, Nancy Y. "The Hard-Hearted Hell of Self-Delusion." *Milton Quarterly* 7 (1973) 11–14.

Holmes, Michael, ed. *The Apostolic Fathers.* Translated by J. B. Lightfoot and J. R. Harmer. 2nd ed. Grand Rapids: Baker, 1989.

Honeygoskey, Stephen R. *Milton's House of God: The Invisible and Visible Church.* Columbia: University of Missouri Press, 1993.

Hooker, Richard. *Of the Laws of Ecclesiastical Polity.* Edited by W. Speed Hill. Binghamton, NY: Medieval and Renaissance Texts and Studies, 1993.

Hooker, Thomas. *The Soules Humiliation.* London: J. Legat for Andrew Crooke, 1638.

Hopf, C. *Martin Bucer and the English Reformation.* Oxford: Oxford University Press, 1946.

Hoxby, Blair. "The Trade of Truth Advanced: *Areopagitica,* Economic Discourse, and Libertarian Reform." *Milton Studies* 36 (1998) 177–202.

Hughes, Merritt Y. "Milton and the Symbol of Light." In *Ten Perspectives on Milton,* edited by Merritt Y. Hughes, 63–103. New Haven: Yale University Press, 1965.

Huguelet, Theodore L. "The Rule of Charity in Milton's Divorce Tracts." *Milton Studies* 6 (1975) 199–214.

Hunter, William B. "Animadversions upon the Remonstrants' Defenses against Burgess and Hunter." *Studies in English Literature* 34 (1994) 195–203.

———. "*De Doctrina Christiana*: Nunc Quo Vadis?" *Milton Quarterly* 34 (2000) 97–101.

———. "The Provenance of the *Christian Doctrine.*" *Studies in English Literature* 32 (1992) 129–42.

———. "The Provenance of the *Christian Doctrine*: Addenda from the Bishop of Salisbury." *Studies in English Literature* 33 (1993) 191–207.

———. "Responses." *Milton Quarterly* 33 (1999) 31–37.

———. *Visitation Unimplor'd: Milton and the Authorship of De Doctrina Christiana.* Pittsburgh: Duquesne University Press, 1998.

Hunter William B., and Stevie Davis. "Milton's Urania: 'The Meaning, Not the Name I Call.'" *Studies in English Literature* 28 (1988) 95–111.

Hunter, William B., Barbara Lewalski, and John T. Shawcross. "The Provenance of the Christian Doctrine." *Studies in English Literature* 32 (1992) 129–66.

Hunter, William B., C. A. Patrides, and J. H. Adamson, eds. *Bright Essence: Studies in Milton's Theology.* Salt Lake City: University of Utah Press, 1971.

Hutton, Ronald. *The Restoration: A Political and Religious History of England and Wales, 1658–1667.* Oxford: Clarendon, 1993.

Hutton, Sarah. "Mede, Milton, and More." In *Milton and the Ends of Time,* edited by Juliet Cummins, 29–41. Cambridge: Cambridge University Press, 2003.

Hutton, Sarah, and Anna Baldwin, eds. *Platonism and the English Imagination.* Cambridge: Cambridge University Press, 1994.

Hyman, Lawrence W. "The Ambiguity of *Paradise Lost* and Contemporary Critical Theory." *Milton Quarterly* 13 (1979) 1–6.

Iannaccaro, Giuliana. *Ombre e Sostanza: La Figura e la Lettera nella Scrittura Radicale e nella Rivoluzione Inglese*. Milan: Unicopli, 2003.

Ide, Richard S. "Adam's Hyacinthine Locks." *Milton Quarterly* 19 (1985) 80–82.

Illo, John. "*Areopagitica*'s Mythic and Real." *Prose Studies* 11 (1988) 3–23.

Interdonato, Deborah A. "'Render Me More Equal': Gender Inequality and the Fall in *Paradise Lost*." *Milton Quarterly* 29 (1995) 95–106.

Jablonski, Steven. "Ham's Vicious Race: Slavery and John Milton." *Studies in English Literature* 37 (1997) 173–90.

Johnson, Samuel. *The Lives of the Poets*. Edited by Roger Lonsdale. Oxford: Oxford University Press, 2006.

Jones, Edward. "'Church-Outed by the Prelats': Milton and the 1637 Inspection of the Horton Parish Church." *Journal of English and Germanic Philology* 102 (2003) 42–58.

———. "'Ere Half My Days': Milton's Life, 1608–1640." In *The Oxford Handbook of Milton*, edited by Nicholas McDowell and Nigel Smith, 3–25. Oxford: Oxford University Press, 2009.

Juhnke, Anna K. "Remnants of Misogyny in *Paradise Lost*." *Milton Quarterly* 22 (1988) 50–58.

Kastor, Frank S. *Milton and the Literary Satan*. Amsterdam: Rodopi, 1974.

Kaufmann, U. Milo. *Paradise in the Age of Milton*. Victoria: University of Victoria Press, 1978.

Keeble, N. H. *The Literary Culture of Nonconformity in Later Seventeenth-Century England*. Athens: University of Georgia Press, 1987.

———. "Milton and Puritanism." In *A Companion to Milton*, edited by Thomas N. Corns, 124–40. Oxford: Blackwell, 2001.

Kelley, Maurice. "Milton's Debt to Wolleb's *Compendium Theologiae Christianae*." *Modern Language Association of America* 50 (1935) 156–65.

———. "The Provenance of John Milton's *Christian Doctrine*: A Reply to William B. Hunter." *Studies in English Literature* 34 (1994) 153–63.

———. *This Great Argument: A Study of Milton's De Doctrina Christiana as a Gloss upon Paradise Lost*. Princeton: Princeton University Press, 1941.

Kendrick, Christopher. *Milton: A Study in Ideology and Form*. New York: Methuen, 1986.

Kerrigan, William. *The Prophetic Milton*. Charlottesville: University Press of Virginia, 1974.

Kerrigan, William, John P. Rumrich, and Stephen M. Fallon, eds. *Paradise Lost*. New York: Random House, 2007.

Kilgour, Maggie. "Eve and Flora (*Paradise Lost* 5.15–16)." *Milton Quarterly* 38 (2004) 1–17.

King, John N. *Milton and Religious Controversy: Satire and Polemic in* Paradise Lost. Cambridge: Cambridge University Press, 2000.

———. "Milton and the Bishops: Ecclesiastical Controversy and the Early Poems." In *Centered on the Word: Literature, Scripture, and the Tudor-Stuart Middle Way*, edited by Daniel W. Doerksen and Christopher Hodgkins, 277–97. Newark: University of Delaware Press, 2004.

———. "Miltonic Transubstantiation." *Milton Studies* 36 (1998) 41–58.

Kirby, R. Kenneth. "Milton's Biblical Hermeneutics in *The Doctrine and Discipline of Divorce*." *Milton Quarterly* 18 (1984) 116–25.

Klemp, Paul J. "Gallagher's *Milton, the Bible and Misogyny*—and Bauman." *Milton Quarterly* 25 (1991) 149–51.

Knight, Wilson G. *Chariot of Wrath: The Message of John Milton to Democracy at War.* London: Faber, 1942.

Knoppers, Laura Lunger. *Historicizing Milton: Spectacle, Power, and Poetry in Restoration England.* Athens: University of Georgia Press, 1994.

———. "Rewriting the Protestant Ethic: Discipline and Love in *Paradise Lost.*" *English Literary History* 58 (1991) 545–59.

Knott, John R. *Milton's Pastoral Vision: An Approach to* Paradise Lost. Chicago: University of Chicago Press, 1971.

Kolbrener, William. "'Plainly Partial': The Liberal *Areopagitica.*" *English Literary History* 60 (1993) 57–78.

Kranidas, Thomas. "Milton's *Of Reformation*: The Politics of Vision." *English Literary History* 49 (1982) 497–513.

———. "Polarity and Structure in Milton's Areopagitica." *English Literary Renaissance* 14 (1984) 174–90.

———. "Style and Rectitude in Seventeenth-Century Prose: Hall, Smectynmuus, and Milton." *Huntington Library Quarterly* 46 (1983) 237–69.

———. "Words, Words, Words, and the Word: Milton's *Of Prelaticall Episcopacy.*" *Milton Studies* 16 (1982) 153–66.

Labriola, Albert C. "Chaos and Creation in Milton Studies: An Editor's Perspective." *Milton Quarterly* 32 (1998) 53–56.

Laud, William. *Works.* 7 vols. Oxford, 1847.

Lawson, Anita. "'The Golden Sun in Splendor Likest Heaven': Johannes Kepler's *Epitome* and *Paradise Lost*, Book 3." *Milton Quarterly* 21 (1987) 46–51.

Lee, Byung-Eun. "Milton and Arianism Reconsidered." *Medieval and Early Modern English Studies* 12 (2004) 211–24.

Lehnhof, Kent R. "'Impregn'd with Reason': Eve's Aural Conception in *Paradise Lost.*" *Milton Studies* 41 (2002) 38–75.

———. "'Nor turnd I weene': *Paradise Lost* and Prelapsarian Sexuality." *Milton Quarterly* 34 (2000) 67–83.

Leigh, Edward. *A System or Body of Divinity.* London: A. M. for William Lee, 1662.

Leonard, John. *Naming in Paradise: Milton and the Language of Adam and Eve.* Oxford: Clarendon, 1990.

———. "'Once Fawn'd and Cring'd': A Song and Dance about Satan's Servility." *Milton Quarterly* 19 (1985) 101–5.

Lewalski, Barbara K. *The Life of John Milton.* Oxford: Blackwell, 2000.

———. "Milton and *De Doctrina Christiana*: Evidences of Authorship." *Milton Studies* 36 (1998) 203–28.

———. "Milton and Idolatry." *Studies in English Literature* 43 (2003) 213–32.

———. "Milton and the Millennium." In *Milton and the Ends of Time*, edited by Juliet Cummins, 13–28. Cambridge: Cambridge University Press, 2003.

———. "Milton's *Christian Doctrine.*" *Studies in English Literature* 32 (1992) 143–54.

———. "*Paradise Lost* and Milton's Politics." *Milton Studies* 38 (2000) 141–68.

———. "*Paradise Lost* and Milton's Politics." In *John Milton: Twentieth-Century Perspectives, Vol. 4: Paradise Lost*, edited by J. Martin Evans, 213–40. New York: Routledge, 2003.

———. *Protestant Poetics and the Seventeenth-Century Religious Lyric.* Princeton: Princeton University Press, 1979.

Lewis, C. S. *The Literary Influence of the Authorized Version*. Philadelphia: Fortress, 1967.

————. *A Preface to* Paradise Lost. Oxford: Oxford University Press, 1942.

Lieb, Michael. "The Book of M: *Paradise Lost* as Revisionary Text." *Cithara: Essays in the Judaeo-Christian Tradition* 31 (1991) 28–35.

————. "Further Thoughts on Milton's Journey through Chaos." *Milton Quarterly* 12 (1978) 126–33.

————. "Milton and Arianism." *Religion and Literature* 32 (2000) 197–220.

————. *Milton and the Culture of Violence*. Ithaca: Cornell University Press, 1994.

————. "Milton's 'Dramatick Constitution': The Celestial Dialogue in *Paradise Lost*, Book III." *Milton Studies* 23 (1987) 215–40.

————. "*Paradise Lost* and the Myth of Prohibition." *Milton Studies* 8 (1975) 233–67.

————. *Poetics of the Holy: A Reading of* Paradise Lost. Chapel Hill: University of North Carolina Press, 1981.

————. "Reading God: Milton and the Anthropopathetic Tradition." *Milton Studies* 25 (1989) 213–43.

————. "'A Thousand Foreskins': Circumcision, Violence, and Selfhood in Milton." *Milton Studies* 38 (2000) 198–219.

Lieb, Michael, and J. T. Shawcross, eds. *Achievements of the Left Hand: Essays on the Prose of John Milton*. Amherst: University of Massachusetts Press, 1974.

Liebert, Elisabeth. "Rendering 'More Equal': Eve's Changing Discourse in *Paradise Lost*." *Milton Quarterly* 37 (2003) 152–65.

Lifson, Martha. "Creation and the Self in *Paradise Lost* and the Confessions." *The Centennial Review* 19 (1975) 187–97.

Lightfoot, J. B. *St. Paul's Epistle to the Philippians*. London: Macmillan, 1913.

Lim, Walter S. H. "Adam, Eve, and Biblical Analogy in *Paradise Lost*." *Studies in English Literature* 30 (1990) 115–31.

Lindenbaum, Peter. "John Milton and the Republican Mode of Literary Production." *Yearbook of English Studies* 21 (1991) 121–36.

————. "Lovemaking in Milton's Paradise." *Milton Studies* 6 (1974) 277–306.

Loewenstein, David. "'An Ambiguous Monster': Representing Rebellion in Milton's Polemics and *Paradise Lost*." *Huntington Library Quarterly* 55 (1992) 295–315.

————. "*Areopagitica* and the Dynamics of History." *Studies in English Literature* 28 (1988) 77–93.

————. "'Casting Down Imaginations': Milton as Iconoclast." *Criticism: A Quarterly for Literature and the Arts* 31 (1989) 253–70.

————. "Milton Among the Religious Radicals and Sects: Polemical Engagements and Silences." *Milton Studies* 40 (2002) 222–46.

————. *Milton and the Drama of History: Historical Vision, Iconoclasm, and the Literary Imagination*. Cambridge: Cambridge University Press, 1990.

————. *Milton: Paradise Lost*. Cambridge: Cambridge University Press, 1993.

————. *Representing Revolution in Milton and His Contemporaries: Religion, Politics, and Polemics in Radical Puritanism*. Cambridge: Cambridge University Press, 2001.

————. "Toleration and the Specter of Heresy in Milton's England." In *Milton and Toleration*, edited by Sharon Achinstein and Elizabeth Sauer, 45–71. Oxford: Oxford University Press, 2007.

Long, Mary Beth. "Contextualizing Eve's and Milton's Solitudes in Book 9 of *Paradise Lost*." *Milton Quarterly* 37 (2003) 100–115.

Lovejoy, Arthur O. "Milton and the Paradox of the Fortunate Fall." *English Literary History* 4 (1937) 161–79.

Low, Anthony. "Siloa's Brook: *Paradise Lost* I, II." *Milton Quarterly* 5 (1971) 3–5.

Lumpkin, William L. *Baptist Confessions of Faith*. Valley Forge, PA: Judson, 1959.

Luther, Martin. *The Complete Sermons of Martin Luther*. Edited by Eugene Klug. 7 vols. Grand Rapids: Baker, 2000.

———. "Luther's House Postils." In *The Complete Sermons of Martin Luther*, edited by Eugene Klug. Vol. 5. Grand Rapids: Baker, 2000.

———. *Luther's Works*. Edited by Jaroslav Pelikan and Helmut T. Lehmann. 55 vols. Philadelphia: Fortress, 1955–76.

———. *Tractatus de libertate Christiana*. In *Martin Luthers Werke: Kritische Gesamtausgabe*. 66 vols. Weimar: Herman Böhlaus, 1883–97.

———. *A Treatise on Christian Liberty*. In *The Works of Martin Luther*, translated by W. A. Lambert, 2:312–48. Philadelphia: Fortress, 1915.

Luxon, Thomas H. *Literal Figures: Puritan Allegory and the Reformation Crisis in Representation*. Chicago: University of Chicago Press, 1995.

———. "Milton's Wedded Love: Not about Sex (As We Know It)." *Milton Studies* 40 (2001) 38–60.

———. "Rough Trade: Milton as Ajax in 'The Place of Punishment.'" *Prose Studies: Literature, History, Theory* 19 (1996) 282–91.

———. *Single Imperfection: Milton, Marriage and Friendship*. Pittsburgh: Duquesne University Press, 2005.

MacCallum, Hugh. *Milton and the Sons of God: The Divine Image in Milton's Epic Poetry*. Toronto: University of Toronto Press, 1986.

Machacek, Gregory. "Of Man's First Disobedience." *Milton Quarterly* 24 (1990) 111–12.

Madsen, William G. *From Shadowy Types to Truth: Studies in Milton's Symbolism*. New Haven: Yale University Press, 1968.

Major, John M. "Eve's 'Experience.'" *Milton Quarterly* 4 (1970) 39–40.

Mannucci, Loretta. *Ideali e Classi nella Poesia di Milton*. Milan: Edizioni di Comunità, 1976.

Marilla, Esmond L. *The Central Problem of* Paradise Lost: *The Fall of Man*. Cambridge, MA: Harvard University Press, 1953.

Marshall, I. Howard. *A Concise New Testament Theology*. Downers Grove, IL: InterVarsity, 2008.

Martin, Catherine Gimelli. "'Boundless the Deep': Milton, Pascal, and the Theology of Relative Space." *English Literary History* 63 (1996) 45–78.

———. "Demystifying Disguises: Adam, Eve, and the Subject of Desire." In *Renaissance Discourses of Desire*, edited by Claude J. Summers and Ted-Larry Pebworth, 237–58. Columbia: University of Missouri Press, 1993.

———. "Fire, Ice, and Epic Entropy: The Physics and Metaphysics of Milton's Reformed Chaos." *Milton Studies* 35 (1997) 73–113.

———. *Milton Among the Puritans: The Case for Historical Revisionism*. Farnham, UK: Ashgate, 2010.

———, ed. *Milton and Gender*. Cambridge: Cambridge University Press, 2004.

———. "The Sources of Milton's Sin Reconsidered." *Milton Quarterly* 35 (2001) 1–8.

Martin, Roberta C. "'Thy Heart's Desire': God-the-Father and the Feminine Ideal in Milton's Perfect World." *English Language Notes* 33 (1996) 43–52.

Martin, Thomas L. "On the Margin of God: Deconstruction and the Language of Satan in *Paradise Lost*." *Milton Quarterly* 29 (1995) 41–47.

Martz, Louis L. *The Paradise Within: Studies in Vaughan, Traherne, and Milton*. New Haven: Yale University Press, 1964.

Marx, Steven. "The Prophet Disarmed: Milton and the Quakers." *Studies in English Literature* 32 (1992) 111–28.

Mascetti, Yaakov. "Satan and the 'Incompos'd' Visage of Chaos: Milton's Hermeneutic Indeterminacy." *Milton Studies* 50 (2009) 35–63.

Matar, N. I. "Milton and the Idea of the Restoration of the Jews." *Studies in English Literature* 27 (1987) 109–24.

Mattison, Andrew. "'Thine Own Inventions': The Environs of Imagination in *Paradise Lost* 7 and 8." *Milton Quarterly* 39 (2005) 23–44.

McBride, Kari, and John C. Ulreich. "Answerable Styles: Biblical Poetics and Biblical Politics in the Poetry of Lanyer and Milton." *Journal of English and Germanic Philology* 100 (2001) 333–54.

McClain, Alva J. *The Greatness of the Kingdom.* Chicago: Moody, 1959.

McColgan, Kristin Pruitt. "'The Master Work': Creation and Education in *Paradise Lost*." *Milton Quarterly* 26 (1992) 29–36.

McColgan, Kristin Pruitt, and Charles W. Durham, eds. *Arenas of Conflict: Milton and the Unfettered Mind.* Selinsgrove, PA: Susquehanna University Press, 1997.

McColley, Diane K. *Milton's Eve.* Urbana: University of Illinois Press, 1983.

———. "Subsequent or Precedent? Eve as Milton's Defense of Poesie." *Milton Quarterly* 20 (1986) 132–36.

McCready, Amy R. "Milton's Casuistry: The Case of *The Doctrine and Discipline of Divorce*." *Journal of Medieval and Renaissance Studies* 22 (1992) 393–428.

McDowell, Nicholas, and Nigel Smith, eds. *The Oxford Handbook of Milton.* Oxford: Oxford University Press, 2009.

McLaughlin, Elizabeth T. "Milton and Thomas Ellwood." *Milton Quarterly* 1 (1967) 17–28.

McQueen, William A. "'The Hateful Siege of Contraries': Satan's Interior Monologues in *Paradise Lost*." *Milton Quarterly* 4 (1970) 60–65.

Mede, Joseph. *Clavis Apocalyptica.* Cambridge: T. and J. Buck, 1627.

Metaxas, Eric. *Bonhoeffer: Pastor, Martyr, Prophet, Spy.* Nashville: Nelson, 2010.

Michals, Teresa. "'Sweet Gardening Labour': Merit and Hierarchy in *Paradise Lost*." *Exemplaria* 7 (1995) 499–514.

Mikics, David. "Miltonic Marriage and the Challenge to History in *Paradise Lost*." *Texas Studies in Literature and Language* 46 (2004) 20–48.

Miller, Anthony. "'Scotus or Aquinas'—and Horace." *Milton Quarterly* 22 (1988) 1–3.

Miller, Leo. "'Siloa's Brook' in *Paradise Lost*: Another View." *Milton Quarterly* 5 (1971) 5–7.

Milner, Andrew. *John Milton and the English Revolution.* London: Macmillan, 1981.

Milton, John. *Paradise Lost.* Edited by Gordon Teskey. New York: Norton, 2005.

Mitchell, J. Allan. "Reading God Reading 'Man': Hereditary Sin and the Narrativization of Deity in *Paradise Lost*, Book 3." *Milton Quarterly* 35 (2001) 72–86.

Mollenkott, Virginia R. "Milton's Rejection of the Fortunate Fall." *Milton Quarterly* 6 (1972) 1–5.

Moore, Jeanie Grant. "The Two Faces of Eve: Temptation Scenes in *Comus* and *Paradise Lost*." *Milton Quarterly* 36 (2002) 1–19.

More, Henry. *An Antidote against Atheism, or An Appeal to the Naturall Faculties of the Minde of Man, Whether There Be Not a God.* Cambridge: J. Flesher, 1653.

———. *Divine Dialogues: Containing Sundry Disquisitions and Instructions Concerning the Attributes and Providence of God.* London: J. Flesher, 1668.

———. *An Explanation of the Grand Mystery of Godliness; or a True and Faithful Representation of the Everlasting Gospel of our Lord and Saviour Jesus Christ.* London: J. Flesher, 1660.

———. *The Immortality of the Soul, so farre forth as it is demonstrable from the Knowledge of Nature and the Light of Reason,* London: J. Flesher, 1659.

Muller, Richard A. *Post-Reformation Reformed Dogmatics: The Rise and Development of Reformed Orthodoxy, ca. 1520–ca. 1725.* 2nd ed. 4 vols. Grand Rapids: Baker, 2003.

———. "The Priority of Jacob Arminius." *Westminster Theological Seminary* 55 (1993) 55–72.

———. "The Problem of Protestant Scholasticism: A Review and Definition." In *Reformation and Scholasticism: An Ecumenical Enterprise,* edited by Willem J. van Asselt and Eef Dekker, 45–64. Grand Rapids: Baker, 2001.

Mulryan, John. "Satan's Headache: The Perils and Pains of Giving Birth to a Bad Idea." *Milton Quarterly* 39 (2005) 16–22.

Murphy, Erin. "Milton's 'Birth Abortive': Remaking Family at the End of *Paradise Lost.*" *Milton Studies* 43 (2004) 145–70.

Musacchio, George. *Milton's Adam and Eve: Fallible Perfection.* New York: Lang, 1991.

Myers, Benjamin. *Milton's Theology of Freedom.* Berlin: de Gruyter, 2006.

———. "Prevenient Grace and Conversion in *Paradise Lost.*" *Milton Quarterly* 40 (2006) 20–36.

Myers, William. *Milton and Free Will: An Essay in Criticism and Philosophy.* London: Croom Helm, 1987.

Nayler, James. *A Collection of Sundry Books, Epistles and Papers.* London: J. Sowle, 1716.

Nelson, Eric. "'True Liberty': Isocrates and Milton's *Aeropagitica.*" *Milton Studies* 40 (2001) 201–21.

Nestle Eberhard, et al., eds. *Novum Testamentum Graece.* Stuttgart: Deutsche Bibelgesellschaft, 1979.

Nichols, Jennifer L. "Milton's Claim for Self and Freedom in the Divorce Tracts." *Milton Studies* 49 (2009) 192–211.

Nicole, Roger. *Moyse Amyraut: A Bibliography with Special Reference to the Controversy on Universal Grace.* New York: Garland, 1981.

Norbrook, David. *Writing the English Republic: Poetry, Rhetoric, and Politics, 1627–1660.* Cambridge: Cambridge University Press, 1999.

Norton, Mary F. "The Praxis of Milton's Truth: *Proairesis* and Qualifications in the Civil Liberty Tracts." *Milton Quarterly* 28 (1994) 47–56.

Nuttall, Geoffrey. "Milton's Churchmanship in 1659: His Letter to Jean de Labadie." *Milton Quarterly* 35 (2001) 227–31.

Nyquist, Mary. "The Father's Word/Satan's Wrath." *Modern Language Association of America* 100 (1985) 187–202.

Nyquist, Mary, and Margaret W. Ferguson, eds. *Re-Membering Milton: Essays on the Texts and Traditions.* New York: Methuen, 1987.

O'Keeffe, Timothy J. *Milton and the Pauline Tradition: A Study of Theme and Symbolism.* Washington, DC: University Press of America, 1982.

Orgel, Stephen, and Jonathan Goldberg, eds. *John Milton.* The Oxford Authors. Oxford: Oxford University Press, 1991.

Osgood, Charles Grosvenor. *Poetry as a Means of Grace.* Princeton: Princeton University Press, 1941.

Ostriker, Alicia. "Dancing at the Devil's Party: Some Notes on Politics and Poetry." In *Conversant Essays: Contemporary Poets on Poetry*, edited by James McCorkle, 399–413. Detroit: Wayne State University Press, 1990.

Owen, John. *Works*. 6 vols. Philadelphia: Leighton, 1860.

Pacchi, Arrigo. *Cartesio in Inghilterra: Da More a Boyle*. Rome: Laterza, 1973.

———. "Hobbes and the Passions." In *Scritti Hobbesiani (1978–1990)*, edited by Agostino Luppoli, 79–96. Translated by Marialuisa Bignami. Milan: Angeli, 1998.

———. *Il Razionalismo del Seicento*. Turin: Loescher, 1982.

———. "*Leviathan* and Spinoza's *Tractatus* on Revelation: Some Elements for a Comparison." In *Scritti Hobbesiani (1978–1990)*, edited by Agostino Luppoli, 123–44. Translated by Marialuisa Bignami. Milan: Angeli, 1998.

———. *Scritti Hobbesiani (1978–1990)*. Edited by Agostino Luppoli. Translated by Marialuisa Bignami. Milan: Angeli, 1998.

Pagitt, Ephraim. *Heresiography; or, A description of the Hereticks and Sectaries of these latter times*. London, 1645.

Parker, William Riley. *Milton: A Biography*. Edited by Gordon Campbell. Rev. ed. Oxford: Oxford University Press, 1996.

Parry, Graham. *The Intellectual and Cultural Context of English Literature, 1603–1700*. London: Longman, 1989.

Parry, Graham, and Joad Raymond, eds. *Milton and the Terms of Liberty*. Cambridge: D. S. Brewer, 2002.

Patrick, J. Max. "Milton and Thomas Ellwood—A Reconsideration." *Milton Quarterly* 2 (1968) 2–4.

Patrides, C. A. *The Cambridge Platonists*. Cambridge, MA: Harvard University Press, 1971.

———. *Milton and the Christian Tradition*. Oxford: Clarendon, 1966.

———. "Milton and the Protestant Theory of the Atonement." *Modern Language Association of America* 74 (1959) 7–13.

———. "The 'Protevangelium' in Renaissance Theology and *Paradise Lost*." *Studies in English Literature* 3 (1963) 19–30.

———. "The Salvation of Satan." *Journal of the History of Ideas* 29 (1967) 467–78.

———. "'Something Like Prophetick Strain': Apocalyptic Configurations in Milton." In *The Apocalypse in English Renaissance Thought and Literature: Patterns, Antecedents and Repercussions*, edited by C. A. Patrides and J. Wittreich, 207–37. Manchester: Manchester University Press, 1984.

Patrides, C. A., and Raymond Waddington, eds. *The Age of Milton: Backgrounds to Seventeenth-Century Literature*. Manchester: Manchester University Press, 1980.

Patterson, Annabel M. "More Speech on Free Speech." *Modern Language Quarterly* 54 (1993) 55–66.

Patterson, Frank A., et al., eds. *The Works of John Milton*. 18 vols. New York: Columbia University Press, 1931–38.

Pecheux, M. Christopher. "Their Place of Rest: *Paradise Lost* XII. 647." *Milton Quarterly* 6 (1972) 73–75.

Penington, Isaac. *Divine Essays; or, Considerations about Several Things in Religion*. London, 1654.

———. *Some Questions and Answers for the Direction, Comfort, Help, and Furtherance of God's Spiritual Israel*. In *Works*, edited by John Barclay. Vol. 1. London: Darton and Harvey, 1837.

————. "The Testimony of Thomas Ellwood Concerning Thomas Isaac Penington." In *Selections from the Works of Isaac Penington*, edited by John Barclay, ix–xxxiii. London: Darton and Harvey, 1837.

————. *Works*. 2 vols. Edited by John Barclay. London: Darton and Harvey, 1837.

Perkins, William. *An Exposition of the Symbole or Creed of the Apostles*. Cambridge: J. Legat, 1595.

————. *A Golden Chaine; or, The Description of Theologie*. Cambridge: J. Legat, 1595.

————. *A Treatise on Gods Free Grace, and Mans Free Will*. Cambridge: J. Legat, 1595.

————. *The Workes of That Famous and Worthie Minister of Christ, in the Universitie of Cambridge*. 3 vols. Cambridge: J. Legat, 1608–1609.

Petty, Jane M. "The Voice at Eve's Ear in *Paradise Lost*." *Milton Quarterly* 19 (1985) 42–47.

Pierce, Thomas. *Autokatakrisis; or, Self-Condemnation*. London: J. G. for R. Royston, 1658.

————. *Corpuscolum Pacificatorium Orthodoxae Thelogiae*. London: S. Roscroft, 1685.

Polanus, Amandus. *Syntagma Theologiae Christianae*. Hanover, 1609; Geneva, 1617.

Polydorou, Desma. "Gender and Spiritual Equality in Marriage: A Dialogic Reading of Rachel Speght and John Milton." *Milton Quarterly* 35 (2001) 22–32.

Poole, William. "Milton and Science: A Caveat." *Milton Quarterly* 38 (2004) 18–34.

————. *Milton and the Idea of the Fall*. Cambridge: Cambridge University Press, 2005.

————. "Theology." In *Milton in Context*, edited by Stephen Dobransky, 478–79. Cambridge: Cambridge University Press, 2010.

Pruitt, Kristin A. *Gender and the Power of Relationship: "United as One Individual Soul" in* Paradise Lost. Pittsburgh: Duquesne University Press, 2003.

Radzinowicz, Mary Ann. "'In Those Days There Was No King in Israel': Milton's Politics and Biblical Narrative." *Yearbook of English Studies* 21 (1991) 242–52.

Raleigh, Walter. *Milton*. London: Arnold, 1900.

Reichert, John. *Milton's Wisdom: Nature and Scripture in* Paradise Lost. Ann Arbor: University of Michigan Press, 1992.

Reid, David. *The Humanism of Milton's* Paradise Lost. Edinburgh: Edinburgh University Press, 1993.

Reisner, Noam. *Milton and the Ineffable*. Oxford: Oxford University Press, 2010.

Revard, Stella P. "The Dramatic Function of the Son in *Paradise Lost*: A Commentary on Milton's 'Trinitarianism.'" *Journal of English and Germanic Philology* 66 (1967) 45–58.

————. *The War in Heaven:* Paradise Lost *and the Tradition of Satan's Rebellion*. Ithaca: Cornell University Press, 1980.

Rewak, William J. "Book III of *Paradise Lost*: Milton's Satisfaction Theory of the Redemption." *Milton Quarterly* 11 (1977) 97–102.

Reynolds, Edward. *A Treatise of the Passions and Faculties of the Soule of Man*. London: R. H. for Robert Bostock, 1640.

Richmond, Hugh M. *The Christian Revolutionary: John Milton*. Berkeley: University of California Press, 1974.

Riebling, Barbara. "Milton on Machiavelli: Representations of the State in *Paradise Lost*." *Renaissance Quarterly* 49 (1996) 573–97.

Riggs, William G. "Poetry and Method in Milton's *Of Education*." *Studies in Philology* 89 (1992) 445–69.

————. "The Temptation of Milton's Eve: 'Words, Impregn'd / With Reason.'" *Journal of English and Germanic Philology* 94 (1995) 365–92.

Ritchie, Daniel E. *Reconstructing Literature in an Ideological Age: A Biblical Poetics and Literary Studies from Milton to Burke.* Grand Rapids: Eerdmans, 1996.

Robins, H. F. *If This Be Heresy: A Study of Milton and Origen.* Illinois Studies in Language and Literature 51. Urbana: University of Illinois Press, 1963.

Rogers, John. *The Matter of Revolution: Science, Poetry and Politics in the Age of Milton.* Ithaca: Cornell University Press, 1996.

———. "Milton and the Mysterious Terms of History." *English Literary History* 57 (1990) 281–305.

Rosenblatt, Jason P. "Milton's Chief Rabbi." *Milton Studies* 24 (1988) 43–71.

———. *Torah and Law in Paradise Lost.* Princeton: Princeton University Press, 1994.

Rosendale, Timothy. "Milton, Hobbes, and the Liturgical Subject." *Studies in English Literature* 44 (2004) 149–72.

Rowse, A. L. *Milton the Puritan: Portrait of a Mind.* London: Macmillan, 1977.

Rudat, Wolfgang E. H. "Godhead and Milton's Satan: Classical Myth and Augustinian Theology in *Paradise Lost*." *Milton Quarterly* 14 (1980) 17–21.

———. "Ovid's *Art of Love* and Augustinian Theology in *Paradise Lost*." *Milton Quarterly* 21 (1987) 62–65.

Rudrum, Alan. "'For Then the Earth Shall Be All Paradise': Milton, Vaughan and the Neo-Calvinists on the Ecology of the Hereafter." *Scintilla* 4 (2000) 39–52.

Rumrich, John P. "Mead and Milton." *Milton Quarterly* 20 (1986) 136–41.

———. "The Milton–Diodati Correspondence." *Hellas* 3 (1992) 76–85.

———. *Milton Unbound: Controversy and Reinterpretation.* Cambridge: Cambridge University Press, 1996.

———. "Milton's Arianism: Why It Matters." In *John Milton: Twentieth-Century Perspectives, Vol. 4: Paradise Lost*, edited by J. Martin Evans, 143–60. New York: Routledge, 2003.

———. "Milton's God and the Matter of Chaos." *Modern Language Association of America* 110 (1995) 1035–46.

———. "Milton's Poetics of Generation." *Texas Studies in Literature and Language* 38 (1996) 191–208.

Ryken, Leland. *The Apocalyptic Vision in* Paradise Lost. Ithaca: Cornell University Press, 1970.

———. "Milton's Dramatization of the Godhead in *Paradise Lost*." *Milton Quarterly* 9 (1975) 1–6.

Ryken, Leland, and James H. Sims, eds. *Milton and Scriptural Tradition: The Bible into Poetry.* Columbia: University of Missouri Press, 1984.

Ryrie, Charles C. *Basic Theology.* Chicago: Moody, 1999.

———. *Dispensationalism.* Chicago: Moody, 1995.

Safer, Elaine B. "'Sufficient to Have Stood': Eve's Responsibility in Book IX." *Milton Quarterly* 5 (1971) 10–14.

Saltmarsh, John. *Free Grace; or, the Flowings of Christ's Blood freely to Sinners.* 1645. Reprint, London, 1661.

———. *Smoke in the Temple.* London, 1646.

Sammons, Todd H. "'As the Vine Curls Her Tendrils': Marriage Topos and Erotic Countertopos in *Paradise Lost*." *Milton Quarterly* 20 (1986) 117–27.

Samuel, Irene. *Plato and Milton.* Ithaca: Cornell University Press, 1947.

Sanchez, Reuben. "'The Middling Temper of Nourishment': Biblical Exegesis and the Art of Indeterminate Balance in *Tetrachordon*." *Milton Quarterly* 29 (1995) 1–12.

Sanesi, Roberto, ed. and trans. *Milton, Paradiso Perduto*. Milan: Mondadori, 1984.

Sauer, Elizabeth. "Milton's *Of True Religion*, Protestant Nationhood and the Negotiation of Liberty." *Milton Quarterly* 40 (2006) 1–19.

———. "Tolerationism, the Irish Crisis, and Milton's *On the Late Massacre in Piemont*." *Milton Studies* 44 (2005) 40–61.

Saurat, Denis. *Milton: Man and Thinker*. New York: Dial, 1925.

Savoie, John. "'That Fallacious Fruit': Lapsarian Lovemaking in *Paradise Lost*." *Milton Quarterly* 45 (2011) 161–71.

Schaff, Philip, ed. *The Creeds of Christendom: With a History and Critical Notes*. 3 vols. New York: Harper and Row, 1919.

———, ed. *A Select Library of the Nicene and Post-Nicene Fathers of the Christian Church*. 14 vols. Grand Rapids: Eerdmans, 1979.

Schleiner, Louise. "Pastoral Male Friendship and Miltonic Marriage: Textual Systems Transposed." *Literature Interpretation Theory* 2 (1990) 41–58.

Schoenfeldt, Michael. "'Commotion Strange': Passion in *Paradise Lost*." In *Reading the Early Modern Passions: Essays in the Cultural History of Emotion*, edited by Gail Kern Paster, Katherine Rowe, and Mary Floyd-Wilson, 43–67. Philadelphia: University of Pennsylvania Press, 2004.

———. "Obedience and Autonomy in *Paradise Lost*." In *A Companion to Milton*, edited by Thomas N. Corns, 363–79. Oxford: Blackwell, 2001.

Schuler, Stephen J. "Sanctification in Milton's Academy: Reassessing the Purposes in *Of Education* and the Pedagogy of *Paradise Lost*." *Milton Quarterly* 43 (2009) 39–56.

Schwartz, Regina. "From Shadowy Types to Shadowy Types: The Unendings of *Paradise Lost*." *Milton Studies* 24 (1988) 123–39.

———. "Milton on the Bible." In *A Companion to Milton*, edited by Thomas N. Corns, 37–54. Oxford: Blackwell, 2001.

———. *Remembering and Repeating: On Milton's Theology and Poetics*. Chicago: University of Chicago Press, 1993.

Scodel, Joshua. "*Paradise Lost* and Classical Ideals of Pleasurable Restraint." *Comparative Literature* 48 (1996) 189–236.

Scott, Jonathan. *Algernon Sidney and the English Republic, 1623–1677*. Cambridge: Cambridge University Press, 1988.

Sellin, Paul R. "If Not Milton, Who Did Write *De Doctrina Christiana?* The Amyraldian Connection." In *Living Texts: Interpreting Milton*, edited by Kristin A. Pruitt and Charles W. Durham, 237–63. London: Associated University Presses, 2000.

———. "John Milton's *Paradise Lost* and *De Doctrina Christiana* on Predestination." *Milton Studies* 34 (1997) 45–60.

———. "Responses." *Milton Quarterly* 33 (1999) 38–51.

———. "Some Musings on Alexander Morus and the Authorship of *De Doctrina Christiana*." *Milton Quarterly* 35 (2001) 63–71.

Senault, J. F. *De l'usage des passions* (1641). *The Use of Passions*, translated by Henry, Earl of Monmouth. London: J. L. and Humphrey Moseley, 1649.

Sewell, Arthur. *A Study in Milton's Christian Doctrine*. Oxford: Oxford University Press, 1939.

Shaheen, Naseeb. "Milton's Muse and the *De Doctrina*." *Milton Quarterly* 8 (1972) 72–76.

Shawcross, John T. "An Early View of Satan as Hero in *Paradise Lost*." *Milton Quarterly* 32 (1998) 104–5.

———. *John Milton: The Self and the World*. Lexington: University Press of Kentucky, 1993.

———. "Milton's *Christian Doctrine*." *Studies in English Literature* 32 (1992) 155–62.

———. "Milton's *Tenure of Kings and Magistrates*: Date of Composition, Editions, and Issues." *Papers of the Bibliographical Society of America* 60 (1966) 1–8.

———. "Misreading Milton." *Milton Studies* 33 (1997) 181–203.

———. *Rethinking Milton Studies: Time Present and Time Past*. Newark: University of Delaware Press, 2005.

———. "'What Is Faith, Love, Vertue unassaid': Some Literary Answers to Our Ever-Present Evil." *Milton Quarterly* 42 (2008) 69–77.

Sherry, Beverley. "'A Paradise Within' Can Never Be 'Happier Farr': Reconsidering the Archangel Michael's Consolation in *Paradise Lost*." *Milton Quarterly* 37 (2003) 77–91.

Shifflett, Andrew Eric. *Stoicism, Politics, and Literature in the Age of Milton: War and Peace Reconciled*. Cambridge: Cambridge University Press, 1998.

Shoaf, R. A. *Milton, Poet of Duality: A Study of Semiosis in the Poetry and the Prose*. Gainesville: University Press of Florida, 1993.

———. "'Our Names Are Debt': Messiah's Account of Himself." In *Reconsidering the Renaissance: Papers from the Twenty-First Annual Conference*, edited by Mario A. Di Cesare, 461–73. Binghamton, NY: Medieval and Renaissance Texts and Studies, 1992.

Shore, Daniel. "Fit Though Few: *Eikonoklastes* and the Rhetoric of Audience." *Milton Studies* 45 (2005) 129–48.

Shoulson, Jeffrey S. "The King and I: The Stance of Theodicy in Midrash and *Paradise Lost*." *Milton Studies* 36 (1998) 59–85.

———. *Milton and the Rabbis: Hebraism, Hellenism, and Christianity*. New York: Columbia University Press, 2001.

Shullenberger, William. "Into the Woods: The Lady's Soliloquy in *Comus*." *Milton Quarterly* 35 (2001) 33–43.

———. "Satan's Death Trip." *Milton Quarterly* 27 (1993) 41–48.

———. "Wrestling with the Angel: *Paradise Lost* and Feminist Criticism." *Milton Quarterly* 20 (1986) 69–85.

Sims, James H. *The Bible in Milton's Epics*. Gainesville: University of Florida Press, 1962.

Skinner, Quentin. *Liberty Before Liberalism*. Cambridge: Cambridge University Press, 1998.

Slotkin, Joel. "Poetic Justice: Divine Punishment and Augustinian Chiaroscuro in *Paradise Lost*." *Milton Quarterly* 38 (2004) 100–27.

Smith, Nigel. *Literature and Revolution in England, 1640–1660*. Princeton: Princeton University Press, 1994.

Snare, Gerald. "Milton's 'Siloa's Brook' Again." *Milton Quarterly* 4 (1970) 55–57.

Spellman, W. M. *John Locke and the Problem of Depravity*. Oxford: Oxford University Press, 1988.

Stacey, W. David. *The Pauline View of Man*. London: Macmillan, 1956.

Stavely, Keith W. F. *The Politics of Milton's Prose Style*. New Haven: Yale University Press, 1975.

———. "Satan and Arminianism in *Paradise Lost*." *Milton Studies* 25 (1989) 125–39.

Stevens, Paul. "Discontinuities in Milton's Early Public Self-Representation." *Huntington Library Quarterly* 51 (1988) 261–80.

Stevenson, Kay Gilliland. "Eve's Place in *Paradise Lost*." *Milton Quarterly* 22 (1988) 126–27.

Stewart, Douglas. "Speaking to the World: The *Ad Hominem* Logic of Milton's Polemics." *Seventeenth Century* 11 (1996) 35–60.

Stoll, Abraham. "Discontinuous Wound: Milton and Theism." *Milton Studies* 44 (2005) 179–202.

Stone, James W. "'Man's Effeminate S(lack)ness': Androgyny and the Divided Unity of Adam and Eve." *Milton Quarterly* 31 (1997) 33–42.

Stone, Lawrence. *Road to Divorce: England, 1530–1987.* Oxford: Oxford University Press, 1992.

Strier, Richard. "Milton against Humility." In *Religion and Culture in Renaissance England*, edited by Claire McEachern and Debora Shuger, 258–86. Cambridge: Cambridge University Press, 1997.

———. "Milton's Fetters, or, Why Eden Is Better than Heaven." *Milton Studies* 38 (2000) 169–97.

Swaim, Kathleen M. *Before and After the Fall.* Amherst: University of Massachusetts Press, 1986.

———. "Milton in 1825." *Milton Quarterly* 22 (1988) 44–50.

———. "Myself a True Poem: Early Milton and the (Re)Formation of the Subject." *Milton Studies* 38 (2000) 66–95.

Swiss, Margo. "Satan's Obduracy in *Paradise Lost.*" *Milton Quarterly* 28 (1994) 56–61.

Tagashi, Go. "Milton and the Presbyterian Opposition, 1649–1650: The Engagement Controversy and *The Tenure of Kings and Magistrates*, Second Edition (1649)." *Milton Quarterly* 39 (2005) 59–81.

Tanner, John S. *Anxiety in Eden: A Kierkegaardian Reading of Paradise Lost.* New York: Oxford University Press, 1992.

Taylor, Jeremy. *Liberty of Prophesying.* London, 1646.

Teskey, Gordon. *Delirious Milton.* Cambridge, MA: Harvard University Press, 2006.

Thickstun, Margaret Olofson. "Milton among Puritan Women: Affiliative Spirituality and the Conclusion of *Paradise Lost.*" *Religion and Literature* 36 (2004) 1–23.

———. "Raphael and the Challenge of Evangelical Education." *Milton Quarterly* 35 (2001) 245–57.

———. "Resisting Patience in Milton's Sonnet 19." *Milton Quarterly* 44 (2010) 168–80.

Tillyard, E. M. W. *Milton.* New York: Barnes and Noble, 1967.

———. *The Miltonic Setting: Past and Present.* Cambridge: Cambridge University Press, 1938.

Toland, John. *The Life of John Milton.* London: John Darby, 1699.

Treip, Mindele Anne. "'Reason Is Also Choice': The Emblematics of Free Will in *Paradise Lost.*" *Studies in English Literature* 31 (1991) 147–77.

Tremelli, Emmanuele. *Latin Translation of the Hebrew Old Testament.* Frankfurt, 1575, 1579; London, 1580.

———. *Latin Translation of the Syriac New Testament.* Geneva, 1569.

Trevor-Roper, H. R. *Religion, the Reformation and Social Change.* London: Macmillan, 1967.

———. "William Dell." *The English Historical Review* 62 (1947) 377–79.

Trubowitz, Rachel. "Sublime/Pauline: Denying Death in *Paradise Lost.*" In *Imagining Death in Spenser and Milton*, edited by Elizabeth Jane Bellamy et al., 131–50. Basingstoke: Palgrave Macmillan, 2003.

Turner, James Grantham. *One Flesh: Paradisal Marriage and Sexual Relations in the Age of Milton.* Oxford: Oxford University Press, 1987.

Turretin, Francis. *Institutes of Elenctic Theology*. Edited by James T. Dennison. Translated by George Musgrave Giger. 3 vols. Phillipsburg, NJ: Presbyterian and Reformed, 1992–97.

Tyacke, Nicholas. *Aspects of English Protestantism, c. 1530–1700*. Manchester: Manchester University Press, 2001.

Ulreich, John C., Jr. "'A paradise within': The Fortunate Fall in *Paradise Lost*." *Journal of the History of Ideas* 32 (1971) 351–66.

———. "'Substantially Express'd': Milton's Doctrine of the Incarnation." *Milton Studies* 39 (2001) 101–28.

———. "'Sufficient to Have Stood': Adam's Responsibility in Book IX." *Milton Quarterly* 5 (1971) 38–42.

———. "Two Great World Systems: Galileo, Milton, and the Problem of Truth." *Cithara: Essays in the Judaeo-Christian Tradition* 43 (2003) 25–36.

Urwick, William. *Historical Skecthes of Nonconformity in the County Palatine of Chester*. London: Kent and Septimus Fletcher, 1864.

Ussher, James. *A Body of Divinitie, or the Summe and Substance of Christian Religion*. London: I. Owsley and P. Lillicrap, 1653.

———. *The Judgement of Doctor Rainoldes*. London: G. M. for Thomas Dovvnes, 1641.

Van den Berg, Sara. "Women, Children, and the Rhetoric of Milton's Divorce Tracts." *Early Modern Literary Studies* 10 (2004) 1–13.

Van Nuis, Hermine J. "Animated Eve Confronting Her Animus: A Jungian Approach to the Division of Labor Debate in *Paradise Lost*." *Milton Quarterly* 34 (2000) 48–56.

Vermigli, Pietro. *Loci Communes*. London: R. Masson, 1576.

Vossius, Gerardus. *De Theologia Gentili*. Amsterdam: I. Blaeu, 1641.

Waldock, A. J. A. Paradise Lost *and Its Critics*. Cambridge: Cambridge University Press, 1947.

Walker, Julia M. "'For each seem'd either': Free Will and Predestination in *Paradise Lost*." *Milton Quarterly* 20 (1986) 13–16.

———. "Free Will, Predestination and Ghost-Busting." *Milton Quarterly* 21 (1987) 101–2.

———, ed. *Milton and the Idea of Woman*. Urbana: University of Illinois Press, 1988.

Walker, William. "Milton's Dualistic Theory of Religious Toleration in *A Treatise of Civil Power*, *Of Christian Doctrine*, and *Paradise Lost*." *Modern Philology* 99 (2001) 201–30.

———. "On Reason, Faith and Freedom in *Paradise Lost*." *Studies in English Literature* 47 (2007) 143–59.

———. "Typology and *Paradise Lost*: Books XI and XII." *Milton Studies* 25 (1989) 245–64.

Warren, Christopher N. "When Self-Preservation Bids: Approaching Milton, Hobbes, and Dissent." *English Literary Renaissance* 37 (2007) 118–50.

Weinfield, Henry. "'With Serpent Error Wand'ring Found Their Way': Milton's Counterplot Revisited." *Milton Quarterly* 37 (2003) 11–20.

Wentersdorf, Karl P. "*Paradise Lost IX*: The Garden and the Flowered Couch." *Milton Quarterly* 13 (1979) 134–41.

Werman, Golda. *Milton and Midrash*. Washington, DC: Catholic University of America Press, 1995.

Wickenheiser, Robert J. "Milton's 'Pattern of a Christian Hero': The Son in *Paradise Lost*." *Milton Quarterly* 12 (1978) 1–9.

Wigler, Stephen. "The Poet and Satan Before the Light: A Suggestion about Book III and the Opening of Book IV of *Paradise Lost*." *Milton Quarterly* 12 (1978) 59–64.

Wilcox, Helen. "'Is This the End of This New Glorious World?': *Paradise Lost* and the Beginning of the End." *Essays and Studies* 48 (1995) 1–15.

Wilding, Michael. *Dragon's Teeth: Literature in the English Revolution*. Oxford: Oxford University Press, 1987.

———. "Milton's *Areopagitica*: Liberty for the Sects." *Prose Studies* 9 (1986) 7–38.

Willey, Basil. *The Seventeenth-Century Background: Studies in the Thought of the Age in Relation to Poetry and Religion*. London: Chatto and Windus, 1934.

Williams, Roger. *The Bloudy Tenent of Persecution, for the Cause of Conscience, Discussed in a Conference Between Truth and Peace*. London, 1644. In *Complete Writings*. Vol. 3. New York: Russell and Russell, 1963.

———. *Queries of the Highest Consideration*. In *Complete Writings*. Vol. 1. New York: Russell and Russell, 1963.

Winegardner, Karl Lewis. "No Hasty Conclusions: Milton's Ante-Nicene Pneumatology." *Milton Quarterly* 11 (1977) 102–7.

Wittreich, Joseph A. *Feminist Milton*. Ithaca: Cornell University Press, 1987.

Wolfe, Don M. *Milton and His England*. Princeton: Princeton University Press, 1971.

Wolfe, Don M., et al., eds. *The Complete Prose Works of John Milton*. 8 vols. New Haven: Yale University Press, 1953–82.

Wolleb, Johannes. *Christianae Theologiae Compendium*. Basel, 1626. Translated by Alexander Ross, *The Abridgment of Christian Divinitie*, London, 1650.

Woodhouse, A. S. P. "Christian Liberty in Milton's Divorce Pamphlets." *The Modern Language Review* 35 (1940) 153–61.

———. *The Heavenly Muse: A Preface to Milton*. Toronto: University of Toronto Press, 1972.

———. "Milton, Puritanism and Liberty." *University of Toronto Quarterly* 4 (1935) 395–404.

———, ed. *Puritanism and Liberty: Being the Army Debates (1647–1649)*. London: Dent, 1938.

Wooten, John. "The Poet's War: Violence and Virtue in *Paradise Lost*." *Studies in English Literature* 30 (1990) 133–50.

Zanchi, Girolamo. *De Religione Christiana, Fides*. Neustadt, 1585.

———. *De Praedestinatione* [*The Doctrine of Absolute Predestination*]. Translated by Augustus Toplady. New York: George Lindsay, 1811.

Index